LIFE ALONG THE SILK ROAD

LIFE ALONG THE SILK ROAD

Susan Whitfield

University of California Press

Berkeley • Los Angeles

To the memory of Sir Aurel Stein,
for his excavations along the Silk Road,
and to Professor Edward Schafer,
for his equally rigorous literary excavations.
This book owes a great debt to the
treasures discovered by each man.

University of California Press
Berkeley and Los Angeles, California
Published by arrangement with
John Murray (Publishers) Ltd

ISBN-13: 978-0-520-23214-3

Typeset in Monotype Bembo 12/13.5
by Servis Filmsetting Ltd., Manchester

Printed and bound in Canada

09   08   07
9   8   7   6

The paper used in this publication is both acid-free and totally
chlorine-free (TCF). It meets the minimum requirements of
ANSI/NISO Z39.48-1992 (R 1997) (*Permanence of Paper*). ∞

Contents

Illustrations	vi
Preface	ix
Note on Names and Romanization	xi
Map	xii
Introduction	I
The Merchant's Tale	27
The Soldier's Tale	55
The Horseman's Tale	76
The Princess's Tale	95
The Monk's Tale	113
The Courtesan's Tale	138
The Nun's Tale	155
The Widow's Tale	174
The Official's Tale	189
The Artist's Tale	206
Epilogue	223
Further Reading	226
Table of Rulers, 739–960	230
Index	232

Illustrations

Colour plates (between pages 82 and 83)

1. 'Women Playing Double Sixes', silk painting by Zhou Fang (fl. 780–804)
2. Uighur prince, ramie painting, Kocho, 9th century
3. 'A Palace Concert', silk painting, Tang dynasty
4. Female heretics being tonsured, Sariputra story, Dunhuang cave 445, 9th century
5. Manichean priests transcribing texts, Kocho, 8th–9th century
6. Camels in the Tsaidam
7. Musicians on a camel, Chang'an, Tang dynasty
8. Merchants surprised by bandits, Dunhuang cave 45, 8th century
9. Road between Tashkurgan and Kashgar
10. Prince's coat, Sogdiana, 8th century
11. General Zhang on the march, Dunhuang cave 156, 9th century
12. Monk's silk patchwork robe, kasaya, Dunhuang, 8th–9th century

Black-and-white plates (between pages 146 and 147)

1. Stone statue of Maitreya Bodhisattva, Gandhara
2. Quilted shoe from Mazar-Tagh, near Khotan, 8th–9th century
3. Printed almanac (detail), Dunhuang, AD 877
4. Sir Aurel Stein's photograph of Islam Akhun in 1900
5. Illustrated manuscript booklet of *Guanshiyin Sutra*, Dunhuang
6. Bundle of manuscripts inside wrapper, Dunhuang
7. Painted stucco figures of tomb-guarding monsters, Astana cemetery, near Kocho
8. Colophon to a printed copy of *The Diamond Sutra*, Dunhuang, AD 868

9. Sketches for sutra illustrations, Dunhuang, 9th–10th century
10. Donors at bottom of silk painting, Dunhuang, AD 892
11. Dunhuang caves as seen by Sir Aurel Stein in 1907
12. Stucco head of a colossal Buddha, Miran
13. Illustrated manuscript copy of *The Sutra of Ten Kings*, Dunhuang

Line Drawings	*page*
Sassanian design woven on silk, Dunhuang, 8th century	29
Sogdian silver wine ewer, 7th–8th century	32
Four-armed Nana on a lion, 7th century	36
Plan of eighth-century Chang'an	52
Plan of Tibetan fort, Miran, 7th–8th century	59
Plan of battle sites in Wakhan and Little Balur	65
The tarpan, *Equus przewalski*	77
Man in *hufu* (foreigner's robe), Chang'an, Tang dynasty	89
Chinese Tang hairstyle and phoenix hair ornaments	96
Chinese girl dressed in *hufu*, Chang'an, Tang dynasty	107
Uighur princess, Bezeklik, 9th century	108
Charm for ensuring order in the house, Dunhuang, 9th century	114
Buddhist temple in Chinese Central Asia, 9th–10th century	129
Vaisravana, Heavenly King of the North, Dunhuang, AD 947	130
Sogdian dancer, Chang'an, Tang dynasty	140
Chinese women's hairstyles, Tang dynasty	145
Musicians on a bullock cart, Dunhuang	153
Tara, Tantric Buddhist deity	160
Frontispiece of *The Diamond Sutra* (detail), Dunhuang, AD 868	162
Demon supporting a heavenly king, Dunhuang, 9th century	164
Demon guarding the gate to Hell, Dunhuang	165
The Star God, Rahu, Dunhuang, 10th century	175
Ploughing scene, Dunhuang, 7th century	177
Cricket from a Chinese printed encyclopaedia	192
The story of Sariputra, Dunhuang, 10th century	213
Pounce, ink on paper, Dunhuang, 10th century	216

Illustrations

Preface

This book is not a comprehensive history but aims instead to offer a glimpse into the character and characters of the eastern Silk Road between AD 750 and 1000. It does so by concentrating on ten individuals who lived at different times during this period, and relates its history through their personal experiences. The stories span two hundred and fifty years and, in order to make what is a very complex history comprehensible, they concentrate only on a few key political events, recounting them through the eyes of one or more characters. Repetition is used deliberately: I assume that many readers will not be familiar with this region, its peoples, culture or history.

The events in the characters' lives are all taken from contemporary sources, and some of the characters – the princess, artist, nun, official and widow – are themselves historical figures. But their surviving biographies range from an account of events in their lives to only a passing mention in a couple of texts, and so I have 'borrowed' the characters and fleshed out their lives with details from the lives of others. The characters are all, in this sense, composite.

Although these tales represent the diversity of life along the Silk Road, they have a Chinese bias. This is partly owing to the relative richness of primary sources in Chinese and partly a reflection of my training as a historian of China. The last four tales, for example, are all set in the town of Dunhuang when it was under nominal Chinese control. But it also happens that China was the only empire which existed at both the beginning and the end of the first millennium AD, and, before the spread of Islam to the eastern Silk Road, it was heavily indebted to Central Asia for much of its culture. This is, I hope, reflected in these tales.

It would not have been possible to write a book such as this without relying heavily on the work of other scholars. I mention only a few of the most important works in English below: in addition to these there are numerous Chinese, Japanese, French, German, Russian, Indian and American scholars to whom I owe thanks but whose works belong in the footnotes of a more academic book. I am indebted in particular to Valerie Hansen, *Negotiating Daily Life in Traditional China: How Ordinary People Used Contracts, 600–1400* (Yale University Press, New Haven and London, 1995); Gregory Schopen, *Bones, Stones and Buddhist Monks* (Yale University Press, New Haven and London, 1995); Stephen Teiser, *The Scripture of the Ten Kings and the Making of Purgatory in Medieval Chinese Buddhism* (University of Hawaii Press, Honolulu, 1994); and Sarah E. Fraser, *Performing the Visual: The Wall Painter in Tang China* (forthcoming). These books have inspired several of the most interesting characters in this book, most especially Widow Ah-long, the Abbess Miaofu, the official Zhai Fengda and the artist Dong Baode. All four are works of the highest scholarship but also very accessible to the general reader, and I recommend them most highly.

For their scholarship, their personal help, their support, or help with specific problems, thanks are also owed to John and Helen Espir, Anne Farrer, Sarah Fraser, Jill Geber, Janice Glowski, Hao Chunwen, John Huntington, Graham Hutt, John Kiesnick, Charles Lewis, Burkhard Quessel, Ursula Sims Williams, Tsuguhito Takeuchi, Muhammed Isa Waley, Rong Xinjiang, Frances Wood and Marianne Yaldiz; and, most especially, to my indefatigable editor, Gail Pirkis, and my ever-helpful and patient partner, Anthony Grayling.

Note on Names and Romanization

I have been consistent in the romanization of Chinese, using the pinyin system throughout; but there is an exception: my name for the Widow Ah-long. In pinyin it would be spelled 'Along' which might mislead readers as to its pronunciation. I have romanized Sanskrit according to convention, using diacriticals where necessary. For Turkic names, however, I have used 'K' instead of the usual 'Q' ('Kumtugh' and 'Kocho' rather than 'Qumtugh' and 'Qocho') because this makes them seem less alien and more readily pronounceable to English speakers. For Turkic, Tibetan and Arab romanization I have followed the standard conventions, but I am not a linguist of these languages and so have relied on secondary sources: I apologize for any inadvertent mistakes.

The names of all the characters are found in contemporary sources. I have not, however, been wholly consistent with names of towns and regions. I use contemporary names where possible, but in some cases strict historical accuracy has been sacrificed to clarity, and the names used are anachronistic (such as the Gansu corridor). In many cases towns have several names, depending on the source; so Beshbaliq, the Turkic name of a town as found in Uighur sources, is called Beiting in Chinese sources (it has yet another name in Tibetan sources). In such cases I have generally used the name given by the people dominant in the town at that period (at the time of the Horseman's Tale the town was ruled by the Turkic Uighurs, so I call it Beshbaliq).

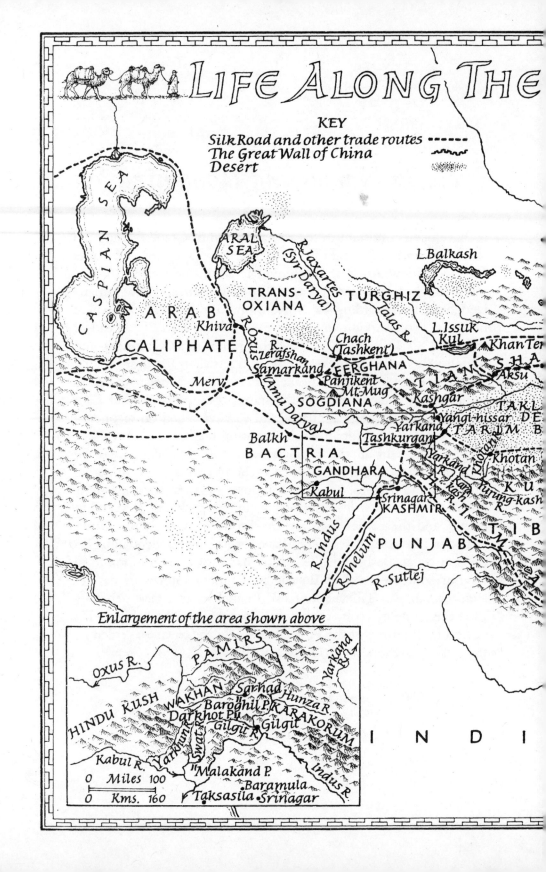

LIFE ALONG THE

KEY

Silk Road and other trade routes - - - - -
The Great Wall of China
Desert

CASPIAN SEA

ARAL SEA

L. Balkash

R. Jaxartes (Syr-Darya)

TRANS-OXIANA

TURGHIZ

ARAB

Khiva

CALIPHATE

R. Oxus

Zerafshan R.

Samarkand

Merv

FERGHANA

Talas R.

L. Issuk Kul

Chach (Tashkent)

Khan Ter

SHA

TIAN

Aksu

Panjikent
Mt. Mug

SOGDIANA

Kashgar

Amu Darya

Yangi-hissar

TARIM B.

TAKL. DE

Balkh

BACTRIA

Tashkurgan

Yarkand

Yarkand R.

Khotan

KU

GANDHARA

Kabul

Srinagar

KASHMIR

Kara-kash R.

Yurung-kash R.

Khotan R.

R. Indus

PUNJAB

TIB

TI

R. Jhelum

R. Sutlej

Enlargement of the area shown above

Oxus R.

PAMIRS

Yarkand R.

HINDU KUSH

WAKHAN

Sarhad

Baroghil P.

Hunza R.

KARAKORUM

Darkhot P.

Gilgit R.

Gilgit

Yarkhun

Swat R.

Kabul R.

Malakand P.

Baramula

Taksasila

Srinagar

Indus R.

0 Miles 100

0 Kms. 160

INDI

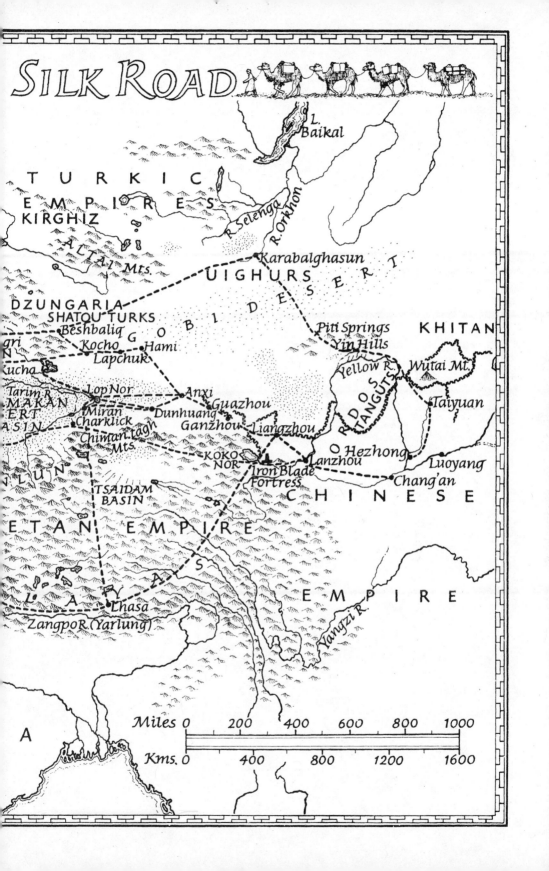

SILK ROAD

L. Baikal

TURKIC EMPIRES
KIRGHIZ
ALTAI Mts.

DZUNGARIA
SHATOU TURKS
Beshbaliq
gri
Kocho Hami
N
Lapchuk
Kucha
Tarim R.
MAKAN
ERT
ASIN
Lop Nor
Miran
Charklick
Chiman.Tagh
Mts.
LUN
TSAIDAM
BASIN
ETAN EMPIRE
L

AYAS
Lhasa
Zangpo R. (Yarlung)

A

R. Selenga
R. Orkhon

Karabalghasun

UIGHURS

G O B I   D E S E R T

Piti Springs
Yin Hills
Yellow R.

KHITAN

Wutai Mt.

Taiyuan

ORDOS
TANGUTS

Anxi
Guazhou
Dunhuang
Ganzhou
Liangzhou

KOKO
NOR
Iron Blade
Fortress
Lanzhou

Hezhong
Luoyang
Chang'an

C H I N E S E

E M P I R E

Yangzi R.

Miles 0   200   400   600   800   1000

Kms. 0   400   800   1200   1600

Introduction

Central Asia is usually defined negatively: as the place that lies outside the boundaries of its neighbouring civilizations. But if we know the region largely through the annals of its neighbours and the accounts of those who passed through it, it is nevertheless misleading to assume that it has always been a place of transience: a land of nomads with neither civilization nor culture, lacking established cities or a history of its own. Evidence uncovered over the past century has revealed a quite different story.

The strategic importance of Central Asia was never doubted by those neighbouring civilizations who fought for its control. During the first millennium AD many of the world's empires – Arab, Chinese, Turkic and Tibetan – had their bases in eastern Eurasia, and it is the story of Central Asia, seen through their eyes, that this book tells. But evidence for that story was not revealed until the nineteenth century, when two quite different empires – those of Russia and Britain – played out their rivalries in the deserts and mountains of the region. Military and political missions were dispatched to Central Asia, and in their wake, drawn by tales of treasures uncovered from lost cities in the sand, archaeologists followed.

Whatever we may now think about the rights or wrongs of these colonial archaeologists, their work has enabled this story to be told, and their finds have inspired, and continue to inspire, scholars to attempt to reconstruct the history of Central Asia for the first time. And perhaps they have also prompted the eastern empires, who owe so much to Central Asia, to reconsider the importance of the region in the modern era. Most of the archaeological work in eastern Central Asia since the 1930s has been

I

carried out by Chinese-led expeditions; India is showing an increasing interest in the land of the Moguls; and Persia's successors are keen to bring eastern Central Asia into a pan-Islamic republic. The archaeologists and adventurers at the start of the century, however, came from Germany, Hungary, Russia, Britain, France, Sweden and Japan.

The geographical focus of this book is not the whole of Central Asia from west to east – the vast lands stretching from the Caspian Sea to China – but only its easternmost half: from the region of Samarkand, now in eastern Uzbekistan, to Chang'an, present-day Xian in China. The northern limits are approximate to the northern border of present-day Mongolia, and the southern limits are marked by the Himalayas. Sir Aurel Stein, perhaps the most famous early twentieth-century archaeologist to explore the heart of this region, coined a French term for it, naming it Serindia ('Ser' being short for Seres or China) to indicate its position between two great civilizations:

> The geographical limits . . . comprise practically the whole of that vast drainageless belt between the Pamirs in the west and the Pacific watershed in the east, which for close on a thousand years formed the special meeting ground of Chinese civilization, introduced by trade and political penetration, and of Indian culture, propagated by Buddhism.

A network of roads crossed this land, along which merchants, mercenaries, monks and others travelled. This network, for the sake of simplicity, is referred to collectively as 'the Silk Road',* though there was in fact no single route and the merchants' cargo also included salt, wool, jade and many other items. The far west of this part of the Silk Road is referred to as Sogdiana – the land between the Oxus river (the Amu Darya) to the west and the Pamir mountains to the east. Its middle section is the Tarim basin – the geographical term for the low-lying desert between the Pamir mountains to the west and Lop-nor to the east. The easternmost section is called the Gansu corridor (after the modern Chinese

---

* Coined by the German Baron Ferdinand von Richthofen in the nineteenth century.

province of the same name), which runs from Dunhuang in the west to Chang'an in the east.

Stein first travelled in these regions in 1900, after many years of preparation and anticipation – he had heard reports of its archaeological possibilities from Count Loćzy, a member of a Hungarian expedition two decades before. Stein himself was Hungarian-born but had adopted British nationality and worked for the Archaeological Survey of India. His modest and understated accounts of his three expeditions in Central Asia over the next fifteen years barely conceal his passion for travel and exploration.

Stein travelled from northern India, through Kashmir and the Hindu Kush and Pamir mountain ranges, a route taken by Buddhist monks throughout the first millennium (see 'The Monk's Tale'). Indeed, one of these monks, Xuanzang, was Stein's inspiration and guide. He had travelled from China to India in the seventh century in search of scriptural texts missing from the Chinese version of the Buddhist canon. On his return, after an absence of over fifteen years, he wrote an account of his travels with descriptions of the lands through which he had passed. His travels fired the imagination not only of Stein but of many others, both at the time and since. A fictionalized account of his journey became a bestseller in China and was made into a traditional Chinese opera, and has subsequently been retold in films, cartoons and television series.

Stein relied on Xuanzang's account to match with towns named in Chinese annals many of the hundreds of ruined desert sites that he excavated. Archaeology in the desert poses particular problems. In the absence of strata of packed earth, dating has to be done by using clues from the architectural features of any remaining buildings, the styles of objects found *in situ* and written sources. The desert does, however, offer one advantage. Its dry, sandy conditions mean that those objects found are extremely well preserved, especially organic materials (corpses, textiles, wood and paper) which in many other places would have decayed. Almost all of the tens of thousands of objects found by Stein – including fragments of wood and silk no larger than a thumbnail – were carefully inscribed by him with a mark indicating the precise location where they were found. We therefore know that the red and black lacquered leather armour scales now in the British Museum were unearthed in the third room within the eastern wall of Miran fort, and we also know, both from Tibetan documents found at the site and from Chinese historical records, that the fort was built and occupied by Tibetans in the latter half of the eighth century (see 'The Soldier's Tale').

Not all finds were quite what they seemed, however. It was on his first expedition in 1900–1 that Stein confirmed his suspicions concerning the authenticity of manuscripts and printed documents sold to the British and Russian consuls in Kashgar from the 1880s onwards. After tracing the main seller, Islam Akhun, Stein subjected him to rigorous questioning, eventually cornering him into a contradiction. Once Islam Akhun realized he had been discovered, he confessed to Stein that the documents had all been forgeries, manufactured by himself and various colleagues from locally made paper, dyed with an extract from the black poplar tree and prematurely aged over fire. Scholars in Europe had spent over a decade trying to decipher the writing and thought it represented a hitherto unknown language. On the contrary, said Islam Akhun, it was entirely fabricated.

Islam Akhun and his colleagues had been successful in their deceit because many genuinely old manuscripts had indeed been discovered in previously largely unexplored ruins in the desert. However, though these were written in many languages and in several scripts – some, such as *kharoṣṭhī* (used to write Indian languages such as Sanskrit, Prakrit and Gandhāri), were unique to northern India and Central Asia – none was new to scholars. What was new was their number, their antiquity and their subject matter. Stein found nearly thirty thousand documents, ranging from fragments of second-century BC woodslips with only a few faint words remaining, to beautifully preserved seventy-foot-long scrolls on paper, complete with the original silk tie and roller made by seventh-century artisans. Among them were Manichean prayers and letters from a Sogdian merchant stranded far from home because of war; contracts for loan of items such as a donkey, a cooking pot and grain for sowing; model letters composed by officials in the Etiquette Bureau making polite enquiries about the weather; poems; educational primers; legal suits; medical prescriptions; almanacs; bawdy tales; Chinese imperial decrees; and much more.

The richest source of these documents was a small cave in a Buddhist cave complex outside the town of Dunhuang, now in Gansu province, China. The cave was a storehouse for copies of Buddhist texts and paintings, and contained over forty thousand documents. It had been sealed up in the eleventh century (we do not know by whom) but was discovered by accident in 1900. When Stein arrived in 1907, having heard rumours of the find, the caretaker of the cave complex, who had already given away some of the manuscripts and paintings to local officials, was happy to part with several cartloads more for a small sum – he was trying to raise funds for the repair of the paintings and sculptures decorating the hundreds of other caves in the complex. Paul Pelliot, a Frenchman and the greatest sinologist of his day, arrived hard on Stein's heels and looked (he claimed) through all the remaining material before persuading the caretaker to part with several more cartloads. After this the Chinese authorities ordered the removal of the remainder of the cave's contents to Beijing, the Chinese capital, although some mysteriously disappeared after being deposited at the Ministry of Education (they later appeared in the collection of a Chinese bibliophile who worked in the Ministry). Despite this, there were still manuscripts for sale when Japanese and Russian expeditions arrived at Dunhuang a few years later, and Stein bought a further 600 scrolls in a neighbouring town in 1913. How many of these later acquisitions are forgeries is still being investigated.

The importance of the Dunhuang documents cannot be overstated. Without them, this book would not have been possible. I have used many of the documents themselves in trying to reconstruct the lives of people on the Silk Road, but I have also relied heavily on secondary scholarship. Study of the Dunhuang documents has spawned its own discipline – Dunhuangology – with university departments, journals, conferences and hundreds of scholars in China and Japan devoted to it. Most of the documents from Dunhuang are in Chinese, but a number are in Tibetan: the town was under both Chinese and Tibetan control during the first millennium. Although the cave seems to have been a repository specifically for Buddhist texts, a shortage of paper meant that some of these texts were written on the back of paper that had previously been used for quite other purposes. Among the texts, therefore, are non-Buddhist works which are unique among Chinese records in giving a glimpse into the everyday lives of ordinary men and women. The texts relating to the case of Widow Ah-long ('The Widow's Tale'), for example, tell us that women had the right to hold land, that Dunhuang was troubled by bandits who kidnapped children, and that the legal system was fairly well organized and – at least in this case – seems to have worked on the side of justice.

This book also relies on scholarship and sources in languages other than Chinese. It is only in recent years, for example, that the history of the early Tibetan empire has been attempted, despite the discovery of the annals of early Tibetan kings among the Dunhuang documents. Soviet-led excavations of Panjikent in Sogdiana have revealed the wonderful murals described in 'The Merchant's Tale'. And the record of an Arab envoy offers rare details of the Uighur empire. It is a great pity that other contemporary accounts, such as that of a Chinese soldier, written on his return to China in AD 762 after being taken prisoner by the Arabs in 751 and sent to Damascus, are no longer extant (we know of its existence only because it is quoted in a contemporary Chinese work).

The tales that follow start in AD 730 and continue to the last years of the tenth century, the end of the first millennium. This is not an arbitrary choice. As pointed out by Christopher Beckwith, the author of a seminal work on early Tibetan history:

> The middle of the eighth century . . . saw fundamental changes, usually signalled by successful political revolts, in every Eurasian empire. Most famous among them are the Carolingian, Abbasid, Uighur Turkic and anti-Tang [Chinese] rebellions, each of which is rightly considered to have been a major watershed in their respective national histories. Significantly, all seem to have been intimately connected with central Eurasia.

The rebellions, which all took place between 742 and 755, were followed by a phenomenal growth in both commerce and culture that provided the basis for great cosmopolitan cities. It is the lives of the people in this burgeoning period that I discuss in these tales, although they offer only a sample of the diversity of the Silk Road; so while, for example, I have included a Manichean and several Buddhists, there are no Nestorians, Jews or Muslims among the characters. The choice was dictated by the evidence available and by the limits of my own knowledge.

The tales come to a close at the end of the tenth century because it was then that the focus of attention shifted to the maritime trade route. For many centuries, Indian and Indo-Malayan merchant ships had been travelling from ports along India's east coast to Guangzhou (Canton) in south China. From the second century BC Greek and then Roman caravans from Petra set sail from Red Sea ports for India, forming what was later called the Spice Route. Later, the Arabs and Persians continued this trade, sailing from the mouth of the Tigris and down the Persian Gulf. By the eighth and ninth centuries, southern China had been extensively colonized and the sea ports were thriving, cosmopolitan cities with considerable populations of foreigners. The merchant ships were large vessels with both sails and oars, which already used the compass as the guide to navigation. (The trade between China and Arabia, via India, was still thriving in the late fifteenth century, when the Europeans joined in. By this time China had also sent an expedition as far as the east coast of Africa and her ships were far larger than the European vessels. But this is to move beyond the scope of these tales.)

To understand the events of the mid-eighth century, when these tales start and when the overland Silk Road was dominant, it is necessary to sketch something of the historical background. What follows is, of necessity, a simplification: the history of Central Asia over this period is characterized by a complex succession of power struggles whose details cannot all be rehearsed here.

Before the start of written sources we know of Central Asia largely through the nomad warriors – Hittites, Greeks, Scythians, Slavs,

Germans and Celts – who came to control much of Europe and Asia from the third millennium BC, after they had domesticated the horse and invented the chariot. Having learnt to ride, they continued to dominate in war and, by the start of the first millennium BC, they were able to control the horse with the lower body, leaving the arms free for wielding weapons. Our earliest written sources for Central Asian history start at this time. The Greek historian Herodotus wrote of the Central Asian Scythians in the fifth century BC, and Alexander the Great marched beyond Samarkand and down the Indus river valley to India a century later, but much of this early history still remains speculative. What is certain is that there were already established trade routes and large urban settlements in Central Asia, and agriculture, mining, manufacturing, metallurgy and commerce were well developed. For example, Chinese silk dating from 1500 BC has been found in Bactria (present-day Afghanistan), and the Scythians worked gold mined in the Altai mountains. We also know that there were great movements of peoples across Central Asia and from Central Asia into Europe. The Aryans had moved into India by 1500 BC, and even further east – possibly into the Tarim basin – within the next 500 years. The movements continued into the first millennium AD, with the Huns (under Attila) arriving in Europe in the fifth century AD, the Turks moving into Anatolia – present-day Turkey – by AD 1000, and, of course, the Mongols pushing west into Europe in the thirteenth and fourteenth centuries.

What is not always certain is whether these peoples originated in the east or the west, and who their descendants were, though these questions are not necessarily insoluble. There are rich archaeological remains which, if systematically excavated, might yield many answers. During the Soviet occupation of western Central Asia, much work was done, but many of the remains now lie in areas of conflict – particularly in north-west Pakistan and Afghanistan – and others remain unexamined owing to lack of resources.

From the end of the third century BC, with the founding of the Chinese empire and its subsequent territorial expansion, we find more systematic written accounts and no longer need to rely so heavily on archaeology. By this time, apart from China, newly united under the Han dynasty, and the empire of a people called the Xiongnu in the Ordos region north west of China, there were a number of other Silk Road powers. Several Indo-Greek kingdoms stretched down from the Oxus river valley into northern India – the legacy of Alexander the Great. The Indian Mauryan dynasty ruled south of the Hindu Kush, its lands including the Punjab and Takṣaśilā (in present-day Pakistan, just west of Islamabad). Parthians ruled what is now Iran, and the Yuezhi – possibly Scythians – dominated the Gansu corridor. In addition, there were many independent kingdoms both in the Tarim basin and on the Tibetan plateau to the south.

But this situation was to change dramatically over the next few centuries. Just as the agents of the 'Great Game' in the nineteenth century ushered in a period of wider cultural interest in Central Asia, so a Chinese envoy of the second century BC, Zhang Qian, kindled his government's interest in Central Asia's riches. In that century the Xiongnu migrated south and east, displacing a people known as the Yuezhi and forming a powerful empire that was maintained by their fast-riding cavalry and which was recognized by the Han dynasty in China. (In response to the Xiongnu's equestrian might, the Chinese adopted the tunic and trousers for battle dress in place of their long robes, and also developed cavalry forces.) In 138 BC Zhang Qian was sent by the Chinese emperor Wudi ('the Martial Emperor') to elicit the support of the Yuezhi in China's battle against the Xiongnu. The mission was unsuccessful, but Zhang Qian returned with vital information about the 'Western Regions', as Central Asia came to be called in China, including details of thirty-six walled cities, their riches and their trade. As a result the existing trade routes were developed further and regular diplomatic contacts began.

The problem with Central Asian history after this period lies not in the paucity of sources, but rather in the fact that most were written by historians of the surrounding empires and thus present an external view. To rely on them is rather like examining the life of the Atlantic Ocean by studying the ecology of Europe and America. To take the analogy further: if Central Asia is viewed as a great sea, then it is one containing numerous currents in complex interaction. The seawaters constantly erode the surrounding lands, making geographical changes on the fringes. Some of these changes have repercussions deeper inland, especially when floods bring in new material – cultures, religions and ideas – which wash away the old. At other times, the currents carry material over vast distances from one land to another and cause long-term changes to these places, just as the warm current of the Gulf Stream gives Britain its temperate climate.

The first Chinese history, compiled by Sima Qian and his father and completed in about 90 BC, tells the story from the Chinese point of view. The Chinese are represented as civilized, and their neighbours – always described as tributary states – as barbaric. The reality is that, starting with the Xiongnu, China had to contend with neighbours who were often militarily superior and sometimes, as in the case of Tibet, also culturally sophisticated. The terms of a peace treaty of 198 BC between the Xiongnu and the Chinese had, for example, stipulated that the Han emperor would give his daughter in marriage to the Xiongnu ruler and that he would also send him annual gifts, including gold and silk. Clearly the balance of military power lay with the Xiongnu, yet the Chinese histories present them as little more than vassals. Nevertheless, from this time on there was regular trade between the two powers. The Yuezhi meanwhile moved further west to Bactria, where Zhang Qian found them in 138 BC (he had been held captive by the Xiongnu for the previous ten years, forced to marry, and had even fathered a son). Their migration in turn displaced many of the Indo-Greek kings ruling north of the Hindu Kush, although it was another century before those south of the mountains lost their power. The Indo-Greek and Mauryan rulers of the kingdoms to the west of Kashmir, in present-day Pakistan and Afghanistan, were similarly displaced by Śākyas (Scythians), who came down through the Gilgit and Swat valleys (see 'The Monk's Tale') and by the Hindu Sunga dynasty.

In 121 BC, a Xiongnu noble defected to the Chinese Han dynasty, and the Chinese thereafter gained control of the Gansu corridor. After this, the Chinese moved into the kingdoms to the west in the Tarim basin, and even extended their campaigns as far as Ferghana, beyond the Pamirs; but the Xiongnu remained powerful in the region of present-day Mongolia until internecine strife led them to split into two factions in 48 BC. The southern faction moved to the Ordos region under the sovereignty of the Han court; the northern faction was finally defeated by an alliance of Chinese, southern Xiongnu and other peoples, in AD 93. One of the members of the victorious alliance, the Xianbi peoples, took control of present-day Mongolia. Some of the Xiongnu escaped and marched westward. Their descendants were later to reach Afghanistan, India and the Roman empire. The Yuezhi in Bactria were displaced again in the beginning of the first century AD by the Kushans, one of their vassal peoples, who then extended their power south across the Hindu Kush mountains into the Punjab and east as far as Kashmir.

By the end of the second century AD, therefore, Central Asia looked very different. The Xiongnu empire had disappeared, replaced by that of the Xianbi, which was to become just as formidable. The Chinese empire was on the verge of collapse and would not be united under one leader again until 589. The Indo-Greeks had all but disappeared, replaced by the Kushans, who were also on the verge of collapse. The Tarim basin and Tibet remained fragmented.

The next five hundred years saw major cultural and political changes among the empires of the Silk Road. Further west in Iran, the Parthian kingdom was replaced by the Sassanians, who also came to dominate the Kushan kingdoms. The Sassanian rulers were Zoroastrians, but during this period Nestorian Christianity, Judaism and Manicheism, as well as Zoroastrianism, all spread eastwards from Iran, reaching as far as China. At the same time, Hinduism, and Buddhism, in both its Hīnayāna and Mahāyāna forms, flourished in the newly established Gupta state in northern India. Buddhism had already reached China, but many more monks now travelled between India and China. Independent oasis states, supported by agriculture and livestock breeding, flourished as a result of the burgeoning trade, among them Sogdiana and Bactria, west of the Pamirs, as well as Tarim basin city-states such as Khotan and Kucha, east of the Pamirs. Sogdian merchants were found all along the Silk Road and in China. North China was now ruled by the Xianbi, who had moved south and founded several kingdoms after the collapse of the Chinese Han dynasty. One of their tribes, the Aza, had moved to the region around Koko-nor, in northern Tibet. Several other tribes also took advantage of the power vacuum that followed the end of the Han dynasty to move into the area, among them the Turks who, from the mid-sixth century, formed an empire in modern-day Mongolia.

At the end of the sixth and the beginning of the seventh centuries changes came about which bring us to the period of the tales that follow. By this time, kings from the Yarlung valley in southern Tibet had succeeded in uniting the previously independent tribes of most of the Tibetan plateau, and had formed the first Tibetan empire, although they were still at war with the Aza tribes around Koko-nor. In 608 they started diplomatic contacts with China, newly reunited under the Sui dynasty. The Tang dynasty succeeded the Sui in 618 and reigned until 907. A confederation of Turkic tribes ruled the area of Mongolia. In Arabia a new religion was founded by Muhammad, and the Arabian Umayyad Caliphate, ruling from Damascus, began their territorial advance eastwards. They reached Afghanistan in the middle of the seventh century and the Oxus river by the 680s, conquering Sogdiana beyond the river in the following century. In the seventh century the Karkota dynasty seized Kashmir and extended their territory west beyond Takṣaśilā. In the Tarim basin, though China established protectorates, the semi-autonomous city-states continued to be fought over by Tibetans, Arabs and other peoples such as the Turghiz.

In 730, the Silk Road was pressed by four empires and their attendant armies. The Arab Caliphate was pushing at the western boundaries of Transoxania. From the south the Tibetan empire sought control of the towns in the Tarim basin, the Ordos and Gobi steppe lands, and the kingdoms of the Pamirs that straddled the routes to Kashmir. Successive Turkic kingdoms held the north, the area now known as Mongolia, with their capitals west of present-day Ulan Bator. And China, in the east, struggled to assert control of what it euphemistically called its 'western garrisons'.

The tales tell of individuals who lived at different times during the next two hundred and fifty years. The merchant, a resident of

Samarkand called Nanaivandak, and Seg Lhaton, a Tibetan soldier, lived at the start of this period when the Tibetan and Chinese empires were at their most extensive. In 715 the armies of these two super-powers clashed in the Ferghana valley, in Transoxania, with the army of another great empire coming from the west, the Arabs, and Arab raiders reached as far as Kashgar in the Tarim basin before being pushed back west of the Pamirs by the Chinese. At a subsequent battle between the Chinese and the Arabs in 751 at the Talas river (in northern Transoxania) the Arabs were victorious. This was also a time when both the Tibetan and Chinese empires suffered internal political upheavals which greatly curtailed their expansionist plans for the rest of the period. Early in 755 the Tibetan emperor was murdered during a revolt by his ministers and there followed serious internal disturbance. In December 755, a general of the Chinese army, Rokhshan, led a rebellion against the Tang dynasty which lasted for nearly a decade. His forces occupied both the main and the subsidiary capitals of China and forced the reigning emperor to abdicate. Rokhshan was finally defeated with the help of a Uighur army, part of whose story is told in 'The Horseman's Tale' by Kumtugh, himself a Uighur.

Over the decade of the rebellion the Chinese had had to recall their forces from the western garrisons, and in their absence Tibetans seized control of most of the Silk Road towns. The Gansu corridor was effectively closed to Chinese trade, although other routes still existed between Tibet and the west. The Tibetans retained their control until the middle of the ninth century, during which time travellers were forced to journey north of the Yellow river into Uighur territory, where the Uighurs taxed them heavily.

At the start of this story the Uighurs were just one of many tribes subject to the Western Turkic empire who occupied what is now Mongolia. But their fortunes were to rise as those of the Chinese declined. They succeeded in deposing the Western Turkic kaghan and set up an empire of their own that lasted nearly a century, during which time they changed from being a nomadic to a largely agricultural people and adopted Manicheism as their state religion. They, too, had expansionist aims: a planned invasion of China in the late eighth century was prevented only by an internal coup. On their north-west frontier they fought to protect themselves against the nomadic Kirghiz tribes, and likewise on their south-west borders against the Turghiz. Tibet, China and the Uighurs all frequently clashed on their common boundaries, most especially along the Gansu corridor and the land bordering the Yellow river as it flowed north from Tibet into the Ordos. In 'The Princess's Tale' Taihe is sent as a bride to the Uighur capital during the final decades of Uighur domination of the Mongolian steppes.

In the west the armies of the fourth great power, the Arab Umayyad Caliphate, were encroaching beyond the Oxus into Sogdiana and Ferghana, partly assisted by money borrowed from Sogdian merchants in Merv. They, too, underwent political upheavals which resulted in a coup in 750 that marked the beginning of the Abbasid Caliphate. The Arab capital was moved east from Damascus, first to Kufa then to Baghdad. As the Arab armies consolidated their gains in Transoxania, they encountered the Turghiz, Tibetan and Chinese armies. The battle at the Talas river in 751 did not radically alter the boundaries between the empires, but it was important in defining the limits of their respective powers. All were fighting over territory that lay thousands of miles from their capitals across difficult and, in places, mainly uninhabitable territory. All relied heavily on locally raised troops: the same troops fought for different sides at different times, and even changed sides in mid-battle on occasion – such an event is credited with giving the Arabs their victory at the Talas river.

In the second half of the period, from the middle of the ninth century onwards, the Uighur empire fell and the Uighurs were driven out of the Mongolian steppes south-east into China and south to the cities of the Silk Road. Islam joined Manicheism as one of their main religions and Turkic–Islamic culture gradually became dominant in these city-states. The period also saw nominal political control of most of the Silk Road towns shift once again from Tibet to China, and the Silk Road reopened. In Tibet a Buddhist hermit assassinated the anti-Buddhist emperor, plunging the country into protracted civil war.

By this time Tibet had become a Buddhist state, an earlier emperor having decided to promote the Indian Tantric form of Buddhism after a debate between an Indian and a Chinese monk. Thereafter, the main cultural influence in Tibet was Indian rather than Chinese, but it was several centuries before Buddhism became widespread among all classes. Skirmishes continued on Tibet's eastern borders with China, but both empires had by now relinquished control of the Pamir kingdoms to the south-west and had largely abandoned expansionist aims in the west, leaving the Arabs a free hand.

In China the Tang dynasty continued to experience internal unrest. There was a major rebellion in the 880s (witnessed by Lariskha, a musician and courtesan from Kucha whose story is told in 'The Courtesan's Tale'), but the dynasty did not finally collapse until 907. There then followed a period of disunity until 960, when the Song dynasty took power. In the interval other regional powers had emerged and made territorial gains, most notably the Khitans, the Tanguts and the Mongolians from the north-east. These peoples were to have a profound influence in the following centuries but are not part of this story. China, which had already been greatly influenced by culture from the west, now turned inwards and sought to reassert its native Confucianism, though over the next thousand years China's imperial rulers were to include two further foreign dynasties. Meanwhile, the Silk Road towns remained nominally under Chinese control and life continued as normal, as related in the final four tales of the book by residents of Dunhuang – a nun, a widow, an official and an artist.

This fascinating period in Central Asian history is sometimes obscured by the current character of the Silk Road. Today the area of the Tarim basin is occupied by Turkic Uighurs and Chinese colonists. Its religion is Islam. In the period covered by this book, however, many of its towns were Indo-European in character and Buddhist in religion. Territory was sought and won not only by armies consisting of hundreds of thousands of armour-clad horsemen, but also by alliances, including marriage alliances, and gifts of titles and goods. The towns along the route were isolated and vulnerable, despite the garrisons of various armies, and even when under the nominal control of one power or another, they acted as semi-autonomous city-states. They were also cosmopolitan. Many languages were heard and many different peoples seen in their market places – Africans, Semites, Turks, Indians, Chinese, Tibetans and Mongolians. And these people practised a variety of religions: Manicheism, Judaism, Zoroastrianism, Islam, Nestorian Christianity, shamanism and, above all, Buddhism.

Buddhism's predominance during this period is reflected in the tales of Chudda, a monk from Kashmir, and Miaofu, abbess of a nunnery in Dunhuang. 'The Widow's Tale' also concerns a Buddhist believer. The founder of Buddhism, the historical Buddha, Gautama, was a prince born to a Śākya – or Scythian – tribe on the border of present-day Nepal and India, south-west of Katmandu, in the sixth century BC (hence his later name, Śākyamuni – Sage among the Śākyas). At the age of twenty-nine, having lived a sheltered life of luxury and pleasure, he first encountered scenes of suffering, old age, disease and death. Although he was married and his wife had given birth to their first son that same evening he decided to leave the palace immediately, determined to seek enlightenment ('bodhi'). At first he sought out Indian philosophy masters, but after only a year he rejected their extreme asceticism and turned to a life of contemplation and meditation. Six years later, though beset by a host of temptations sent by Māra, the god of evil, he achieved enlightenment while meditating under the Bo tree (*Ficus religiosa*).

Śākyamuni's enlightenment consisted of the realization of the Four Noble Truths: life is suffering; suffering is caused by desire; the end of desire means the end of suffering; and the end of desire is achieved by following the Noble Eightfold Path: right view, thinking, livelihood, speech, conduct, effort, mindfulness and meditation. Each sentient creature in the world of suffering – 'saṃsāra' – suffers according to the karmic debt from its past lives. If a man is evil in one life, then his debt increases. If he commits more bad deeds than good, he may not have sufficient merit to achieve rebirth as a human, and on dying he will be born again as an animal or a lower form of life. If, on the other hand, his good deeds outweigh his bad, his debt from past lives is decreased. When the debt is finally paid he is ready for enlightenment or 'nirvāṇa'. Monks who have reached a level of understanding comparable to that of Buddha himself are called 'arhats' – 'worthy' or 'perfected beings', and will be released from the cycle of rebirth at their death, but in their final lifetime they retain traces of their former unenlightened selves and also differ from Buddha in having attained their enlightenment through instruction, rather than by their own insight. Buddha further taught that individual souls are not immortal, as held by Hinduism, and that when a person dies only the karmic debt remains.

Buddha spent his life lecturing on these themes and, after his death at the age of eighty, councils were held at which his disciples met to discuss doctrinal issues, and his lectures were passed down orally from generation to generation. Tradition holds that at the Third Council, during the reign of the Mauryan king Aśoka, they were transcribed to form the Buddhist canon. Aśoka sent Buddhist missionaries from his kingdom in north-west India as far afield as Sri Lanka, Syria, Egypt, Crete and possibly China, and although his death in 232 BC signalled the collapse of the Mauryan dynasty, the four centuries of stability and tolerance that characterized the succeeding Kushan empire provided the ideal circumstances for trade and, with it, the dissemination of Buddhism.

By this time there were many sects among the adherents of Buddhism, and followers of one such sect called it 'Mahāyāna' ('Greater Vehicle'), to be distinguished from 'Hīnayāna' ('Lesser Vehicle') or Theravada Buddhism by its promise of complete enlightenment – buddhahood – for all. It became the prominent form of Buddhism in much of north India, Central Asia and China, while the Theravada tradition is represented by Sri Lankan Buddhism. This difference between Mahāyāna and Theravada is exemplified by the bodhisattva ('enlightened being') and the arhat, the former unselfishly seeking to help others to attain enlightenment, the latter only concerned with their own liberation. Mahāyāna also holds that Śākyamuni is only one of many manifestations of Buddha, and its iconography therefore contains many different buddhas. Tantric Buddhism, which became dominant in Tibet, is a sect of Mahāyāna in which ritual and meditation are held to be paramount in attaining enlightenment. During the same period, several other religions – Judaism, Zoroastrianism, Manicheism and Nestorian Christianity – were also carried by missionaries along the Silk Road to Samarkand and China.

A short-lived persecution of Jews under the Sassanian empire in the mid-fifth century led some Jews to migrate east and by the sixth century there were Jewish communities in India and Samarkand. In the eighth and ninth centuries Judaism spread further, reaching China and gaining converts among the Turkic Khazars who lived north of the Caspian Sea. Zoroastrianism was the religion of the Sassanians and it, too, had gained converts in Samarkand by the sixth century; from whence it was carried into China by merchants and missionaries, a Zoroastrian temple being built in Chang'an in the early seventh century.

Zoroaster, or Zarathustra, lived in eastern Iran in the sixth century BC and there preached a reformed version of the older Iranian Magian religion. Zoroastrianism shared many ideas with Judaism, which was developing at the same time, namely a belief in a messiah, a resurrection, a last judgement and a heavenly paradise, and was later to influence Christianity. The messiah in Zoro-astrianism is the god Ahura Mazda, the incarnation of light, life and truth. The incarnation of darkness, death and evil, Angra Mainyu, has always existed alongside him and the two are engaged in a con-stant struggle. Although man was created by Ahura Mazda, he was given free will and so can choose either good or evil: Zoroastrianism urges that man must resist evil in his thoughts, words and deeds, but that a saviour will come to the world and that good will triumph over evil. The symbol of Ahura Mazda is the eternal fire, and the Sassanians worshipped at fire altars situated throughout their empire, in which the flame was never allowed to die.

In the third century AD during the reign of the Sassanian emperor Shapur I, Zoroastrianism was challenged by a prophet from Babylon called Mani, who had received a divine revelation showing that there are two principles, good and evil, manifested in Light and Dark particles. All things including the Earth itself, contain various amounts of Light particles trapped within Dark matter, except for the Sun and Moon which were created from undefiled Light. To prevent Light achieving its liberation, man was created by the Prince of Darkness from the copulation of devils, in order to perpetuate the confinement of Light (the soul) in Dark (the body) through his lust and procreation. When the liberation of Light is almost complete the Earth will degenerate into a war made inevitable by the sin and strife of the matter left behind. The

Prince of Darkness and his followers will then be sealed in a great pit by a stone, and the universe will, as in Former Time, be divided into separate realms of Light and Dark.

The Manichean faith taught abstinence from blasphemy, meat, alcohol, and, as in Buddhism, the clergy were not allowed to till the soil, harvest any plant, or kill any animal. While Buddhist concern with life stopped at the animal kingdom, so that the most rigorous monks would sweep the ground in front of them as they walked in order to avoid stepping on an insect and thereby inadvertently taking a life, Manicheans were not even supposed to walk on ground which had been planted in case they harmed a plant and the Light contained within: in fact, plants contained more Light than animals and so their survival was more important. Walking itself harmed the Light in the ground and the strictest adherents therefore tried to avoid this as well. Mani realized that only a few would be able to observe all these strictures and so he divided believers into two classes, the Elect and the Hearers – the clergy and the lay community. The Elect, because of their adherence to the rules, were the earthly agents for the release of captive Light, refining the Light particles in the fruit and vegetables they ate and releasing them through the act of belching. (Melons and cucumbers, in particular, were thought to contain very high concentrations of Light.) The Hearers were urged to engage in fasting, prayer and alms-giving to support the Elect. They were allowed to own property and marry, although procreation was not encouraged, and they could also eat meat, although they were not permitted to kill the animals themselves. But while at death the souls of the Elect returned directly to the Kingdom of Light, those of the hearers remained on earth and only reached the Kingdom of Light through a series of reincarnations leading to a final reincarnation in the body of an Elect.

Manicheism was first brought to Sogdiana in Mani's lifetime by Mar Ammo, the 'Disciple of the East'. Legend had it that on encountering the spirit who guarded the Sogdian frontier, Mar Ammo said he had come to teach abstinence from wine, flesh and women. The spirit replied that there were many such men in her lands, probably referring to the Buddhist community in Sogdiana. Mani then appeared to Mar Ammo in a vision and instructed him to read to the spirit from one of his books. When Mar Ammo did so the spirit realized that he was a 'bringer of the true faith' rather than simply a man of religion, and she let him pass.

Mani himself lost favour with the Sassanians after the death of Shapur I and was imprisoned and tortured to death. Thereafter his followers were persecuted and fled east, soon forming a strong community in Sogdiana which broke ties with the mother church in Babylonia. The Sogdian Manicheans considered Mar Ammo the founder of their sect and called themselves 'The Pure Ones'. By the eighth century the centre of this eastern diocese was Kocho, on the northern Silk Road, and there were Manichean monasteries all the way from Samarkand to Chang'an. The schism with the mother church was healed in the eighth century, and the votaries of the eastern diocese recognized the jurisdiction of Mihr, head of the Babylonian community. Nanaivandak, the merchant in the first tale, is a follower of Mani.

Christianity also spread eastwards in the centuries following Christ and by the third century there was a Christian community in the city of Merv, south-west of Samarkand. In the fifth century a group called the Duophysites split from the main Christian church over their belief that Christ had both a human and a divine nature. One of the apologists of this view was called Nestorius, hence the name, Nestorianism, later given to this belief. The Nestorians fled east to escape persecution by the dominant Monophysites (who held that Christ had a single, divine nature), although Iranian Christians confirmed Nestorianism as the dominant sect in the late fifth century. By the seventh century Nestorianism had gained converts among the Turkic tribes then ruling Bactria and by the early eighth century it had reached China.

Thus by the time these tales begin in 730, there were communities of all these religions in the great cities of Samarkand and Chang'an, and in the towns in between. Islam had also spread east and older native religions still persisted, Bon among the Tibetan nobility, shamanism among Tibetan and Turkic tribal peoples, and Hinduism among groups resident to the north-west of India as far as Bactria.

★

Religion was not alone in contributing to the diversity of the Silk Road. Trade and the expansionist plans of the surrounding empires, who sent diplomats, officials and soldiers to carve out territory, also played their part. In the eighth century, Samarkand and Chang'an were enormous cities, far larger than any in Europe at the time, and their size and wealth derived from trade along the Silk Road. Indeed, in terms of both commerce and culture the Silk Road was then the centre of the world.

Trade routes have existed in Central Asia as long as there have been people to buy and sell. The discovery in Bactria of Chinese silk dating from 1500 BC, for example, has already been noted, and when Zhang Qian went on his mission to the Yuezhi in the second century BC he found Chinese bamboo, brought through Tibet and India. But trade burgeoned after diplomatic links were established, especially as the Romans started to develop a taste for silk and other Eastern luxuries. In the first century BC silk was so rare in Rome that even the wealthiest citizens could only afford small strips which they sewed in a prominent position on to their cotton, linen or wool togas, but stocks started to increase in the first century AD as the sea route between China and the west was developed, an expansion that whetted the Romans' appetite for oriental luxury items, as lamented by Pliny the Elder in his *Natural History*:

> . . . we have come now to see . . . journeys made to Seres [China] to obtain cloth, the abysses of the Red Sea explored for pearls, and the depths of the earth scoured for emeralds. They have even taken up the notion of piercing the ears as if it were too small a matter to wear those gems in necklaces and tiaras unless holes were also made in the body into which to insert them . . . at the lowest computation, India and Seres and the [Arabian] Peninsula together drain our empire of one hundred million *sesterces* every year. That is the price that our luxuries and our womankind cost us.

In AD 14 the Roman senate forbade the wearing of silk by men, but the trade continued undiminished. At this time Rome paid in gold and silver for silk from China and gems from Central Asia, but soon goods started to travel in both directions, especially after the Kushan dynasty came to power in Central Asia and ensured stability along the overland route. At this time a Chinese envoy was sent to western Central Asia. Although probably prevented from reaching Rome by Parthian guile (the Parthians wished to keep their lucrative position as middlemen and it was therefore in their interests to deceive both sides as to the extent and nature of the territory between China and Rome), he discovered several desirable commodities which China then started to buy, among them glass and asbestos. Interestingly, China developed glass-making skills in the fifth century, at about the same time as the west learned the secrets of silk production, but even after the establishment of local industries, both continued to import these products. The technique of casting iron, developed in China by Roman times, was also unknown in the west, and therefore ironware formed part of China's early export trade. Central Asia was the main source of jade and certain gems, such as lapis lazuli, while India provided spices, cottons and ivory to both China and the west. Numerous other goods were traded locally along the Silk Road. Astrakhan fur was bought in Dzungaria and sold in Liangzhou, a town in the Gansu corridor. Merchants bought salt from the Tibetan plateau, and gold from the Altai mountains in southern Mongolia was sold in Chach (present-day Tashkent) and Samarkand to artisans skilled in fashioning beaten gold ornaments.

In the first millennium AD Sogdians became the recognized merchants of the eastern Silk Road, and Sogdian cities, such as Samarkand, Balkh and Chach, contained thousands of warehouses stockpiled with goods from both east and west. Many of the merchants did not travel themselves but instead sent agents along sections of the Silk Road, from one major market town to another. However, there were also those, like Nanaivandak, who made the complete journey from Samarkand to Chang'an.

This journey was a considerable undertaking, not solely in terms of the distance (over 3,000 miles), but also because of the geographical obstacles along the way. From Samarkand, the easternmost edge of the Eurasian plains, there were several roads east, but all had to negotiate the great mountain ranges which divided Transoxania from the Tarim basin. One route traversed the foothills of the Pamirs to the Jaxartes river (the Syr Darya). Following the river upstream the road then passed through a fertile, oval-shaped valley – breeding-ground to horses prized along the Silk Road who were fed on the valley's waist-high alfalfa. The Ferghanan valley, source of the Jaxartes river, lies between two great mountain ranges, the Tianshan to the north-east and the Pamirs to the south-east. At the valley's head the road crossed the Terek Davan pass, where these two ranges join, and then dropped down into the city of Kashgar in the Tarim basin. The glacier and detritus-filled valley floors of the Pamirs lie at between 12,000 and 14,000 feet above sea level. Above them tower boulder-strewn peaks of over 20,000 feet. Although the valleys are green in summer, during the rest of the year, when not covered with snow, they present an expanse of sand, clay and stones, virtually unrelieved by trees or cultivation. The Tianshan are almost as formidable, with several peaks over 18,000 feet. Extending from Chach to Hami they mark the dividing line between the central and northern tracts of Central Asia.

Once past the natural barrier of the Pamirs and the Tianshan, the traveller was confronted with the Tarim basin, which, as its name suggests, is a great pear-shaped depression extending for about 900 miles from Kashgar in the west to Lop-nor in the east, and over 300 miles from the Tarim river in the north to the gravel glacis of the Kunlun mountains in the south. The greater part of the basin is occupied by the Taklamakan desert – not, in fact, a desert of sand but of fine, disintegrated particles of rock. Although there is little precipitation, the alluvial loess is very fertile and so at the desert's margins, where water flows from the mountains, the use of irrigation makes agriculture possible: the oasis towns are still famous for their fruit. On the borders of the desert there are areas of vegetation – tamarisk, wild poplar and reeds – but in the centre the soil is blown by the wind to form dunes a thousand feet or more high.

From Kashgar, the westernmost point of the Tarim basin, the Silk Road divided to skirt the desert either to the south or to the north. For 300 miles along the southern route the ridge of the Kunlun mountains rises to a height of 20,000 feet and therefore presents a practically impenetrable barrier to the south. The few streams which reach the Tarim basin flow through deep-cut, inaccessible gorges, and the outer slopes of the Kunlun are utterly barren and forbidding. The only major oasis along this route is Khotan which lies on the sole water course to cross the desert from the south, and then only in summer. The Kunlun continue for another 400 miles, bearing north-east towards Lop-nor where they become lower and merge into the Nanshan. Throughout their course a barren glacis of gravel extends for as much as 70 miles beyond their northern slopes. The northern route from Kashgar passes through more fertile land and the major oases of Aksu and Kucha, lying at 3,000 to 4,500 feet above sea level. The route is fringed to the north by the Tianshan but along this stretch there are several passes that give access to Issuk-kul and the Mongolian steppes.

At the eastern end of the Tarim are more basins, starting with the Lop, a series of marshes which disappear into the great salt-encrusted, dried-up inland sea, Lop-nor. Continuing eastward from the Lop basin is another river basin, extending for over 200 miles between the eastern continuations of the Kunlun to the south and the Tianshan to the north. This is the site of the town of Dunhuang, fed by the Dang river, and this is where the northern and southern routes rejoined, the northern route having veered south-east from the last major town of Hami to cross a particularly desolate region before reaching the safety of Dunhuang. A series of smaller basins continuing to the east of Dunhuang form what is now called the Gansu corridor; low, uniform desert hills lie to their north, and north of them again is a huge desert area, a vast, stony, waterless tract, devoid of life and swept by icy north-easterlies even in the summer. This is part of the Gobi. The floor of this desert consists of sand and tamarisk only where it joins the Taklamakan on its south-western edge: the rest is rock covered with a thin layer of sand and gravel, supporting only short, wiry grass, camel sage and low, thorny bushes. No young trees are found here, only the long-dead remains of elms in the few dessicated river beds, but when it rains the whole surface becomes tinged with green. In winter the temperature drops to minus 50°F.

Routes also led out of Samarkand to the north-east and south. The north-eastern route crossed a belt of desert known as the Red

Sandy Wastes, although it actually consists of patches of desert with small ranges of mountains, stretches of grassy steppe and further areas of fertile soil which are covered with vegetation in spring. After crossing the Jaxartes, the route continued north-east to the sizeable walled city of Chach and then followed valleys in the northern Tianshan to Issuk-kul, a brackish lake between the Tianshan and the Altai. This northernmost branch of the Silk Road continued north of the Tianshan, passing Beshbaliq (near present-day Urumqi in China) and thence across the low eastern foothills of the mountains of Hami, where it rejoined the northern Tarim basin route. It was also possible to continue north-east from Beshbaliq, across the Dzungarian pastures and the Mongolian steppes to the Orkhon river, the site of several Turkic capitals during this period. Dzungaria was a natural basin, protected by mountains used by the Turks for grazing their vast herds of live-stock — horses, cattle, yaks, sheep, goats and camels — and for mounting attacks on the Silk Road towns. And there was a south-eastern route that connected the Turkic capitals with China and a south-western one that led back to Issuk-kul across the steppes. This is a region with rolling topography, few water courses and an almost complete absence of trees, where temperatures fall to below freezing in the winter and rise to over 70°F at the height of the summer.

The route south from Samarkand led along a low plain between the western fringes of the Pamirs and the Oxus to Balkh in the land of Bactria. From here the traveller could go east, crossing the Pamirs at the headwaters of the Kashgar river and dropping into the Tarim basin or going south-east into the north Indian states. This latter route crossed the Hindu Kush, entirely barren and uninhabited mountains with few points of access, whose main peaks, always snow-covered, stand at over 18,000 feet and whose average height is over 15,000 feet.

There were also routes north and south that crossed the Samarkand–Chang'an Silk Road at several points. The roads south — many of them old salt-trading routes — led across the eastern Kunlun and Nanshan passes to the Tibetan plateau, a huge stretch of upland plains generally lying more than 12,000 feet above sea level and surrounded by walls of mountains rising to even greater heights. From here it was a thousand miles south via Koko-nor to Lhasa, where more routes led in all directions – east to south China; south and south-west into India; west into Kashmir; and north to other points on the east–west road. West of Koko-nor lies the Tsaidam, another natural basin which, like Dzungaria, provided ideal conditions for grazing large herds of livestock and mounting armed raids across the Kunlun on the Silk Road towns.

These stories start with Nanaivandak, a Sogdian merchant from Samarkand and an experienced traveller. He has braved the Silk Road many times in his twenty years as a trader but, as he bargains with buyers in Chang'an's markets and toys with dancing girls in a city restaurant, he little realizes that this will be his last visit to China. It is the 750s and control of the Silk Road is about to change hands.

The Merchant's Tale

Nanaivandak, 730–751

> The country of Samarkand is about 500 miles in
> circumference and broader from east to west than from north
> to south. The capital is six miles or so in circumference,
> completely enclosed by rugged land and very populous. The
> precious merchandise of many foreign countries is stored
> here. The soil is rich and productive and yields abundant
> harvests. The forest trees afford a thick vegetation and
> flowers and fruit are plentiful. *Shen* horses are bred here. The
> inhabitants' skill in the arts and trades exceeds that of other
> countries. The climate is agreeable and temperate and the
> people brave and energetic.
>
> Xuanzang, *Buddhist Records of the Western World*, AD 646

IT WAS THE year 751 in the Western calendar, 134 by Islamic reck-
oning, the second year of the reign of al-Saffah, the first of the
Arabic Abbasid caliphs, and the ninth in the Tianbao (Heavenly
Riches) reign period of the Tang dynasty emperor Xuanzong in
China. The merchant Nanaivandak was from Samarkand, a city-
state formerly independent but now, since the advance of the
Arab-led armies east of the Oxus river (Amu Darya), under the
rule of the Baghdad Caliphate. He had travelled for several months
along the Silk Road from the great trading city of Samarkand, over
the towering Pamirs and along the fringes of the Taklamakan
desert to Chang'an, the capital of Tang dynasty China.

Nanaivandak's family hailed from the town of Panjikent, about
forty miles east of Samarkand in the region known as Sogdiana.
The Arab armies coming from the west referred to Sogdiana as

'the land beyond the Oxus,' or Transoxiana, but it was really a continuation of the great Eurasian steppe lands. Panjikent was at the easternmost edge, tucked in the Zerafshan valley between two fingers of mountains which extruded from the great Pamir ranges to the east. Panjikent, like all Sogdiana cities, was built with thick fortified walls on a small hill. The land sloped away on the western side of the city to the Zerafshan river, and the foothills of the Pamirs could be seen across the plain. On clear days at the height of summer their snow-capped peaks were also visible in the far distance.

The area enclosed within the walls was quite small, little more than thirty acres, and only the ruler, nobles, merchants and richer tradesmen had their houses there. Before Nanaivandak's time, people lived in large, two-storey apartment blocks, although each dwelling was spacious and had its own entrance. More recently the aristocracy and merchants had started to build individual, three-storey houses. Indeed, space had become so tight, that the second and third storeys were partially built over the maze of small lanes which ran between the houses, supported by stone arches. Small workshops occupied the ground floor facing the main street and these were rented out to shopkeepers and artisans. There was no space for courtyards, gardens or parks, and few trees grew within the walls, although the valley floor was criss-crossed with irrigation canals which fed the fields and numerous gardens. The small lanes of the city were crowded and dirty with refuse, and the smell was sometimes unbearable in the summer when the temperature soared to 80°F and the air was still. After a few days the heat of the unrelenting sun would even scorch the summer grass on the plain, but then after a few days of oppressive heat a northerly wind would herald a rainstorm, and the city lanes were washed clean.

The city did not stop at the walls. Next to the main gate leading west to Samarkand there were scores of caravanserai, stopping places for itinerant merchants, which provided lodgings for the merchants and their servants, warehouse space for their goods, and a courtyard for their animals. The bazaar was held here and the area was always bustling with people and animals. Ten or more languages might be heard at any one time, as people haggled over the silks, spices and other luxuries, which dazzled the senses with

Typical Sassanian design woven on silk found at Dunhuang, eighth century

their colours and smells. Beyond the caravanserai, smaller houses sprawled down the hill and over the valley floor.

Nanaivandak wore distinctive Sogdian clothes: a Phrygian hat, conical with the top turned forward; a knee-length, belted over-jacket of deep-blue silk brocade woven with decorative roundels enclosing two deer facing each other; and narrow trousers tucked into calf-length brocade boots with leather soles. His dress and heavily bearded face distinguished him from the Chinese, Turks and Tibetans in Chang'an's Western Market, but he was not the sole representative of his community in the Chinese capital. The Sogdians were the recognized traders of the Silk Road: their language was its *lingua franca* and there had been Sogdian communities in all its sizeable towns for several centuries.

Nanaivandak profited handsomely from the sale of his cargo of wool, jade, and gems in Chang'an, despite having to pay a considerable bribe to customs officers at the Chinese frontier. During the long journey he had opened gaps in several of the large bales of wool in order to allow the desert sand to seep in, thus increasing their weight. It was a risk – an experienced buyer would spot the trick immediately – and he had therefore avoided the stalls run by his fellow countrymen. Since sellers always lied, buyers would demand to feel the wool for themselves, smelling and kneading a handful torn from the bale. He knew that, like him, some could tell immediately which sort of sheep had produced the wool, where they grazed – on steppes, in valley pastures or on high mountain passes – and even whether the pastures lay on a north- or south-facing slope.

Nanaivandak took care to offer an unopened bale for testing. The others weighed only a little more – too little to arouse suspicion – but by the time the transaction was complete he had made a larger profit than expected. The rest of his goods he sold to his agent in the capital and through him he also bought the fine silk beloved by his countrymen and by the Turks who lived on the northern borders of his homeland, to whom he would sell it on his return to Samarkand. The Chinese had retained the secret of silk production for many centuries before the west finally mastered the technique of delicately unwinding the gossamer-fine thread from cocoons produced by silkworms reared on the tender, young leaves of the white mulberry tree. By Nanaivandak's time, silk was being made in Sogdiana and exported west to Europe, but a market still persisted for the finer and more varied Chinese silks. While Nanaivandak was in Chang'an, Chinese prisoners-of-war captured after a recent clash between the Arabs and the Chinese were being escorted east to Damascus, the site of Arab silk production. There their silk-weaving skills would be exploited. Prisoners from the same battle with paper-making skills were sent to Samarkand, providing the impetus for the transformation of the Arab book, long written on parchment or papyrus.

In Chang'an, Nanaivandak also bought ornaments, jewellery and drugs to trade on his return journey. Finally he organized presents for his wife and grandchild. He had brought with him a piece of unworked lapis lazuli from Bactria which he now took to a jeweller to be fashioned into an ornament for his wife. For his young grandson he went to a tailor to have a traditional Sogdian suit made, a short jacket with narrow sleeves, a mandarin collar and front, central fastening, flared slightly from the waist. The outer silk, which he had brought with him from Sogdiana, was woven in blue, yellow, green, red and white with a pattern of paired facing ducks inside roundels, a typical Sogdian pattern, while he chose a brown Chinese damask with a large-scale floral pattern for the jacket lining and trousers. He also ordered a pair of matching boots. Then, having completed his business, he joined his agent and others for an evening of dining and entertainment: there were many Sogdian singers and dancers in the hostelries and wineshops of Chang'an. Nanaivandak had been travelling the Silk Road for twenty years and knew the city well.

They went to one of the many restaurants lining the 500-foot-wide avenue leading south from the imperial city. After some discussion about what sort of food they wanted, they chose a place renowned for its spicy noodles, mare's teat grape wine and dancers. Three girls, heavily made-up with elaborate coiffures and smelling of jasmine, leaned over the first-floor balustrade and beckoned them in. The men removed their shoes and were shown upstairs to the most expensive part of the restaurant which was divided into compartmentalized seating areas. The floor was covered with reed matting and they sat on low benches, another Central Asian import to China, at a lacquered table. Waiters appeared with silver trays bearing the delicacies of the house, and the wine was served in a Sogdian-style silver jug decorated with an elaborate pattern of a winged camel.

Mare's teat grapes were grown in Kocho and made into the finest wine. Both the wine and grapes were imported into China, the grapes packed with ice into thick, leaden containers to keep them fresh. The wine was expensive, but Nanaivandak and his fellow merchants had no trouble affording it with the profits from their trade. Drinking was an accepted part of social life in both Samarkand and Chang'an, and it was not unusual to see parties of drunken men and their attendant courtesans staggering out of the wineshops and restaurants late at night.

After they had eaten their fill they called for dancers, and two girls, sixteen or seventeen years old, appeared to the rapid beating of the musicians' drums; left hands on hips and their bodies bent slightly like lotus stems, they twirled around, keeping their left legs almost straight and their eyes firmly fixed on the men. They wore tight-sleeved blouses of fine silk and long, gauze flowing skirts, embroidered in many colours and held at their waists with broad, silver belts, and peaked hats decorated with golden bells whose jingling provided a contrast to the rhythmic, deep drum beat. The men shouted encouragement and clapped in time with the music

Sogdian silver wine jug showing a winged camel,
late seventh – early eighth century

and the girls' red-slippered feet moved more and more quickly. Suddenly the drummers stopped, the girls stood still facing Nanaivandak's table and both pulled down their blouses to reveal their small, bare breasts. After this one of the girls sat on Nanaivandak's lap and persuaded him to order more wine, which he drank while fondling her breasts. She was from Chach (present-day Tashkent) and they spoke together in Sogdian, but he was soon too drunk to remember much.

Nanaivandak was a Manichean, a follower of Mani, although he did not always strictly adhere to the prohibition on alcohol. Though the Manicheans had once formed a strong community in Sogdiana there were now few of them left in Samarkand and Panjikent. Nanaivandak had been brought up as a Zoroastrian but had been converted to Manicheism by his uncle, who had learned about the religion during his trading trips to Balkh, a thriving centre of Manicheism south of Samarkand. Apart from the Zoroastrian and Manichean communities, there were also Buddhists, Jews and Nestorian Christians in Panjikent and Samarkand but, since the Arab conquest of Sogdiana, Islam had become dominant and many of Nanaivandak's countrymen had already chosen to be converted.

Before the advent of the Abbasid Caliphate in Baghdad in 750 the Arabs had been ruled by the Umayyad Caliphate, their capital the city of Damascus. Their armies had crossed the Oxus river as early as the 680s, but it was not until the first decades of the eighth century, after a long period of internecine strife, that Arab leaders turned their attention seriously to the east. Thereafter their armies moved steadily eastwards, exploiting rivalries among the kings of the semi-independent city-states to turn their enemies into allies. They reached Samarkand in 712 and besieged the city for a month, until the residents were forced to surrender and agree to a peace treaty. Then they continued their eastward invasion, reaching Chach and Ferghana, the lands to the north-east of Samarkand, in 713 and 714.

The nomadic Arab nobles were then encouraged to settle in these lands and promote Islam. The rewards for conversion were not only spiritual: converts were exempted from the poll tax. This inducement proved so tempting that large numbers of Sogdians converted, thereby drastically reducing the tax revenue. In consequence, the exemption was withdrawn, and a new law stipulated that converts also had to be circumcised and were expected to be familiar with Islamic scriptural texts. These changes provoked anger among a population already resentful of their Arab rulers and convinced that the Umayyads protected only the interests of their own aristocratic elite. Between 720 and 722 there were several serious rebellions in Sogdiana.

Nanaivandak's father and uncle were among the rebels. With the help of their northern neighbours, the Turghiz, the Sogdians succeeded in destroying the Samarkand garrison and driving the Arabs out of the city. The defeated Arab governor, unable to regain control, was replaced by a man infamous for his complaints about the leniency with which his Arab countrymen had treated their Sogdian subjects. Determined to retake the rebel cities, the new governor advanced from the west with a large army and, realizing that they would probably not be able to hold out, the rebels retreated. Nanaivandak's uncle and his fellow rebels from Samarkand negotiated refuge in the valleys of Ferghana to the east, unaware that the Ferghanan king had already betrayed them. There they were forced to surrender to the Arab army, and most of the nobles and thousands of commoners were executed. A few nobles escaped and fled north to Chach, where they established themselves as an elite corps in the Turghiz army. Otherwise only four hundred merchants, among them Nanaivandak's uncle, survived, spared because of their great wealth which their captors hoped to exploit. Indeed, loans from Sogdian merchants to the Arabs had made earlier Transoxanian campaigns possible.

Nanaivandak's father had fought with a second band of rebels under the ruler of Panjikent, Devashtich. This group took refuge in the fortress of Mount Mug, in the mountains to the south-east of Panjikent and, in the same year, 721, the Panjikent Sogdians advanced to meet the Arab army at a nearby gorge, hoping that geographical advantage would give them victory. But they were heavily defeated and their ruler killed. Nanaivandak's father did not return from the battle.

Nanaivandak and his mother hoped that perhaps his father had survived and had joined his countrymen among the Turghiz forces to the north. The Turghiz had originally ruled a kingdom stretching from Chach along the northern fringes of the Tianshan – the Heavenly Mountains – as far as Dzungaria, the southern edge of present-day Mongolia. Already under threat from their northern and eastern neighbours when the Arab armies started to push at their southern boundaries, they were determined to repel any full-scale Arab invasion, and therefore welcomed the escaped Sogdian rebels into their ranks. Thereafter the Sogdian corps took every opportunity to seek battle with the Arab army in revenge for the earlier slaughter, and their exploits were spoken of in the market-places at Samarkand – though not within hearing of the Arabs.

On his return from battle, Nanaivandak's uncle adopted Nanaivandak, and the boy and his mother moved from their large, three-storeyed house in Panjikent to the uncle's house in

Samarkand. Merchants belonged to the second of four classes in Sogdian society, directly below the nobility and above artisans and commoners, and they could afford to build solid, flat-roofed houses of compressed clay and mud bricks, plastered with finer clay. Nanaivandak's old house in Panjikent had friezes in all the rooms depicting traditional tales: when he was small his mother and father had often told him their stories, and his favourite was that of the fight between Rustam and the demons. After the hero Rustam had chased the demons into the city and they had closed the gate to stop him catching them, the demons said to each other: '"It was a great shame on our part that we took refuge in the city because of a single horseman. Why do we not strike?" The demons then began to prepare their heavy equipment and donned strong armour before opening the city gate. Numerous demon archers and demon charioteers rushed out, along with demons mounted on elephants, pigs, foxes, dogs, snakes and lizards. Others were on foot and yet others flew like great vultures, or upside down, with their heads facing earthwards and their feet in the air. The demons all bellowed out in a great roar, causing immense showers of rain, snow and hail and violent claps of thunder, and they released fire, flame and smoke from their mouths . . . Rustam's horse came to wake him from his sleep and he quickly donned his leopard-skin robe, tied on his quiver and hastened towards the demons.'

The paintings depicting this story were in two registers along the side walls of the main ceremonial hall of the house. Covering the wall at the end, behind the altar, was a large painting of the patron goddess of their home, the four-armed Nana, astride a lion. Nanaivandak was named after his life-giving mother-goddess, Nanaivandak meaning 'slave of Nana'. The hall had a high, vaulted brick ceiling lined with plaster, with carved wooden pillars. Here Nanaivandak's extended family performed religious rites, held meetings to discuss family business and hosted large banquets on holidays and festivals. The family were very wealthy. They owned land in the valley which was worked by serfs and which produced a sizeable income, and they also received a share of the tolls on the bridge across the river and income from water mills on their land.

Nanaivandak's uncle's house in Samarkand was just as large but

Four-armed Nana on a lion in a Panjikent house, seventh century

less richly decorated than the Panjikent home. Samarkand was a large city on a low hill further down the Zerafshan valley than Panjikent, but just as heavily fortified, with eight miles of 50-foot-high walls punctuated by bastions and barbicans. The streets were no less crowded and, in addition to hundreds of caravanserai, large garrisons of Arab soldiers lay just outside the city walls. It was usual for Sogdian boys to be educated from the age of five, and so Nanaivandak had little time to enjoy the city, as he was soon being tutored each day in the ways of trade and the languages he would need as a merchant – Arabic, Chinese and some Turkic and Tibetan. It was now that he was taught to be a follower of Mani, a departure from the Zoroastrian faith of his parents with its fire worship and numerous deities. His uncle tried to convert Nanaivandak's mother too, arguing that Mani had proclaimed a religion to supersede all earlier religions, but she continued to attend a Zoroastrian temple in the city with its eternally burning fire. Zoroastrianism had been dying out, however, since the arrival of Manicheism in Sogdiana. Not long after the Arab invasions its priests fled persecution in Sogdiana and established thriving communities in India, now known as the Parsees. Manichean texts were written in a different script from official documents, and Nanaivandak had to learn this as well, so that he could copy religious texts for his uncle and read to him.

As he grew up Nanaivandak accompanied his uncle on short trading trips to Merv to the south-west, Chach to the north-east and Balkh to the south whenever the political and military situation allowed. Unlike his uncle, who travelled simply to make money, Nanaivandak loved the journeys themselves. He found the mountain scenery endlessly fascinating, and his uncle would often come across him in the morning sitting outside as the dawn light suffused the great hulks of the distant Pamirs with a pink glow, or in the evening, when he should have been helping to supervise the unloading of the camels, staring into the distance as dusk fell across the great plains and the mountains turned purple before disappearing into the shadows of the night. This love of travel never left Nanaivandak and sometimes he even prolonged his journey in order to linger among his beloved mountains.

He especially enjoyed his visits to Balkh, the main Bactrian city situated on a tributary of the Oxus at the head of the route south to India. The residents were proud of their city's history, insisting that it was the real birthplace of Zoroaster (not everyone agreed) and boasting how Alexander the Great had chosen a Bactrian bride and married her in the city over a thousand years before. Nanaivandak's uncle was among a group of merchants from Samarkand who had established caravanserai in the major market cities in Transoxania and Bactria for themselves and their fellow countrymen, and the largest establishment was at Balkh. There were thousands of caravanserai in and around the city, many managed by such groups of merchants who were thereby assured of home comforts when on a trading mission.

In 728 there was another rebellion against the Arabs among the citizens of Samarkand and other Sogdian cities, after the rules on conversion to Islam had once more been changed. This time, both the Turghiz to the north and the Tibetans to the south sent forces to help the rebels and almost succeeded in driving the Arabs out of Sogdiana. Many Sogdians who had escaped the Ferghana massacre and joined the Turghiz now returned, but Nanaivandak's father was not among them.

Even after Arab forces regained Samarkand and, in 732, finally defeated the Turghiz, there were frequent uprisings. From time to time the Sogdians would drive the Arab forces out of one or another city, but the armies of the Caliphate would always regroup and retake it. Sogdiana was traditionally a land of city-states and its forces were rarely united.

In the late summer of 751, as Nanaivandak rode around the now familiar streets of Chang'an, he recalled his first visit to the Chinese capital. It was 730 and his uncle had decided that he was old enough to accompany him to China on a trading mission. There were reports of Tibetan incursions into the nominally Chinese-controlled Pamir kingdoms to the south and his uncle therefore decided to take the north-eastern route, past Lake Issukkul, rather than the southern route via Kashgar, enabling them to avoid the Tibetan armies. Most of the goods they carried would be traded at markets on the way, but some items, such as brass, amber and coral, were destined specifically for Chang'an. Brass was used by Chinese court artisans to ornament the girdles of officials of the two lowest grades of the civil service, and the Buddhists also used it to make statues of Buddha and would buy any excess at a good price. Amber from the shores of the Baltic and red coral brought from the Mediterranean were likewise highly prized in China. In Samarkand they also bought gold and lapis lazuli, both much sought after by the Tibetans, Turks and Chinese, and they would trade some further east for the wool which was to be their main cargo. Much of the gold was already beaten and worked into filigree ornaments in Persian style by artisans in Samarkand. Turkic men commonly wore golden belts, often decorated with animal motifs, and in Tibet skilled artisans worked the metal into mechanical toys and ornaments: many of these were presented as gifts to the Chinese emperor.

Preparations for the journey were elaborate and meticulously planned. It was over 3,000 miles to Chang'an. Nanaivandak and his uncle would have to pass through Turghiz and Chinese territory, as well as the *de facto* independent city-states in the Tarim basin. On the mountain passes they would encounter freezing temperatures, in the desert searing heat. Special footwear and warm furs were required for the former, and head and face coverings for the latter. They carried a variety of currencies, some of which might be needed to hand out as bribes to border guards, and they were also armed: bandits preyed on rich travellers.

The road from Samarkand led east, following the Zerafshan river before veering north to cross the easternmost stretch of the Red Sandy Wastes to the Jaxartes, or Syr Darya, river. The land of Chach, the summer home of the ruling Turghiz chief – the kaghan – started on the far bank. The kaghan and his army had assisted several rebellions by the residents of Samarkand and other cities in Sogdiana and relations between their peoples were friendly. The city of Chach was not as large as Samarkand but nevertheless considerable in size, supported by farming in the temperate valleys and stockbreeding in the mountains. Like Samarkand it had a citadel, a large palace for the kaghan and temples of several religions as well as numerous houses, shops and workshops. Nanaivandak and his uncle stayed in their usual lodgings run by their countrymen and prayed four times a day, facing the sun during daylight and the moon in the evening, at the main Manichean temple within the city walls. They also presented alms to the clergy.

They did not linger in Chach for they had to reach the winter pastures of the kaghan before he returned to the city, so that they could purchase the newly shorn sheep-wool, and the pastures were still several weeks' journey away. But they had time to listen to a storyteller in the marketplace. Though they both knew the tale – it was the epic of Rustam – they still enjoyed the telling, which was accompanied by colourful paintings as a backdrop.

From the city of Chach they took the road east, along the valley of the Talas river into Tianshan, leaving behind the familiar Transoxanian plains. Then there was a long but easy trek through low mountain valleys and passes to Issuk-kul, the warm lake. As its name suggests, owing to its brackish waters and sheltered position between the Tianshan and Altai mountains it never froze, even in the coldest winters, and there were tales of great monsters which lived in its deeps. Each winter the kaghan moved his court, his army and his herds here for the winter so the pastures on either side of the road were filled with tens of thousands of horses, sheep, cattle and camels.

Nanaivandak and his uncle had set out at the start of spring and it was now almost summer. Having just finished shearing, the kaghan and his army were preparing to leave for their summer residence at Chach, along the road which Nanaivandak and his uncle had just taken. There was plenty of wool for sale, but his uncle was interested only in the wool from the fat-tailed dumba sheep, not found further east. He also brought skins from lambs slaughtered when fourteen days old, known as astrakhan, which he intended to trade at a specialist market in a town further east.

The land to the north and north-east of Sogdiana was occupied by various Turkic tribes, who fell in and out of alliances. One such alliance was known as the Western Turks, because the region to their east was originally controlled by another alliance of Turks, named the Eastern Turks. In the seventh century the Eastern Turks had been defeated by the Chinese and hundreds of thousands of them had resettled in the Chinese capital. The Western Turk alliance had then spread both eastwards, into the land thus left unoccupied, and westwards into Chach. The Turghiz had only driven them out of Chach and the rich pastureland surrounding Issuk-kul three decades previously. The Turghiz leader then assumed the title Kaghan of the Ten Arrows and, like the Western Turkic kaghan, established twenty tribal leaders called tutuks, to rule over the areas that owed him allegiance. Each tutuk could muster 5,000 warriors, mounted and armed. This army was essential, for the Turghiz were constantly fending off attacks from the west by the Arabs, from the south by Tibetans, and from their east by pretenders to their throne from other Turkic tribes, supported by Chinese troops. The Turghiz kaghan had fought many battles, and had conducted a successful siege and attack on Kucha to the south a few years before, but he also made use of more peaceable solutions, marrying daughters of both the Western Turkic kaghan and the Tibetan emperor to prevent further attacks from these old foes.

The Turghiz kaghan's winter camp on the northern banks of the lake consisted of hundreds of white felt tents, distinctive against the green of the valley floor. That of the kaghan himself was the largest, adorned with rich silks and brocades. When Nanaivandak and his uncle went to pay their respects they were dazzled by the gold and silver ornaments covering its walls and roof. The kaghan's officials sat in rows on either side of him dressed in embroidered silk robes, their hair worn in long plaits. The soldiers wore coarser clothes of felt and carried bows and other weapons. All the men also wore daggers at their belts. The kaghan was in a long, green robe of the finest silk, slit up the sides. His long hair lay loose down his back and a broad silk ribbon, tied around his head, reached down his back to his waist.

The mood in the valley was festive. The shearing had been successful and everyone was glad to be going back to Chach where they could trade their wool for the many luxuries in the city's bazaars. The horses were sleek and fat from the new grass and the men spent their last few days hunting with their falcons and dogs in the mountains, galloping back every evening across the valley in a great swoop of noise and colour with their kills. During the day the valley was full of noise and laughter as the children held pony races and the women packed for the move, and in the evenings the sound of drunken singing echoed among the flickering lights of the numerous campfires. Then the tents were loaded on to wooden carts so large that it took several rows of yaks to pull them and the encampment started its long journey back west.

Nanaivandak and his uncle were headed east, but from Issuk-kul they had a choice of routes to Chang'an. The northern route – skirting the northern edge of the Tianshan rather than crossing them, and passing through the Turghiz pasturelands – was the easiest but also the least populated, and inaccessible to many of the goods found in the markets beyond the mountains. Instead Nanaivandak's uncle had decided he wanted to visit the markets along the western stretch of the Tarim basin route to China. It had been several years since he had last travelled that way, and he was eager to meet old acquaintances and to see what was for sale. Accordingly, they now had to head south and negotiate the road through the Tianshan. The route was barely passable in winter and was extremely dangerous in spring when melting snow caused great avalanches and ice falls. But Nanaivandak and his uncle met travellers who had just come from the south and who assured them that the worst of the spring thaw was over and that the road south was clear. They stayed for several more days in the valley to rest their animals, then made arrangements for the next leg of their journey, hiring yaks and more horses to carry the large bales of wool. The animal keepers would be paid off when they reached the desert to the south, and there camels would be hired as replacements. Camels were slower but more reliable desert travellers.

The road south followed one of the river valleys up into the mountains. There were four passes to negotiate before they reached the watershed, and the journey, if all went well, usually took two weeks. The glacial peak of Khan-Tengri, over 22,000 feet high, towered to the east, but after a couple of stages the view was obscured by the encroaching valley walls. The mountain peak would become a familiar sight on Nanaivandak's later journeys along the Silk Road.

Nanaivandak's uncle was used to high mountain passes. Samarkand was divided from the trading markets to the east and south by some of the highest ranges in the world – the Pamirs and the Hindu Kush – and the routes across them demanded considerable endurance from travellers. The Tibetans and the peoples who lived in the kingdoms of the Pamirs between Samarkand and Kashmir were acclimatized from birth to high altitudes, but in battle many of the recruits from the desert towns experienced shortness of breath and headaches: the Tibetan army even had a special corps devoted to the treatment of altitude sickness among its soldiers. The Tianshan were not so huge as the Pamirs, but even so, the final pass on the road south, just west of the headwaters of the Bedal river, lay at almost 14,000 feet. On reaching its flat, snow-covered saddle, the weather cleared and they were offered a spectacular view of the Bedal valley and, in the distance, the start of the great sand-filled depression of the Tarim basin.

Nanaivandak and his uncle negotiated the descent through the melting snow cover and down into the valley. The track ran along the eastern bank of the river, perched high above its boulder-strewn waters. After travelling for three more days along a gradually widening valley they reached the caravan town at the valley's mouth. Here they stopped to pay off their yak drivers and horsemen who soon found other customers wanting to travel back across the pass. Nanaivandak's uncle then negotiated the hire of camels for their cargo. Camels were expensive – an animal in its prime might cost fourteen bolts of silk – and the hirers were responsible for the injury or death of any camel during its period of hire.

The caravanserai did not provide food, fuel or fodder: the purchase of these was negotiated separately with provisioners in the town. The inn itself was a crude affair to Nanaivandak's eyes compared with the well-kept structures in Transoxania. The walls surrounding the large open courtyard where the animals were housed and the single-storey rooms to the side were made of tamped earth without any plaster or decoration, and the open windows allowed in all the dirt and dust of the desert. Moreover, the innkeeper was surly and unhelpful, and they pressed on as soon as the camels were ready.

Nanaivandak remembered learning from his uncle on this first journey the unfamiliar names of the Silk Road oases. The stages led first to Aksu, a smallish town compared to Samarkand but important because of its position at the crossroad of the north–south road between the Bedal pass and Khotan, and the east–west road from Kashgar to Chang'an. The road changed at every stage, and even during a single stage. Some of the most difficult stretches occurred when the route traversed marshy ground, but then suddenly the surface would change to gravel glacis and, a few miles further on, to bare rock. The snow-covered peak of Khan-Tengri to the north, however, was a constant companion, while to the south lay an expanse of grey-yellow sand.

Their next major stop was Kucha, a thriving city-state. The last couple of stages before they entered the triple walls of the city passed through fertile and well-farmed country, and the road was lined with poplar trees and fringed with fruit orchards, apricot, pear, pomegranate and peach all growing in abundance. The river running to the south of the city plain acted as a natural barrier against the drifting desert sand, providing a welcome relief from the dustiness of the previous stages. Nanaivandak had heard that the dancing girls in Kucha were almost as good as those in Samarkand. The country was ruled by a king who lived in a palace decorated with gold from mines in the Tianshan to the north and jade from the river beds in Khotan to the south. He and his queen were both Buddhists and their patronage of their religion was much in evidence: the streets were full of monks and nuns with their begging bowls, a large monastery abutted the main market square, and stupas, it seemed, stood at every corner. Several of the stalls in the market were run by monks. Apart from scriptures, prayers and charms, they also sold drugs and told fortunes. Nanaivandak heard many languages, including Turkic, Chinese – a language he could recognize though not yet really speak – and something else which his uncle told him was Kuchean.

Kucha was one of four Chinese garrison towns along the Silk Road. For years the Tibetans and the Chinese had fought for control of this vital corridor of land and, not long before, the Chinese had gained the upper hand. Now their garrisons were manned by 30,000 troops, many of them Turks or local men. At Kucha Nanaivandak and his uncle heard of the recent peace treaty signed between the Tibetans and the Chinese, its terms inscribed in both Tibetan and Chinese on a stone stele in Tibet to symbolize its permanence. Nanaivandak's uncle hoped that the peace would last: the past years of conflict had not been good for trade. The Turghiz had also negotiated peace with the Chinese, which meant that the southern route through Khotan and Kashgar would be safe, and Nanaivandak's uncle decided to travel back that way, as both towns had Chinese garrisons and were lively, independent cities. Most important for his uncle, Khotan was famous for its jade and jewel markets and attracted merchants from the routes south into India. It would also be an opportunity for Nanaivandak to see these towns for the first time and to be introduced to the resident Sogdian agents.

By this point in their journey the caravan had settled into the dull routine of desert travel: long, hot stages through a featureless landscape with an indifferent inn at the day's end if they were lucky; problems with sick camels; cold desert nights; searing daytime heat; dust storms and floods that arose without warning; and the continuing threat of bandits. Staging-posts were vital and during the period of Chinese control care was taken to keep them open. Some nights found Nanaivandak and his uncle lodging in an inn which was the only building left occupied in an otherwise deserted hamlet. The innkeeper and his wife, often colonists from distant Chinese lands, had stayed on because they were paid and given free supplies by the government. At other halts there was only a well and perhaps a few trees to give shelter from the sun. And occasionally there was no water at all, because the surveyors who had built the road were unable to find a source at the end of a single stage. Then Nanaivandak and his uncle would set out before dawn or even late at night to try to complete a double stage, but it was wearing on both animals and men. When the heat became unbearable they started to travel at night.

It was always a relief to reach one of the larger towns where they could be sure of a good inn and fodder for their animals. Summer nights in the walled towns were punctuated by the rumble of caravan trains embarking on the next stage of their long journey. The dull clang of the bells around the camels' necks warned pedestrians to get out of the way, since the narrow streets were barely wide enough to accommodate a loaded camel. In the desert the bells alerted caravans coming in the opposite direction. When they met, the lead camel-drivers would stop briefly to exchange a few words about their destination and conditions on the road, the state of the wells, or the presence of robbers. Then they would press on: they might have a thirty-mile stage to complete before dawn.

The camels travelled nose to tail in a long line. A large caravan would consist of hundreds of camels, with each string of between five and fifteen beasts tied together by a rope looped through wooden nose pegs. The cameleers, usually Chinese, Turks and Tibetans, wore shoes made of felt or thick wool stitched with a scale design, the toes and heels reinforced with leather and turned up to reduce friction with the ground. The soles were sometimes lined with several sheets of paper – a precious commodity – and a drawstring pulled the shoe tight around the ankles to prevent sand entering. The insides were lined with soft red cloth.

The cameleers carried water flasks fashioned from hollowed-out gourds, light in weight but thick enough to prevent too much evaporation. If their supply of water ran out or a well was dry they used the camels to help them find water. The two-humped Bactrian camel is not renowned for its speed – it travels at about two and a half miles an hour – but its life-saving skills as storm-detector and water-diviner are famous, as a fifth-century chronicler noted:

Occasionally the old camels would roar, huddle together in a group and bury their noses in the sand. This gave warning of fierce, sudden winds which were dreaded along the northern route. They would whip up the sands and, although over in a matter of minutes, those without protection over their faces might be left for dead.

At the site of underground water the older camels would stop and paw the ground, a skill inherited from their wild cousins who still roamed the desert in large herds. The wild camels were generally smaller and difficult to train, so working camels were bred rather than caught. The Bactrian camel is better suited to the extremes of temperature found in the deserts and mountains of the eastern Silk Road than its single-humped Arabian cousin, for although both have double-lidded eyes and the ability to close their nostrils against the sand, the Bactrian camel is short and stocky and grows long, thick fur in the winter. The Chinese imperial herds which grazed on the steppes to the north numbered hundreds of thousands, many having been received in exchange for silk. There was even a special government department devoted to their care and breeding, and cameleers were paid well for their expertise with clothing and grain. In China the fastest camels were reserved for the 'Bright Camel Envoys' who were dispatched if there was a military crisis on the frontier.

The camel had many other uses for travellers and residents of the Silk Road. A Chinese general marching into battle used one to carry a large tank of fresh water filled with fish to keep him supplied during the campaign: only a camel had the strength and steadiness for the task. And these same qualities were put to use by entertainers. In the marketplaces of the Silk Road young boys would perform acrobatics on a camel's back, while princes and the nobility were often accompanied on their travels by a troop of musicians, all eight of them seated on a large, wooden cradle atop a camel. In war, armies used up to two hundred camels to carry their heavy whirlwind guns into battle. Mounted on a wooden frame, the guns revolved, able to shoot in all directions in rapid succession. Camels were also eaten, the hump being considered the choicest cut.

Apart from wild camels, Nanaivandak saw wolves, wild horses and herds of asses, antelope and gazelle on his first and subsequent desert journeys, as well as gerbils and lizards. Like present-day travellers, he also came across the ruins of long-abandoned towns. There had been people living in the oases fringing the Tarim basin for two millennia, but invasions and changes in the water table or the course of rivers meant that settlements sometimes died. Once the exodus had started, there was soon not enough manpower to maintain the complex irrigation systems, and over even just one or two generations the area of cultivable land might shrink so much that it was no longer sufficient to support the remaining population. The town would then be left, to be reclaimed by the constantly drifting desert sands.

Whenever possible, Nanaivandak and his uncle travelled with other merchants. Sometimes they were passed by small groups of travellers on donkeys which were both faster and cheaper than camels. The aristocracy and high officials preferred to ride horses, especially Ferghanan horses. Their qualities had been recorded by the Greek historian Herodotus, and the Chinese believed them to be part-dragon. But these animals were in short supply and Turkic horses, although less prized, were more frequently seen. It was these that Nanaivandak and his uncle rode. The breed's Arab ancestry had given it two thick bands of muscle on either side of the spine which made bare-backed riding more comfortable, although Nanaivandak and his uncle used saddles. But by far the most common horse, especially along the northern Silk Road, was the steppe pony, the tarpan.

The horror stories which circulated among travellers about the desert stages were not false, although they were sometimes exaggerated, and Nanaivandak's uncle taught him about the stages renowned for their ferocity. The northern route between Anxi and Hami, for example, had few wells and was prone to sudden winds which would sweep down from the north. Nanaivandak's uncle described it as a stretch with no landmarks other than the bones of travellers and their camels. He also warned Nanaivandak never to be tempted to take a short-cut or travel along lesser-used ways, for by doing so he would put himself at the mercy of the desert. Sometimes a small family group, unable to keep up with a large caravan, would branch off on to a seemingly well-trodden camel path. Then the path would peter out or a sandstorm would blow up. In either case the inexperienced would become hopelessly lost and might wander around for days until, weakened by hunger and thirst, they were unable to go any further and would simply lie down and die. Soon only their bones would be left, scoured by the wind and sand, and bleached by the sun. Nanaivandak's uncle also told him of the whistling wind that sounded like the fabled desert sirens who lured men to their death.

Though the dangers of the desert were real enough, Nanaivandak and his uncle were more at risk from robbers than from thirst, being otherwise well equipped and using the main routes. On one journey Nanaivandak's uncle had been travelling with a group of merchants. When he woke in the morning he found that several of the group had set out secretly before dawn, hoping to reach the next town ahead of the others and thus secure the best prices for their goods. Nanaivandak's uncle and the remainder of the party came across the bodies of their former travelling companions two hours later at a narrow defile. They had been ambushed and killed, and all their goods taken.

Nanaivandak saw plenty of evidence of death on this first journey: ruined and abandoned towns, carcasses in varying states of decay, petrified trees, and old human and animal bones. Flash floods were another hazard of desert travel: they would rise in spring and summer without warning and sweep everything away, dashing the unwary against boulders. But of the thousands of travellers who made their way along the Silk Road each year most survived.

On this first journey Nanaivandak and his uncle stopped over for several days at the city of Kocho, east of Kucha. This was the centre of their church and his uncle wanted to introduce him to the community, to worship, to make confession and to offer alms to the Elect. The last was easily achieved, a donation of newly ripened melons, silk and other goods being distributed to the several monastaries. The city itself was situated in the Turfan basin, smaller in size but much deeper than the Tarim basin, in parts lying almost 1,000 feet below sea level. It was now summer and the heat was so intense that the wealthiest residents had retreated to special apartments, built in the basements of their houses. The nomads who camped on the plain during the summer had moved into the mountains to the north, and everyone else tried to avoid any exertion, sitting next to the irrigation canals where the shade of the trees and the constantly flowing spring water offered some respite. Nanaivandak soon saw why the route here was called the 'road through the willows'.

The travellers had now left the Taklamakan desert but had to cross the end of the Gobi before reaching the haven of the Gansu corridor. Up to Hami there were numerous wells, but then after a couple more stages the road left the protection of the northern mountains and veered south-east towards Anxi. Nanaivandak soon understood why this tract of the route was spoken of with such dread: though their camels were well fed, they were still exhausted when only half-way into each stage, and there was no chance of respite. The bleached animal bones along the path were a constant reminder of what happened to those who had to be left behind. Moreover, all the well water along this stretch of the route was brackish and only induced a greater thirst, but Nanaivandak's uncle had brought along a sack of dough-strings which, when boiled in the water, absorbed much of the salt, making the water more palatable. They had also purchased extra gourds for carrying fresh spring water from Hami.

The next few stages took them through granite hills riddled with holes left by gold prospectors. The road's surface was a mixture of huge boulders and granite grit whose myriad colours were echoed by the skin of the small desert lizards. Five days on from Hami they reached a narrow ravine, where a well whose water was purer than the rest on this route supplied a small village; but they did not linger. They had another six days to Anxi across the 'Black Gobi', so called because the constant winds had swept away any covering of sand and left a surface of grey grit, mixed with small, black pebbles. Their most difficult day was the third, when the desert was covered with a thick, salt crust. The camels hated this soft, spongy surface and were constantly stopping and spitting when the cameleer tried to get them to move on, and the sun was already high in the sky before they reached the inn at the end of the stage. When they caught sight of the Chinese defensive walls north-west of Anxi, two days later, they were all extremely relieved – even Nanaivandak, who normally relished the hardships of travel. They were now less than two months away from the great city of Chang'an, their destination, along a road protected from bandits by the wall and its garrisons of Chinese soldiers, from thirst by the streams flowing from the Nanshan – the southern mountains, and from the sand-filled desert winds by the Beishan – the northern hills. The landscape became greener and they gradually left the sere-yellow earth behind.

The main Chinese border post was at Liangzhou, another crossroads, with routes leading north to the Ordos and steppes beyond, and south to Koko-nor and the Tibetan plateau. After showing their papers and paying the necessary customs duty on their goods, along with a little extra to facilitate the paperwork, they found a caravanserai in the town and traded the astrakhan lamb skins they had bought from the Turghiz at Issuk-kul. They then entered the great plains of the Yellow river, winding its loess-laden, sluggish course from its source in Tibet, far to the south. The countryside here was well cultivated and dotted with farms and villages, and there was plenty to divert Nanaivandak on the last few stages to Chang'an. After crossing the final mountain pass, only 9,000 feet and well guarded by Chinese soldiers, they passed through the deeply ravined loess typical of north-western China and then, finally, descended into the plain of Chang'an with its groves of persimmon and fields of summer wheat.

They entered the Chinese capital through the western gate from which the road led directly to the Western Market, where most of the merchants from Central Asia conducted their trade. Over two hundred merchants' guilds were represented in the vast, walled market area and there was even a lake under the walls in the northeastern corner, fringed with willows and blossoming fruit trees. His uncle had an agent in Chang'an who arranged for the sale of their goods and, because the Silk Road had been closed for a while, they received good prices. The goods were taken to warehouses built against the market's enclosing walls. The day after their arrival Nanaivandak's uncle showed him around. Over 3,000 shops lined the market's small lanes, each displaying the goods of its guild: silver and goldware, ginger, silk gauze, fresh fish, dried fish, crabs, goldfish, sugared cakes, saddlery, ironwork, scales and measures, medicine, flowers, vegetables, and much else besides. There were also streets of shops offering various services – printers, pawnshops, safe-deposit shops, moneylenders, brothels, teahouses and restaurants. It seemed to Nanaivandak that anything could be had in Chang'an.

Twenty-one years after his first journey, as Nanaivandak completed his transactions, he would have noted that the market and the city of Chang'an had changed little, only becoming more familiar with long acquaintance. But there had been many changes in Sogdiana and elsewhere along the Silk Road. For much of these two decades the Arab conquerers of Samarkand had been distracted by internal rivalries further west. These had only been resolved the year before Nanaivandak embarked on his most recent journey, with the fall in 750 of the Umayyad Caliphate and the rise of the Abassids who moved the Arab capital from Damascus to the village of Baghdad.

Along the land north of the Silk Road, too, things had changed. By 750 the Western Turk confederation had broken up and had been driven out of the steppes north of the Silk Road (in what is now Mongolia). It was replaced by another confederation of Turkic tribes, the Uighurs, who were to rule for almost a century. The Turghiz, after signing a peace treaty with the Chinese to protect their eastern flank, had formed an alliance with the Tibetans – sealed with a marriage between a Tibetan princess and the Turghiz kaghan in 734 – and combined to fight the Arabs on their western flank. The peace with the Chinese did not last long, however. After the execution of one of their envoys by the Chinese, the Turghiz besieged the Silk Road garrisons in 735. Twice heavily defeated, they again sought peace with the Chinese

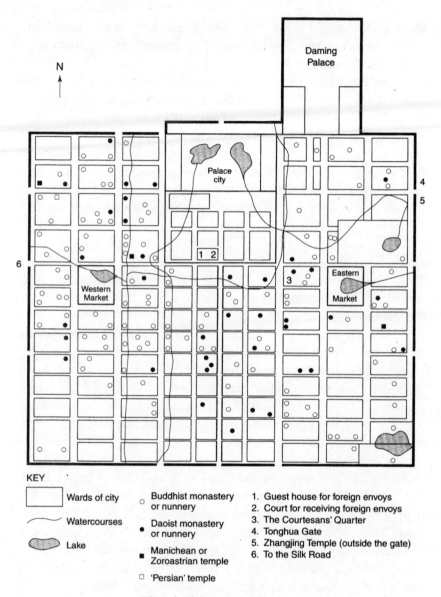

N

Daming
Palace

Palace
city

1　2

3

Eastern
Market

Western
Market

4

5

6

KEY

☐ Wards of city

〜 Watercourses

▨ Lake

○ Buddhist monastery
or nunnery

● Daoist monastery
or nunnery

■ Manichean or
Zoroastrian temple

☐ 'Persian' temple

1. Guest house for foreign envoys
2. Court for receiving foreign envoys
3. The Courtesans' Quarter
4. Tonghua Gate
5. Zhangjing Temple (outside the gate)
6. To the Silk Road

Plan of eighth-century Chang'an

and it was accepted in 736. They were more successful against the Arab armies, inflicting heavy defeats in Transoxania throughout the 730s, until rivalry between two Turghiz chiefs put an end to their unity and power.

The Chinese–Tibetan peace treaty, signed in 730 during Nanaivandak's first visit to Chang'an, lasted seven years but was followed by decades of bloody battles between these two old foes. They fought for control of the Silk Road and of the route into India across the Pamirs. In the eastern arena – the Gansu corridor – the Chinese usually had the upper hand in summer, but the Tibetans would raid the Chinese army camps every autumn just after the harvest and steal the grain, so that the land became known as the 'Tibetan grain estates'. The Tibetans were dominant in the western arena – the Pamirs; but by the late 740s the Chinese emperor Xuanzong, at the height of his power and determined to inflict defeat on the Tibetans, was finally successful in both arenas. The last Chinese counter-attack in the Pamirs took place in 747. The Chinese routed the Tibetan forces and the successful general – a Korean called Gao – was nicknamed Lord of the Mountains of China. In the east the Chinese armies also started to gain the upper hand under the leadership of a half-Turkic general who, Nanaivandak had heard, had Sogdian blood. There was certainly another Sogdian–Turkic general in the Chinese forces called Rokhshan and word had it that he was in favour with the emperor despite his recent defeat on China's northern frontier. By 751, therefore, the Chinese empire seemed pre-eminent, though it was soon to become clear that it had reached the limits of its expansion and power.

On his journey to Chang'an in 751 Nanaivandak had encountered a Chinese army on its way to meet the Arab forces north-east of Sogdiana. They were led by the famous General Gao who, after his success in the Pamirs, had inflicted a heavy defeat on Turghiz and other forces in Sogdiana. Now the Arabs were threatening to conquer the Chinese Silk Road garrisons and so Gao was sent west again to confront them. The two forces met at the Talas river to the north-west of the Tianshan, on the fault-line of Chinese and Arab power. The battle lasted five days and was only decided when one of the tribal armies supporting the Chinese changed its allegiance. The

Chinese fled in disarray but, as has been seen, many were captured and sent either to Samarkand or Damascus. One of their number, Du Huan, returned to China in 762 and wrote an account of his travels to the heartland of the Arab Caliphate. Sadly, it is no longer extant.

Nanaivandak had been travelling for two decades and was accustomed to armies on the march. They usually left merchants and other travellers alone, though their requisitions from the local community sometimes meant that it was difficult to find supplies. He had travelled alone after his uncle's death. The journey to China was always long and arduous but he had retained his love of the mountain landscapes and his zest for trade: the markets in the Silk Road towns and especially in Chang'an still fascinated him. He was fortunate to live in a period of relative stability on the Silk Road and at a time when China still welcomed foreigners. He did not imagine then that the journey of 751 would be the last he would make to China.

The Soldier's Tale

Seg Lhaton, 747–790

The Tibetan men and horses all wear chain mail armour of
extremely fine workmanship. It envelops them completely
leaving openings for only the eyes so that strong bows and
sharp swords cannot injure them. When they do battle they
must dismount and array themselves in ranks. When one dies
another takes his place. To the end they are not willing to
retreat. Their lances are long and thinner than those in
China and their archery is weak. Even when not in battle the
men carry swords.

Du Yu, *Tongdian*, AD 801

IN THE 780s Seg Lhaton, a Tibetan soldier, was quartered in a fort
near Miran on the southern branch of the Silk Road, over a
thousand miles from his home. His countrymen had retaken
Miran and many other towns and army garrisons from the Chinese
over the past two decades, and they now controlled the route
between Sogdiana and China, blocking trade and diplomatic missions between Samarkand and Chang'an and thereby stopping one
source of China's wealth and power. A few merchants had recently
managed to get through by going north of the Tianshan, but this
was Uighur-held territory and the merchants had had to pay a
toll for safe passage. Most did not attempt the route: even
Nanaivandak, a consummate traveller and trader, had had to rest
content with making deals closer to Samarkand. His 751 trip to
Chang'an had been his last to the Chinese capital.

The vassal tribes under the Uighurs in the north resented their
rulers, and the Tibetans were currently debating whether to send

troops to assist them in rebellion. The Tibetans were also keen to retake Khotan, an independent city-state to the west of Miran that still owed nominal allegiance to the Chinese. The loyalty of Khotan to China was largely an irrelevance since Chinese troops and officials could no longer reach it, but occupation of the state would be of strategic use to Tibet, and its grain and food supplies would help feed the Tibetan soldiers garrisoned on the Silk Road.

It was harvest time and the Tibetan army camp at Miran was stocking up on grain for the winter and for the possible Uighur campaign for which extra provisions would be required. Local farmers gave a portion of their crops to the military in return for protection, labour and the loan of animals and implements, but the fort was also sent extra supplies of barley and animals from Tibet. The camp commander assigned his men to provisions duty – checking and recording existing stores. Seg Lhaton, a squad leader and a veteran, was among them. It had been years since he had last seen his family, who were farmers in southern Tibet, the home of the founders of the Tibetan empire. Kings of this region had defeated the nomadic peoples in the north and west of Tibet during the late sixth and early seventh centuries in a series of victories referred to as 'the southern bamboo defeating the northern yak', and thereafter they founded a vast mountain empire. Diplomatic relations with China were established in 608, but it was not until a decade later that the Tibetan ruler's consolidation of his empire was complete and only in 633 that the capital was established at Lhasa. The emperor then had to turn his attention to his neighbours, especially the Chinese, and over the next century relations were conducted by both diplomacy and war. The Tibetan emperor required a strong army to back up his diplomacy and to deal with internal and external enemies, and for Seg Lhaton, as for all his countrymen, military service was obligatory. The Tibetan armies were huge, the adult male population of the Tibetan empire being augmented with recruits from their many colonies, which ranged from the Aza kingdom near Koko-nor and the Indo-European city-state of Kucha on the northern Silk Road to the Pamir mountain kingdoms of Wakhan and Little Balur in the west. Earlier wars, however, had taken their toll. Tens of thousands of soldiers had died in the battles against the Chinese and it was only in recent years that the Tibetans had gained dominance of the Silk Road.

The Tibetans chose Miran as the site for their main eastern garrison because of the town's strategic importance and access to Tibet. Miran lay at the point where two direct routes from the Tibetan plateau beyond the Kunlun mountains to the south debouched on to the main east–west Silk Road. One route over the Kunlun led directly to Lhasa, across the Chiman-tagh mountains and over the Tibetan plateau. The other headed first east, in the direction of Dunhuang, before turning south to the great grazing grounds of the Tsaidam basin across Nanshan, the eastward continuation of the Kunlun. There was also a direct route from Tibet to Khotan but the road passed through terrain too poor to support an attacking army.

The main road east from Miran to Dunhuang traversed a belt of gravel which extended for as much as seventy miles beyond the foot of the Kunlun before the salt-encrusted desert wastes took over. In ancient times the road had bifurcated a short march east of Miran, one route hugging the Kunlun, the other crossing the Lop desert. Travellers were advised to attempt the latter only in winter when there was still ice available at the salt springs south of the dried-up inland sea, Lop-nor, to cut as supplies for the next stages of the journey: water was otherwise extremely scarce. But after the fourth century an increasing lack of water forced the small villages servicing even this route to be abandoned and it soon ceased to be a regular thoroughfare. After this, the population of Miran, once a town of eight or nine thousand people, dwindled.

By the time Miran was occupied by Tibetan forces – from the mid-eighth century – it had shrunk to a small settlement. The soldiers and their camp followers gave it a new lease of life. The Miran river flowed down from the Kunlun over uncultivatable gravel beds, and much of the water evaporated or was dissipated *en route*, but when it emerged in the loess deposits at the edge of the desert it was carefully channelled into a large canal with branches and sub-branches feeding the fields. The main canal was sixty feet at its widest and over thirty feet deep, and it flowed five miles beyond the river before branching into seven main divisions. When they were first built, several centuries previously, the branch canals continued on for two or three more miles, subdividing into smaller and smaller channels. The fan of irrigation had then supported a fertile area of ten square miles. Beyond the fields, the water continued underground, feeding the ubiquitous desert tamarisk. Sand would build up around the tamarisk, resulting in large mounds, some up to fifty feet high, which could be seen stretching into the immediate distance. Beyond this there was only sand.

When Seg Lhaton was quartered in Miran, the canal system was no longer all in use. The town's population was now too small to maintain it and many of the sub-branches had become clogged so that sand and then tamarisk had encroached into the once fertile fields of wheat. Seg Lhaton and his squad were on a rota to keep the remaining canals clear under the direction of the irrigation officer. One of the main problems, ironically, was flooding. There were two flood periods: early spring when the ice in the river-bed itself and the snow in the lower mountains melted; and early summer, when the snow and ice on the higher ranges did the same. The summer floods were often uncontrollable. Great quantities of water surged over the ends of the canals, inundating the fields and turning them into marshy quagmires, ruining the crops. In winter the river froze, spreading out in a large sheet of ice.

Other than irrigation and agricultural work the soldiers had various everyday duties. They were required to make bricks from the local soil and mud in order to repair the fort and build new quarters. The fort, which had only been built a few decades earlier when the Tibetans reoccupied the Silk Road, was an irregular quadrangle, its longest side measuring 240 feet, with projecting bastions at each corner and in the centre of each wall. The southern bastion was the largest, over forty feet high topped with a seven-foot parapet, and made of stamped earth which was strengthened by layers of tamarisk stalks.

Soldiers were also sent to collect bundles of wood from the long-dead corpses of poplar trees in the desert and from the stunted poplar, willow and juniper trees growing in the gorges of the Kunlun. Young trees which occasionally grew up after the summer floods were soon chopped down. Some of the wood was cut into strips for tallies of supplies or to record reports on local

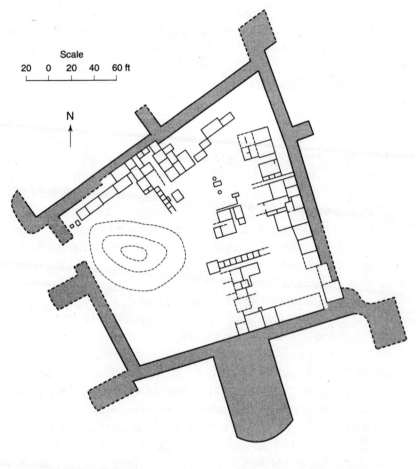

Plan of Tibetan fort, Miran

Fort wall of stamped clay and walls of quarters and store rooms

Walls of quarters and store rooms barely traceable

conditions which were sent to nearby watch stations and other forts. The rest was used, along with tamarisk, as firewood and building materials. When there was no wood for fires the soldiers would use animal dung, yak being the best. The soldiers all had ponies, and yaks were used as pack animals and for agricultural work. Seg Lhaton, like his fellow soldiers, did most of the repairs to his clothes and kit himself, and when his armour and clothing were beyond repair they were thrown, like everything else, on to one of the rubbish heaps. He also helped maintain the watch of eight three-hour periods and provided relief for soldiers stationed at the network of beacon forts and watch stations at strategic points on the roads out of Miran.

Being posted to one of the beacon forts was considered a hard-ship. The men had to spend long hours in cramped quarters below the beacon tower, ready to light the carefully prepared firewood at a moment's notice. There were three raised fire brackets on the tower. An incendiary fuse enclosed in a tube ran from each bracket down to the soldiers on duty below. To light the fuses they used a fire drill and tinder made from local inflammable material such as wormwood. Two fires signalled an alert, and three the appearance of enemy troops. A single fire was the all-clear signal. Each small tower was manned by only six soldiers, equipped with the company's standard and battle drums as well as weapons and left with all the supplies necessary for several weeks' duty.

The commander at Miran had recently dispatched a squad of men to relieve a remote watch station on a mountain pass to the south. Several of the soldiers there had fallen ill and were being sent back to the fort to recuperate under its resident doctor (who also acted as the camp veterinarian). The watch station leader sent a message with the returning soldiers confirming the safe arrival of the relief troops, and adding that since 'there was not a single female companion for the soldiers, the commander is begged to send at once many serving women'. There were not that many serving women in the fort at Miran but a few were rounded up: the only prostitutes available at these remote stations were those kept for this purpose by the army. In smaller camps they doubled as maids and general skivvies.

When he was not on duty outside Miran, Seg Lhaton lived in a small room built inside the eastern end of the fort. The room was barely ten feet square but here he both ate and slept. There was no means of disposing of rubbish or sewage in this outpost – where would it be taken? The soldiers simply threw garbage into a corner and when the room became too odorous and messy to be used as quarters, it was turned into a latrine. When eventually the room was full to overflowing with human and other camp waste, it would be abandoned, and new rooms would be progressively built along the insides of the fort walls to provide replacement quarters. Sand encroached into the gaps of the rubbish-filled rooms and this, coupled with the dryness of the desert, controlled the stench while also preserving the rubbish – a mixed blessing for archaeologists excavating the site over a thousand years later.

It was a rudimentary existence and Seg Lhaton would have much preferred to be farming his own land far to the south in the Yarlung valley. Though it did not offer rich living, the valley was green and lush, set amid the backdrop of the Himalayas. At Miran the earth was sere-grey and the Kunlun mountains to the south were hidden in an almost permanent haze of dust. There was little entertainment on offer in Miran. Caravans with their attendant storytellers, dancers and acrobats no longer passed. A few of the soldiers played instruments or sang, but the time was mostly spent in recounting former battles. Seg Lhaton was often asked to tell of his experiences in the Pamir and Koko-nor campaigns against the Chinese.

The peace treaty of 730 between Tibet and China had been broken in 737 by a Chinese invasion and since then relations between the two countries had deteriorated. Another peace treaty was not agreed until 783. In between, many bloody battles were fought which concentrated on two fronts: the north-eastern border between Tibet and China, and the route from the Silk Road into India across the Pamir mountains to the west of Tibet. By the 740s the Chinese had predominated, owing to the leadership of two outstanding foreign generals and the wholehearted support of the Chinese emperor, Xuanzong, who was at the height of his powers. He poured men and resources into the campaigns, determined to defeat the Tibetans and take control of the Silk Road.

In the east, the Chinese and the Tibetans met several times around Koko-nor, a great inland sea 10,000 feet above sea level and home to the Aza people. Long before, China had fought the Aza for control of this land, which lay on the main route between

China and Tibet. However, the Aza were fierce warriors and had taken advantage of the change in dynasties in China in 618 to regain control of their land. The Chinese took it back in 634, thus effectively removing the buffer between Tibet and China. Several years of war and diplomacy between the two followed, with the Aza as pawns in the power struggle, until in 641 a *modus vivendi* was reached, following which a Chinese princess was sent to marry the Tibetan emperor and the sons of Tibetan noblemen were sent to China to study. In fact, the princess was not in the direct imperial line, but she was of royal blood. The two countries recognized each other as equals, though the Chinese insisted on referring to their relationship as that between an uncle and a nephew. But hostilities broke out again in the 740s and those around Koko-nor were among the fiercest. The battles went one way and another until eventually the Chinese were driven back, forced to relinquish all but an island in the lake. Both sides were seeking control of a fortress twenty-five miles east of the lake and, according to the boundaries agreed in the 730 treaty, in Chinese territory. The fortress was called Stone Fort by the Chinese and Iron Blade by the Tibetans and it lay on high ground between the valleys of the Yellow and Huang rivers, controlling the main road between Lhasa and Chang'an as well as access to the rich meadows of Koko-nor. When the Tibetans retook Iron Blade in 741 the Chinese emperor was furious, demanding that the military governor of the region mount a counter-attack. In an act of great courage he refused, replying that: 'The fortress is strongly defended by the whole Tibetan nation. If we array our troops below we cannot capture it without incurring several tens of thousands of deaths among our men. I am afraid that what would thereby be gained is not comparable to what would be lost.' He almost lost his own life for this insubordination but was spared execution on the intervention of a rising young general, Koso Khan, who was appointed as military governor in his place. When the emperor later ordered Koso Khan to attack Iron Blade he could hardly refuse.

Seg Lhaton had been among the Tibetan ranks that faced this Chinese attack. He would relate that story another day. For now, he wiled away the time with his companions in the lonely fort at Miran by telling them of another battle which had taken place in the Pamir mountains to the west, two years before the attack on Iron Blade. Tibetans had established their rule over the small valley kingdoms that controlled the route between the Silk Road and the Gilgit river valley which led to northern India. During the 740s the Tibetan army had encountered the Chinese army several times in these valleys and had always been victorious. But they were not so fortunate in the summer of 747. Seg Lhaton remembered the battle vividly.

His division was with the main forces of the army, 9,000 men, deep in the mountains. They had marched to the town of Sarhad on the Oxus river in the kingdom of Wakhan between the Pamirs and the Hindu Kush. The Oxus runs west from its source in the Pamirs south of Kashgar, then turns northwest and emerges from the mountains to skirt Sodgiana before reaching the Aral Sea. Not far from its source it has already become a great grey-brown river, flowing in a deep gorge through the mountains until just east of Sarhad, where the mountain sides retreat slightly and the river spreads out over the flat valley floor. One of the tributaries leading into it from the south here flows along a valley wide enough for pack animals and humans to traverse it. At the valley's head lie two high glacial passes in succession, the Baroghil and the Darkhot. The second leads to the mountain-enclosed kingdom of Little Balur, then also controlled by the Tibetans, and to the high reaches of the Gilgit river valley which in turn leads to Kashmir, Tibet and India.

Tibetan spies brought back reports to the army camp at Sarhad of Chinese forces, estimated at 10,000 men and led by General Gao, approaching from the Silk Road to the north. These spies had tracked the Chinese army's progress over the past three months from Aksu to Kashgar, and then to the Chinese military bases north of the Pamirs. On hearing the intelligence, the general at Sarhad was sanguine: he did not expect all these men with their horses to negotiate the passes from Kashgar. And even if they did, their progress would be slow because they would be encumbered with supplies for both men and beasts: the grazing in the Pamir valleys was woefully insufficient to support a large number of horses and the single supply line would be overextended. More-over, he had already taken advantage of the terrain at Sarhad.

Should the Chinese forces reach them, his own forces were well protected. He had ordered his men to build palisades at a point where the road south to Little Balur along the tributary valley narrowed a few miles distant from the Oxus and where the sides of the valley were sheer rock. The ground here was marshy and the palisades, made from wood obtained higher up the valley, were easily driven into the soft ground. When the advancing Chinese forces met the palisades they would be unable to advance further or climb around them. The main Tibetan forces were positioned south of the palisades. Seg Lhaton and his fellow soldiers could all see how the approaching Chinese army would thus be trapped in the narrow defile. Moreover, the Tibetan archers could send volleys of arrows over the palisades and into the confused mass of Chinese soldiers on the other side where they were easy targets.

Seg Lhaton used a stick to draw the positions of the two sides on the clay wall of his room. Many of the soldiers at Miran were too young to have seen service in the Pamirs, but most understood mountain terrain. He drew the Oxus river and showed the position of a squad of 1,000 men left to hold its southern bank. Their role, he explained, was to harass and delay the Chinese forces crossing the river from the north and to provide the main Tibetan army with advance warning of an attack. They would also draw the Chinese army towards the tributary valley and into the trap. Over the past seven years, the Tibetans had defeated three other Chinese armies sent to take the kingdoms of Wakhan and Little Balur and they were confident that they could defeat another. Seg Lhaton was a veteran of those campaigns and had been promoted through the ranks to deputy squad commander.

The Oxus was in flood and therefore the Tibetan squad did not attempt to cross to confront the Chinese soldiers arriving from the north. In any event, the Tibetans had a perfect defensive position on the southern bank. Moreover, Seg Lhaton explained, they expected the Chinese to reach the opposite bank in disarray: there would be plenty of time to choose the day for battle, and any delay, the Tibetans believed, would be to their advantage. 'We thought that the Chinese supply lines would be stretched and that the enormous Chinese army could not survive long in the Pamirs, while our forces had an assured supply line through Little Balur to

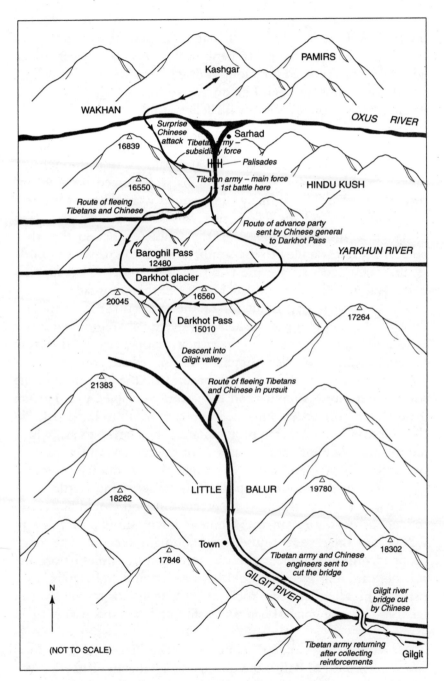

Plan of battle sites in Wakhan and Little Balur

the south.' He then told how the large Chinese army approached and set up camp on the north bank of the Oxus over several days. The Tibetans prepared for a long wait while the river subsided.

The next morning Seg Lhaton awoke to noise and confusion. At first he was only aware of his fellow soldiers beyond the palisades to the south in battle with Chinese troops, but then he saw Chinese soldiers behind him as well. None of the Tibetan commanders was prepared for this and panic spread through the ranks. Seg Lhaton and his companions were forced back against their own palisades and many of his squad were killed or injured. That night he and his fellow survivors scrambled up the steep valley sides and found breaks in the Chinese lines so that they could flee up the valley to the south, towards the passes and Little Balur. They had to leave most of their spare horses and supplies behind, along with the mutilated bodies of their comrades.

The following day remnants of the Tibetan army were still crossing the Baroghil pass. When they eventually regrouped it was estimated that they had lost half their troops, over a thousand horses and much of their supplies. An immediate counter-attack was out of the question, but the Tibetans held the kingdoms to the south where fresh supplies and men were available. The Tibetan general therefore ordered his men to retreat south to Little Balur in the Gilgit valley, a Tibetan protectorate. The Darkhot pass, which led to this valley kingdom, was one of the highest in the range – over 15,000 feet – and led over a huge glacier squeezed into the gaps between the mountain peaks. The descent into Little Balur on the other side of the pass was precipitous and would be certain to encourage dissent in the Chinese forces should they try to follow, for they were unused to mountain terrain. The track dropped almost 6,000 feet in little more than five miles before any suitable camping ground could be reached and the terrain consisted of moraine and bare rock, made treacherous by the layer of ice. No Chinese general had successfully crossed this pass with an army.

Moreover, Seg Lhaton continued, the Tibetans had loyal supporters in Little Balur: the queen was a Tibetan princess, given as a bride to the king in 740, only seven years before. Twelve miles beyond the town to the south was the bridge across the Gilgit river gorge, through which the road then continued on the right bank, following the winding river to the town of Gilgit and, beyond, to the Indus valley. There the Tibetans could resupply and obtain more horses to mount a counter-attack while the Chinese forces were still undecided at the top of the Darkhot pass. Seg Lhaton scratched another sketch on the clay wall of the room. The Gilgit river, he explained, was impassable in the summer beyond this bridge because of the ice melt from the mountain peaks, so the Tibetans could be assured that if they held the bridge – the only one across the river accessible from Little Balur – the Chinese could not advance further south that season. But they planned to meet the Chinese soon after they had crossed the Darkhot pass and before they reached the town of Little Balur, and drive them back across the pass. The Chinese army would certainly not be able to retain its discipline up the precipitous mountain track and there would be ample opportunity to launch waves of attacks. Furthermore, the Chinese would probably have to leave much of their supplies and many horses behind in a forced retreat, which would compensate for those the Tibetan forces had just lost.

It was almost thirty miles south to the foot of the Darkhot pass from the Baroghil pass, and another thirty from its summit to Little Balur. The Tibetan commanders expected that the Chinese would take at least seven days to cover the distance. Encumbered with pack animals, they would be lucky to cover more than ten miles a day, and then there was the Darkhot pass itself to negotiate. The Tibetans did not bother to post men in the town but, after assuring themselves of the loyalty of its officials, they crossed the bridge over the Gilgit river and established camp where the valley widened some miles beyond. At the same time men were sent ahead to obtain reinforcements and supplies from the next garrison. The general planned to attack as soon as the reinforcements arrived, taking the Chinese by surprise.

The extra soldiers arrived quickly. Only eight days had passed since the original Tibetan forces had fled in disarray from Wakhan. Now they returned along the Gilgit river, freshly prepared for battle. Seg Lhaton described his eagerness to confront the Chinese again: he had lost many friends in the previous encounter and wanted revenge. 'We were not used to defeat,' he said. In his three previous encounters with Chinese armies the Chinese had been routed and their generals shamed. The Tibetans' only fear now was that the Chinese might have advanced more quickly than expected and that there would be insufficient time for all the Tibetan forces to cross the precarious rope bridge and form up in battle ranks. The columns of thousands advanced as rapidly as they could along the mountainside paths. In front were the cavalry – mainly non-Tibetans – followed by divisions of archers. The elite Tibetan spearmen, dressed from head to toe in fine iron chain-mail, brought up the rear.

By evening they arrived at the bridge. As they rounded the bend of the road, Seg Lhaton heard the soldiers in front of him cry out in surprise. It was difficult to make out the bridge in fading light, but then he realized why: it was no longer there. On the opposite bank, only an arrow-shot away, stood a detachment of the Chinese army. They had just cut the bridge. Seg Lhaton and the Tibetan army had no choice but to retreat, giving up all hope of retaking Little Balur and Wakhan that year.

Seg Lhaton had finished his account but his audience immediately asked what had happened. How had General Gao supplied his army? How had they crossed the Oxus? How had the general persuaded Chinese troops to descend the Darkhot pass? Everyone knew the Chinese army's weakness in the mountains. How had they reached Little Balur and the Gilgit river so quickly?

General Gao, Seg Lhaton replied, was a Korean and a wily opponent. But how had he succeeded where three other Chinese generals had failed before him? His first master-stroke had been to divide his force of 10,000 men into three columns at the northern foot of the Pamirs. These he sent south to Wakhan along three different routes, so maintaining three supply lines. The three columns met in August on the northern banks of the Oxus opposite Sarhad and the Tibetan camp.

Instead of being defeated by the spate waters spreading over the valley floor, the general made an offering to the river god to encourage his troops and they crossed the Oxus stealthily and without difficulty a few miles downstream, out of sight of the

Tibetan troops. From here they followed a path south up the mountainside, which had been found by a reconnaissance team sent the previous night, travelling parallel to the tributary valley where the main Tibetan force was encamped. After a few miles they reached a spur from which there was a fairly easy descent to take the main Tibetan forces at the rear and by surprise. 'The last thing we were expecting', explained Seg Lhaton, 'was an attack from the rear. We were forced back against our own palisades.' Meanwhile, another Chinese detachment engaged the Tibetans encamped on the southern bank of the Oxus.

In pursuing the fleeing Tibetans, General Gao did not try to take a full force with him to Little Balur. He left behind the wounded, the weak and the sceptical, and pressed on at great speed to the Darkhot pass. He knew of the descent into the Gilgit valley and did not have great faith in the willingness of his troops to negotiate it without some inducement: most were not mountain men. He therefore chose ten reliable soldiers – all non-Chinese – and ordered them to ride ahead secretly by another route, cross the pass and disguise themselves as residents of the town on the other side. There they were to wait until they saw the general and his troops appear on the saddle of the pass. Then they were to ride up as if they were a delegation from the town and report that the townspeople had sent them to welcome the Chinese and that the bridge over the Gilgit had been cut by the townspeople to prevent a Tibetan counter-attack.

The ruse worked. His soldiers, as the general predicted, were unwilling to descend into the valley but the delegation reassured them. The army advanced in optimistic spirits, certain they had already won the war. Next the general sent a party ahead to the town to capture the royal family and the chiefs of the kingdom. With the king and his entourage as prisoners, he entered the town unopposed and immediately executed the officials loyal to the Tibetans. Then, without wasting any time, he dispatched an advance party of engineers to cut the bridge across the Gilgit river to the south. They had barely succeeded in their task when Seg Lhaton and the rest of the Tibetan army appeared in the dusk along the road on the far side. General Gao's speed, strategy and guile had won the war.

One of Seg Lhaton's audience asked what happened to the king and the Tibetan queen of Little Balur. 'They were sent to the Chinese capital where the king was given an honorary position in the palace guards.' Seg Lhaton did not know what had happened to the queen. The slope near Sarhad by which General Gao's forces had gained the heights above the Tibetan army was fortified with a bastioned stone wall, several feet wide and faced with brick and brushwood, and 2,000 Chinese troops were left to garrison Little Balur. General Gao was richly rewarded by the emperor, and from then on Tibetan commanders treated him with more respect.

After the campaign of 747, Seg Lhaton and his fellow tribesmen from the Yarlung valley were allowed home for a brief period of leave before a tour of duty on the eastern front. It was one and a half thousand miles to their home south of Lhasa, and another thousand north to the next posting. They had been paid and given authorization to levy supplies on the journey.

Their route first took them south along the Gilgit river until it joined the Indus. The stages after this were relatively easy, despite the summer flood waters which at times made the lower roads impassable. They kept to the mountains through northern Kashmir, climbing the Indus river valley south-east into Tibet, from whence the road followed a succession of river valleys along the northern foothills of the Himalayas to the Zangpo or Yarlung river. But Seg Lhaton did not have long with his family on their valley farm before he took the road north to his next posting. His armour and weapons had all been repaired and cleaned, and he had a string of fresh ponies. He was headed for the former stronghold of the Aza tribes, the area around Koko-nor.

On another evening Seg Lhaton was persuaded to relate his account of the Koko-nor campaign. All the soldiers at Miran knew the terrain around Koko-nor as most of them had passed through it on their way to Miran from Tibet. Seg Lhaton told how, on approaching the lake, he saw a mass of large, polygonal, black yak-hair Tibetan tents, surrounded by tens of thousands of horses and livestock. The land around the lake is extremely fertile and that summer the grass reached to the yaks' stomachs, which were distended by their rich diet. The camp stretched as far as Seg Lhaton could see and it took him some time to find his own division and set up camp.

Many of the servants in the Tibetan camp were prisoners-of-war, among them Chinese and Uighurs. When first captured all prisoners were kept in a large pit. The more important were questioned and sometimes tortured before being tattooed and assigned duties. Literate prisoners were appointed as interpreters and advisers and tattooed on the arm, while ordinary prisoners received face tattoos. Escapes were not uncommon, but it was a long journey across the mountains to safety. A century later a Chinese officer who managed to escape after six years in captivity lost part of his foot from frostbite during his flight home. Those who were recaptured were flogged with a leather whip. The bodies of high-ranking prisoners on both sides who died in captivity were returned in coffins under the conditions of various treaties between Tibet and China. Neither Chinese nor Tibetan officials relished being sent to the enemy's capital: envoys were sometimes taken hostage and used as pawns in the continual peace negotiations.

When Seg Lhaton arrived in 749 there was an expectant air in the camp. Spies returning from the Chinese army camps on the Yellow river had confirmed that the half-Turkic military governor, Koso Khan, was mustering his forces. The Tibetan commanders wanted to send more troops to the west to retake the Pamir kingdoms. Since the Chinese victory there, Tibetan soldiers had succeeded in disrupting the supply routes from Kashmir of the Chinese garrison in Little Balur, and they had even encroached back into Wakhan. But a full-scale attack to retake these two kingdoms was delayed because of the need to concentrate Tibetan troops on the eastern front where Chinese aggression was escalating. In fact, later that year General Gao again marched west to confront Tibetan forces in the Pamirs. And again he was successful. Seg Lhaton did not take part in that battle, but there were veterans at Miran who had.

Koso Khan raised a special army of 63,000 men for the attack on

Iron Blade, naming it the Divine Prestige Army. He was determined to succeed against the Tibetans and had drawn men from four commands, all battle-hardened soldiers. Many of the divisions were Turks, loyal to the Chinese but especially pleased to be fighting under a Turkic general. The appointment of non-Chinese generals for the frontier commands was a recent and deliberate policy decision: the Chinese chief minister had advised the emperor that they were better soldiers and had only military, rather than political, ambitions. Apart from the Korean general Gao, who commanded the western regions, and the Turkic general Koso Khan in the Gansu corridor, the north-west was commanded by two Turkic–Sogdian generals, Rokhshan and his cousin. All proved their worth in battle, but six years later Rokhshan showed that being non-Chinese did not preclude him from having ambitions beyond the military sphere: he staged a rebellion, toppled the emperor and took China into a protracted and costly civil war. But all this still lay in the future.

Seg Lhaton described to his audience the first confrontation between the two armies. It was a fine clear day. The Tibetan army drummers started their beat as the two armies advanced. The drums of the Chinese side grew steadily louder as the front lines approached each other. Iron Blade fortress rose behind the ranks of Tibetan soldiers. It was heavily guarded, but the main battle was to take place on the plains below, where there were no trees to obscure the view. As the two armies lined up in opposing ranks, they both sent lone horsemen to gallop up and down close to each other's lines in an attempt to provoke them.

As usual, the Tibetans put non-Tibetan cavalry in the vanguard: both sides used foreign divisions as battle-fodder. Then came the lightly armoured and mounted archers, with pouches of poisoned arrows which they let loose among the Chinese soldiers. In their iron chain-mail, the ranks of Tibetan foot soldiers in the rear were almost impregnable to Chinese swords and arrows. Only the long, steel-tipped arrows of the Chinese archers could hope to pierce it. Each Tibetan foot soldier carried a sword, a lance, daggers and catapults, and the Chinese were similarly equipped. Behind the lines lay the heavy artillery – a row of catapults. Chinese archers made liberal use of fire arrows, and some of the foot soldiers carried heavy lances tipped with combustible material which they set alight and projected from flexible bamboo poles into the Tibetan forces.

The battle continued day after day in the bright sunlight of the high plateau. The tall grass was soon trampled by the tens of thousands of men and horses, and the air was thick with dust and death. Still the Chinese could not break the Tibetan lines. As one soldier fell another would replace him. A Tibetan fatigue-relieving corps collected the soldiers near to collapse and took them back behind the lines, where they would be revived and then ordered back to the front. Every night the dead and the wounded were collected by both sides from the field of battle.

After several days of fighting with thousands of casualties among his soldiers, the Chinese general Koso Khan called his deputies into his tent. He laid down an ultimatum: he would have them all executed unless they broke the Tibetan lines and took Iron Blade fortress within three days. Seg Lhaton and his fellow soldiers did not hear of this until later, but they noticed the renewed determination of the enemy troops. Though line on line of Chinese soldiers fell, the pressure became too great for the Tibetans. Eventually they were forced back into the fortress. Now the Chinese sent battering rams to knock down the gates and catapults to hurl boulders to break down the walls. Toxic smoke bombs, made from powdered lime and arsenic stuffed in thin earthenware pots with broken matting, were lobbed into the heart of the fort to poison its inmates. The Tibetan archers continued to do their work, but still the Chinese advanced.

At last the fortress was taken but at a tremendous cost. In the final Chinese advance, the Tibetan general and four hundred of his men were captured. The rest of the Tibetan army retreated south, leaving the bloody land behind. A Chinese poet expressed what must have been a common feeling on both sides:

> Kites and ravens peck men's guts,
> Fly with them dangling from their beaks
> And hang them high on boughs of barren trees.
> The troops lie mud-smeared in the grass
> And the generals acted all in vain.

Now I see that weapons are the tools of evil.
The Sage will only use them when he cannot do otherwise.

Seg Lhaton finished his story. He did not reveal to his audience that he had lost his taste for battle after this, although he had had to fight in several more encounters against the Chinese before being posted to Miran. He was only prevented from returning home for good by loyalty and fear of reprisals – deserters were executed. He could not read Chinese, but he may have sympathized with the sentiments of the many anti-war poems produced by Chinese poets in reaction to the frontier campaigns:

> I have learned that bearing males is bad,
>   but bearing girls is good.
> If you bear a girl you can marry her to a neighbour
> But a boy will end up buried out on the prairie grass.

> Haven't you seen on Koko-nor's shores
> White bones from ancient days that no one gathers?
> The new ghosts are tormented with rage,
> The older ghosts just weep.
> When the sky grows shadowed and rain pours down,
> You hear their voices wailing.

Many more evenings were spent in the desert fort talking of former battles and exchanging stories before Seg Lhaton finally received orders that he could return home and was exempted from further military service. He had been fighting since he was fifteen. It was not unusual to see men of fifty or older in battle, but Seg Lhaton had incurred several injuries that made active service difficult. One leg wound, received at Koko-nor, had left him partially lame and every winter he suffered from arthritis in his knee-joints and could ride only with difficulty. During his brief home leaves he had married and had children, but his wife and sons had done most of the farm work over the past two decades. He consulted a local astrologer who chose a good day to begin his journey, packed his belongings and set off south for the Kunlun mountains. He was not sorry to leave the fort at Miran: it has been a poor home.

A long journey through a landscape of memories lay ahead of him. He travelled quickly, from one Tibetan camp to another, across the great grazing grounds of the Tsaidam to Koko-nor, now back in Tibetan hands. Here the memories were especially bitter. He rode around the former fields of war, recalling the battle of long ago. The new grass showed little trace of those bloody days with only just a few rusty, broken weapons left as a grim reminder of what had happened here. Before he left he pulled up some roots of liquorice to take back for his grandchildren. Their father was also away on military service on the Silk Road. Seg Lhaton had been fortunate to have survived twenty-five years of fighting. Who knew if his son would be so lucky?

The Horseman's Tale

Kumtugh, 790–792

A green-eyed Uighur goshawk treads his brocaded gauntlet.
With piebald horse and white ermine furs
He comes and goes in the three markets, but knows no one;
Throwing down his gold-handled whip, he ascends the tower of wine.

Xue Fang, 'Xia shao nian', 9th century AD

IT WAS 790 and the beginning of the short steppe summer when the land is all too briefly green and the sky a constant, unrelenting blue, a respite from the grey and white of winter's snow-laden clouds and frost-bitten earth. The camels and horses of the caravan crossing the steppe numbered thousands, but to the horseman approaching from afar at the head of a herd of ponies they were barely a speck in the rolling landscape.

The horseman Kumtugh was a Uighur Turk, with a characteristically broad face, thick eyelashes and deep-set, green eyes. His language, Uighur, was close to modern-day Turkish. He was dressed in a short-belted blue tunic with narrow sleeves, and trousers tucked into soft leather boots. His ponies were tarpans (*Equus przewalski*), age-old travellers of the Eurasian steppe. They had lived in this land since the Pleistocene era – long before man – and they were better-adapted to its rigours. (Their wild cousins, though now driven almost to extinction, are still to be found on the western steppe of Dzungaria in southern Mongolia.) The tarpan has a large head and a distinctive mane that stands up in summer, although in the winter both its mane and hair grow long and shaggy to ward off the bitter cold of the steppes. Kumtugh's

The tarpan, Equus przewalski, *with its erect mane but no forelock*

herd of ponies comprised several hundred head, and with it he was
joining the larger caravan that he could see in the distance. This
caravan was an embassy headed for the Chinese capital by way of a
trading post on the Uighur–Chinese border. There the horses
would be sold to the Chinese government.

The Uighurs were a confederation of Turkic tribes, the same
peoples who later migrated west into what is today Turkey. Before
744, when they seized the steppes north of the Tianshan, the
region had been divided between two other confederations: the
Eastern and Western Turks. At the height of their power an adviser
to the Eastern Turkic kaghan had observed:

> The Turks number but one to every hundred of the Chinese.
> When they feel strong they advance. When weak, they retreat
> and hide. In this way they compensate for their lack of
> numbers. If you establish your peoples in a walled town and are
> beaten by the Chinese, albeit only once, you will become their
> prisoner.

The Turkic kaghan had heeded this advice and the Eastern Turks
had continued to be difficult neighbours, constantly making raids
across the borders into Chinese territory. The Chinese Tang
dynasty believed the Turks to be descendants of the Xiongnu,

while a Turkic legend tells of a young boy injured by the enemy and left to die, whose subsequent union with a she-wolf produced ten sons, forebears of the Turks, who were to rise to tribal supremacy in AD 552. The Turkic standard bore a golden wolf's head and every year the Turkic kaghan offered a sacrifice at the cave believed to have sheltered their ancestors.

By the seventh century, the two confederations of Eastern and Western Turks were increasingly beset by internal conflict. The Chinese Tang dynasty, founded in 618, encouraged and inflamed their arguments, eventually in 630 defeating the Eastern Turks and resettling tens of thousands of their people, in both the Chinese capital, Chang'an, and the Ordos region to the north. An inscription on a stone erected at the Turkic capital on the Orkhon river expressed the Turks' bitter feelings on Chinese policy:

> Because of discord between nobles and commoners, because of the cunning and deceitfulness of the Chinese who set against each other younger and older brother, nobleman and commoner, the Turks brought about the disintegration of their own empire, and caused the downfall of their kaghan.

The Western Turks then expanded their territory so that it stretched across the whole of the steppe, and they made several incursions into Chinese territory in the early years of the eighth century, but they too were weakened by internal dissension, and the Uighurs, one of three vassal tribes in the north, took the opportunity to rebel. After success on the battlefield they moved south from their base on the Selenga river, seizing control of the land as far east as the borders of China and south to the Tianshan, beyond which lay the Silk Road. Contrary to nomadic tradition, the Uighurs then built a walled capital called Karabalghasun on the Orkhon river in the north of their new empire, established in 744. The Uighur kaghan kept a traditional felt tent erected on the roof of his palace, perhaps to remind him of his nomadic origins. The tent, covered in gold, was a permanent structure from which the kaghan could see his domain stretching away beyond the city walls. For miles around, the land was cultivated by Uighur farmers. Sogdian and Chinese architects had already been at work designing fine buildings for his city and had been directed to build another town, named 'Rich Town', on the Selenga river to the west. Kumtugh's grandfather had been sceptical about these changes and Kumtugh remembered his constant boast: 'When we Uighurs fight our neighbours, we generally destroy several thousand of their cavalry with but five hundred of our men. It is as if we were simply sweeping up leaves.'

At first the new Uighur kaghanate looked set to be a better neighbour to the Chinese, both states being united against the Tibetan threat to their respective borders. During the late 740s and the early 750s Chinese forces, under the leadership of the generals Gao and Koso Khan, seemed to be gaining the upper hand over the Tibetans. A third foreign general, a Turkic–Sogdian named Rokhshan, had been less successful in his northern campaigns against the Khitan peoples but remained a favourite of the Chinese emperor Xuanzong and, most especially, of the emperor's consort, the Lady Yang. In 751, following one of his defeats, she adopted Rokhshan as her son and scandalous stories were soon circulating in Chang'an's tea-houses about her more than maternal affections. Matters were not helped when they both took private lessons in the Sogdian 'whirling' dance, considered by conservative Chinese officials to be highly immoral. Rumours also circulated that she had sent Rokhshan presents given to her by her husband, such as the ten pieces of best camphor from Borneo, presented as a tribute by a delegation from that country. She demanded use of the Bright Camel Envoy to carry the camphor, even though this was normally reserved for military emergencies.

But Lady Yang retained the favour of the emperor who was, by this time, no longer young. When the emperor first became infatuated with her, Rokhshan had given him a hundred tiny red pills from essence of passion flower and advised him to place one in his mouth every evening before entering Lady Yang's bedroom so as 'to help his passions develop into excitement and the strength of his sinews not to flag'. Lady Yang also knew many other ways to keep the emperor happy. She would perform Central Asian dances in a multi-coloured gauze blouse and feathered skirt in the style of the legendary immortal ladies of the west, and was also an adept musician:

The copper tongues in the mouth organ resound in the cool
    bamboo tubes,
As slowly she plays new tunes with her jade-like fingers.
Her eyes look at me invitingly – as autumn waves, swiftly
    changing.
We knew the 'rain' and 'clouds' in the intimacy of the curtained
    chamber,
Where our passions united us. Now, after these feats, how empty
    is the room!
There is nothing left but to lose myself in dreams of spring.*

When the emperor was losing at a game of double sixes she would
release one of her pets, her Samarkand lapdog or her white cocka-
too, and shoo them in the direction of the gaming board in order
to distract his opponent. Every year they would go to hot springs
just outside the city which the emperor had built specially so that
he could enjoy watching her bathe: she was reported to have had
skin of snowy whiteness and was plump, as demanded by the
fashion of the day. The emperor was totally infatuated with her.

Later in 751, Rokhshan lost most of his army in yet another
battle against the Khitans, but he retained his position and, in 754,
was even promoted, much to the consternation of Koso Khan, one
of his many critics. But feeling against Rokhshan was mounting in
Chang'an, fostered by the chief minister, Lady Yang's cousin.
Having refused orders to attend the emperor at the capital and
knowing that in the chief minister he had a bitter enemy,
Rokhshan decided to take matters into his own hands. In
December 755 he rebelled.

Initially he met with success. Within little more than a month he
had taken the secondary capital of China, Luoyang, which lies two
hundred miles east of Chang'an. To stem the tide of rebellion the
emperor recalled all the military garrisons on China's north-west
borders. This withdrawal of troops was to signal the beginning of
the end of China's influence along the Silk Road.

Rokhshan spent the winter of 755–6 consolidating his gains and

---

* Poem by Li Yu (937–78), ruler of the Southern Tang dynasty. 'Rain and clouds' was a traditional
Chinese literary expression for sexual intercourse, the *locus classicus* a text of the third century BC.

driving further south, but then he began to suffer setbacks as local prefects returned to the loyalist cause and his armies endured defeats. The rebels were weakening and when the emperor ordered Koso Khan to attack them, he refused, arguing that his troops held an impregnable position defending the capital which it would be foolhardy to surrender. Unwisely the emperor insisted and Koso Khan had no choice but to comply. In the sixth month of 756 the general's fears were borne out: his advancing army was ambushed and destroyed, and Koso Khan was forced to surrender to Rokhshan by his own men.

When news of the defeat reached the emperor he promptly fled the capital with Lady Yang, and headed for the safety of the mountainous south-west. But the troops in his escort blamed the Lady Yang for Rokhshan's rise and threatened to mutiny there and then. He could only appease them by ordering Lady Yang's strangulation. She was buried at the site of her execution and the imperial party continued their flight. Meanwhile, the heir apparent had fled north to the border regions and there he usurped the throne, declaring himself emperor in the summer of 756. The Chinese empire, at the height of its power only a few years before, was now in disarray.

The new emperor lost no time in sending embassies to the Uighur court at Karabalghasun to plead for their help against the rebels. The main Uighur contingent of 4,000 men arrived in July 757 under the leadership of the kaghan's eldest son. By this time, Rokhshan had been assassinated by a fellow rebel who had then assumed command. The Uighur army prepared for battle and Chang'an was retaken by the end of the year. In return for their aid, the Uighurs had demanded the right to plunder the city if they were successful, but the Chinese chief minister persuaded them to wait until Luoyang, too, was retaken. The Uighur army did so in the same month and many of the rebels surrendered. Then they exercised their right to plunder Luoyang and for the next three days the city was the scene of appalling carnage.

The rebellion continued to simmer for several more years, in the course of which two more of its leaders were assassinated and its armies took Luoyang a second time. On this occasion the rebels themselves tried to enlist the support of the Uighurs. When in desperation the Chinese emperor sent his heir apparent and three top officials to plead his cause, the Uighur kaghan demanded that they perform the ceremonial dance expected of all subordinates attending the kaghan. The heir apparent refused and both he and the three officials were beaten, two of them so badly that they died the same day. Nevertheless, the Uighurs decided to support the Chinese and, in late 762, again drove the rebels out of Luoyang and again plundered the city. Kumtugh's grandfather was among the veterans of this campaign and he often boasted of how frightened the Chinese had been of the Uighur forces. Other veterans spoke of the tremendous riches of Luoyang and of the young women of the city, many of whom were raped and killed by Uighur soldiers. Some residents took refuge in Buddhist buildings, but these were burned to the ground with the people still inside. Much was destroyed but even more was loaded on to camels and taken out of the city and back to Karabalghasun.

The Uighur army camped around the city in their tents, seizing supplies from local farmers and granaries until nothing was left for the local populace. People fled into the surrounding hills where they survived as best they could. The veterans did not tell of the terrible famine which forced people to eat soil and the bark of trees while the soldiers grew fat on their plunder. The city, once a rival to Chang'an for its broad, tree-lined avenues, fine buildings and bustling lanes, lay in charred ruins.

As a further reward for their services, the Uighurs demanded that border markets be established for the trade of horses and silk. From this time on, the Uighurs and the Chinese had an uneasy alliance. The Uighurs regularly brought herds of thousands of ponies for sale to the Chinese government at a fixed price of forty bolts of silk each, though a pony could be bought for as little as one bolt elsewhere. The ponies were euphemistically referred to as 'Uighur tributes to the court' by the Chinese annalists but were really Chinese payment for Uighur military assistance and security against future Uighur attack. The Uighurs benefited most from these transactions, although the Chinese limited their financial losses by regularly defaulting on payment.

While in Luoyang, the Uighur kaghan met a group of Manichean priests from Samarkand and was himself converted.

1. 'The women sat in the dappled shade of the courtyard . . . hunched intently over the delicately carved double-six table' (p. 183)

2. *(left)* 'Ever since Larishka could remember, Kucha had been under the jurisdiction of the Kocho Uighurs' (p. 141): Uighur prince, Kocho

3. *(right)* 'The eighth-century emperor Xuanzong . . . housed thirty thousand musicians and dancers in the imperial palace' (p. 139)

4. *(below)* Female heretics being tonsured after their defeat in the contest with the Buddhist Sariputra (pp. 210–13)

5. *(far left)* 'Manichean clergy traditionally dressed in white and did not cut their hair' (p. 135)

6. *(above)* 'West of Koko-nor lies the Tsaidam . . . which provided ideal conditions for grazing large herds of livestock and mounting armed raids across the Kunlun on the Silk Road towns' (p. 26)

7. *(left)* 'The nobility were often accompanied on their travels by a troupe of musicians . . . seated atop a camel' (p. 47)

8. 'The party came across the bodies of their former travelling companions two hours later at a narrow defile. They had been ambushed and killed, and all their goods taken' (p. 48)

9. From Tashkurgan to Kashgar: 'To the north-west they could see the snowy peak of the Mustagh-ata among the continuation of the Pamirs northwards' (p. 125)

10. 'For his young grandson he went to a tailor to have a traditional Sogdian suit made, a short jacket with narrow sleeves . . . woven with a typical Sogdian design' (p. 30)

11. General Zhang after his victory over the Tibetans at Dunhuang: 'Fengda's father had taken him to see a painting of the general with his victorious army' (p. 190)

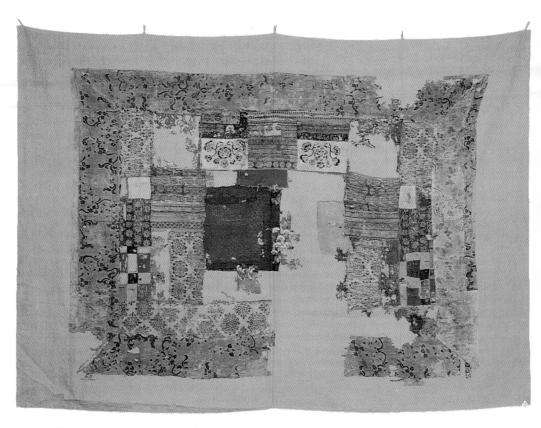

12. 'Some of the monks had their assembly robes, or kasaya, made for them out of the most luxurious silk from central China . . . a mockery of the robe's significance and the monks' vows' (p. 172)

On his return to Karabalghasun he ordered the propagation of the new religion in his kingdom, though many of his subjects, among them Kumtugh's family, retained their shamanistic beliefs. Manichean teachers were dispatched throughout the land and the kaghan decreed that one in ten of his subjects would be responsible for the spiritual education of the other nine. Monasteries were established, even as far south as Dzungaria, and the white-cloaked Manichean monks became a common sight. At first they were full of missionary zeal, burning all the statues they found of the local gods and spirits. Kumtugh's own tribal leader flirted with Manicheism for a time: groups of priests would hold day-long prayer sessions in his tent. But Kumtugh's family would have nothing to do with the new religion, and his grandmother, herself a shaman, did not lose customers. Even their neighbours, who professed a belief in the new religion, would attend seances and make their offerings and requests along with everyone else. It was not long before many of the new converts were lapsing, reverting to agricultural labour in defiance of monastic rules, returning to their traditional meat diet, and making offerings to local gods and spirits. There was also considerable antipathy towards the Manichean Sogdians among some of the kaghan's courtiers.

However, Sogdian influence extended beyond the spiritual: they were the merchants of the Silk Road and also fine builders, craftsmen and agriculturists. Sogdian architects and artisans helped transform the capital into a thriving commercial centre with metallurgists, potters, engravers, blacksmiths, sculptors, stonemasons and weavers. Many Uighurs now abandoned their nomadic lifestyle altogether, while others farmed in the summer but still travelled with their livestock to the winter pastures. The Uighurs also adopted the Sogdian script, an alphabet of seventeen letters with two special characters. Sogdian is an Iranian language, and therefore its alphabet was not perfectly adapted to Uighur, a Turkic language, but it sufficed. The Uighurs in turn passed the script on to later inhabitants of the steppes, the Mongols.

Sogdians also played a political role. In 779 they urged the kaghan to mount an invasion of China while her court was in mourning for its emperor Taizong. The kaghan's nephew disagreed with the policy and, failing to win his argument by persuasion, arranged for his uncle's murder along with that of his Sogdian advisers. There followed several years when the Sogdians were less welcome at court.

Sogdians travelled with the Uighurs on their frequent embassies to the Chinese capital and many stayed and settled there and in other Chinese cities. Some even married Chinese women or took Chinese concubines. During the last part of the eighth century they had an excuse to stay, for the Silk Road to the east of Sogdiana was not passable, being held by the Tibetans, and during their residence in Chang'an they received Chinese government aid which amounted to half a million strings of cash (copper coins) annually. One Chinese minister suggested that the merchants be granted status as Chinese subjects and given jobs, and although his proposal was not implemented the aid was ended. In 780, a Uighur embassy was ordered to take both Uighur and Sogdian merchants back with them to Karabalghasun, from whence the Sogdians could travel through Uighur-held territory almost to the borders of Sogdiana. Fearing that their Chinese wives and concubines would not be granted permission to leave, the merchants smuggled them out in sacks loaded, along with their other goods, on camels. The caravan stayed three months on the border just north of the Yellow river, waiting for the travelling season. Since they were still in Chinese territory their rations were supplied by the Chinese government. The unusually large bill soon came to official notice, the caravan was searched, and the stowaways discovered.

The story did not have a happy ending. The Sogdian merchants were reluctant to go to Karabalghasun because of the recent murder of the pro-Sogdian kaghan and his advisers. They therefore sought a secret agreement with the Chinese general accompanying them whereby they would assist in massacring the Uighurs in the embassy in exchange for being allowed to stay in China. The Chinese general thought that on the whole it would be less trouble-some to massacre both the Uighurs and the Sogdians and duly sought permission from the emperor, arguing that this would be a means of diminishing the influence of both. When his request was refused for the third time, the general engineered a breach of protocol to provide him with the necessary excuse. He then arranged a great banquet, wined and dined his guests into a helpless state, and had them killed. Two Uighurs were spared and sent to Karabalghasun to report the event, and the Chinese wives and concubines were returned to Chang'an. The Uighur kaghan took revenge in characteristic fashion: instead of murdering the Chinese envoys sent to accompany the coffins of the merchants back to Karabalghasun, he kept them waiting in the capital for two months before granting them an audience. We must presume that they were by then in a state of some anxiety. The kaghan then demanded payment in full of all outstanding debts on the purchase of horses, amounting to two million strings of cash (suggesting that the Chinese were inveterate defaulters). The Chinese emperor realized he had escaped lightly and paid the debt, using state reserves of gold, silver and silk.

A Chinese imperial decree of 779 had ordered non-Chinese to wear their national dress in China so as to be distinctive, but the Uighurs stood out anyway. Groups of young men would ride into Chang'an's Western Market in search of a tea-shop, the latest fashion or simply some excitement. There were complaints from market officials about the Uighur's loutish behaviour and their harassment of traders, many of whom were in debt to Uighur moneylenders though it had been illegal for Chinese subjects to borrow money from Uighurs ever since a famous general's son had defaulted on a loan. The Uighur moneylender had taken the case to law and a scandal had ensued, with the general being dismissed from his post. The law had little effect, however, and Uighur moneylenders continued to thrive for at least another century.

The horse trade also flourished. The land and water in Central China contains too little calcium for successful horse-breeding and ever since the Chinese had learned the arts of horsemanship from their Central Asian neighbours, these neighbours continued to be their main source of new stock. As China expanded her territory to include the steppe pasturelands to the north-west, traditional home of many of the horses, they were able to breed more success-fully. They preferred horses with Arab ancestry to the pure tarpan pony, but the herds always contained a mixture of the two. Arab blood gave the tarpan a smaller head and flowing mane and, most importantly, its ridge of muscle on either side of the backbone that made bareback riding more comfortable: Chinese soldiers and horsemen, however, rode on saddles with stirrups – a Central Asian invention. But the herds were always vulnerable to looting by the Turks and Tibetans who made frequent raids across the borders, and to disease. In one particularly bad epidemic, the Chinese lost 180,000 horses, causing a minister to proclaim: 'Horses are the military preparedness of the country; if Heaven takes this preparedness away, the state will fall.' When the Chinese Tang dynasty came to power in 618 there were only 5,000 horses left in the imperial pastures. By mid-century their numbers had increased to over 700,000, divided among eight pasturelands. But after Rokhshan's rebellion, Tibetan raids on the pastures increased and the Chinese came to rely on the Uighurs for replacement mounts – although they did not need all that were sent, especially since many of them were old nags. It was nevertheless an in-dication of Chinese fear of Uighur military strength that they continued to buy them.

The Uighurs were consummate horsemen and, despite the more sedentary lifestyle of some of the population after the found-ing of their empire, their equine skills were not neglected. Kumtugh was a typical horseman. He knew how to pick the best pony for each job and season, skills he had been taught while still a child. For summer it was essential to choose a mount with a thin hide that had not been worked too hard in the previous months, since even the toughest ponies found the unrelenting heat difficult and a good-natured mount was a great asset. The best pony for winter, by contrast, had a thick hide, long hair and a round stomach, with legs that rose straight from the ground, showing no hint of splaying. For lassoeing, a short-bodied mount was required, stout but swift. Kumtugh and his peers had been riding since before they could walk and were more at home on horseback than on foot.

Kumtugh was riding one of his favourite mounts as he approached the large caravan across the steppe in the summer of 790. The horses already in the caravan had been taken from the summer grazing grounds near the Uighur capital. Kumtugh was bringing several hundred head more from the southern grazing grounds in Dzungaria to join them. There were many old nags among them and others that would barely make the journey, and so Kumtugh carried various horse medicines with him, including a recipe which helped relieve colic caused by cold water from desert wells. The mixture comprised wormwood, fennel, apricot kernels, rhubarb, ground ginger and a tree-growing fungus. Kumtugh knew that the Chinese overseer would complain about the state of the horses, but also that he could do nothing about it. He would pay for them all and the Uighurs would return with fine silks for trade with their western neighbours. The horse-trade was a good opportunity for the Uighurs to get rid of poor stock, and if horses died *en route*, then they could always be eaten.

Before he had left with his horses to join the embassy to China, Kumtugh had asked his grandmother for advice about the journey. As a respected shaman she had chosen Kumtugh's name, which means 'lucky', and she always advised the family whenever there were important decisions to be made. Kumtugh, his relations and neighbours now crowded into the family's tent and settled themselves around its walls. Each brought small offerings, mainly of food, which they gave to his grandmother as she encountered hungry spirits on her journey through the spirit world. When she awoke from the trance she explained to Kumtugh that one spirit had told her of a good day for him to embark on his travels, and others had offered warnings about situations and people to avoid.

Kumtugh's family lived in the south of the Uighur kaghanate, beyond the Altai mountains in the great steppe basin now known as Dzungaria. They belonged to one of ten Uighur tribes, each of which owed allegiance to its own leader, the tutuk. The kaghan was drawn from one of the tribes. Several other non-Uighur Turkic tribes also offered allegiance to the kaghan and frontline troops were usually chosen from among these. Dzungaria had excellent pasturage and shelter for vast herds of camels, horses, yaks and sheep, and when one area of pasture was cropped, Kumtugh and his family would pack up their tents and belongings, load them on to camels and horse-driven carts and move on. The richer among the tribe had at least two tents or yurts, substantial round dwellings made of thick felt supported by a collapsible wooden frame, with a smoke hole in the centre of the domed roof.

Felt played an important role in Uighur life. It was used not just for tents but also for saddle-pads, boot linings, clothes and furnishings, and new batches were made very autumn. A piece of old felt, called 'the mother', was laid on the ground and soaked with water. Three layers of sheep wool and a layer of grass were placed on top, each soaked in turn, and then the bundle was rolled up tightly inside hides that had also been soaked, and fastened with leather straps. More water was poured in at either end, and ropes were tied to the bundle and to two mounted horsemen on opposite sides. They both stood on their horses next to the bundle so that the ropes were slack. One then walked his horse away until his rope was taut and then dragged the bundle along the ground until the other horseman's rope was taut. This continued, first one way and then the other, perhaps thirty or forty times. The whole soggy bundle was then unwrapped, unrolled and the grass removed. The resulting piece of rough felt, formed from the amalgam of the layers of sheep wool, was called 'the daughter'. But the process was not yet complete. Next the daughter felt was rolled up with another three layers of wool and the process repeated. The resulting felt was soaked again and laid against the side of a tent to dry. Different types and grades of wool were used to make different qualities of felt. The best was made from the downy fleece of the unshorn sheep, collected by hand.

Kumtugh had spent most of his life with his family in Dzungaria. He regarded the tribal head, the tutuk, as his leader: the kaghan was a distant figure. The tutuk was responsible for raising an army, and all males between the ages of fifteen and fifty could be called up. To hone their military skills, Kumtugh and his fellows played many games and sports, among them archery competitions in which they would ride at full speed with the reins between their teeth and then fire a volley of arrows at various targets. They also went on hunting expeditions into the mountains in search of wolves and deer. But Kumtugh's greatest joy was his goshawk. He and his fellow tribesmen would catch young hawks in passage using decoys and nets dyed with *toghruga*, a yellow-

Man in hufu *(foreigner's robe) with falcon and dog, from
a mural in an imperial Tang dynasty tomb near Chang'an*

brown dye from the bark of the black poplar, which meant the nets could not been seen against the earth. Or they might raid nests for chicks, fitting them with jesses, leashes and leather hoods, and training them to catch small mammals and birds. A group of men often hunted their hawks together, riding with their birds and hounds into the Altai mountains and taking watch on a circle of peaks which afforded a clear view of the valley below. As soon as prey was sighted, their birds were released. A group of eagles, which were also used for falconry, could take a wolf this way.

Kumtugh was excited when he learned that he had been chosen to join the embassy bound for Chang'an, for even members of the leading families in Karabalghasun vied with each other for the opportunity to travel to China. Kumtugh had visited neither the Uighur nor the Chinese capitals, but stories told by veterans of the wealth of Chang'an, and more recent accounts from fellow tribesmen who had been on earlier embassies, had aroused his curiosity. They spoke of all the goods in Chang'an's Western Market and of how they had ridden in on horseback and 'persuaded' cowering merchants to make presents of their wares. In the wine-shops and tea-houses they were entertained by beautiful Kuchean girls and afterwards they had visited the famous courtesan quarter by the Eastern Market. This abutted a rich residential area, and they laughed when they recalled how Chinese scholars had veered off down side streets when they saw the Uighur youths approaching. The Uighurs considered themselves masters of the city.

Kumtugh and his herd caught up with the large caravan and settled into its rhythm. Its progress was slow, its speed dictated by the plodding camels and the need to graze the enormous herds. As soon as suitable pasturage was reached each day the camels were unloaded, tents erected, and cooking fires prepared, while the horses and camels were left to graze on the thin grass that covered the rocky steppe. The Uighurs carried noodles and dried fruit with them, but their main food was meat. Mares' milk was also used extensively, to make butter and cheese, or fermented to make a slightly alcoholic drink that could in turn be distilled into a clear liquor. When there was no firewood they cooked with camel or yak dung.

The caravan was in high spirits as it approached the Chinese border and trading-post, although also vigilant: there were often Tibetan raids in this area. Kumtugh learned that not everyone would be allowed to continue to Chang'an. The main party of high officials and members of the kaghan's family, including two princesses, carried letters for the emperor and further 'gifts'. Kumtugh hoped to accompany them, but the Chinese border guards always limited the number of Uighurs allowed into the capital. They had been particularly strict since an incident involving a previous embassy in which drunken Uighur youths, in a rage at some perceived slight, had tried to hack down the gate to the court for receiving foreign envoys in the Imperial City. The Uighur men looked forward to a few encounters with their Chinese counterparts: they considered the Chinese scholar–official with his feminine demeanour and refusal to carry arms a contemptible sort of person, a victim to bully. Such encounters did not always stop at verbal abuse: drunken brawls were commonplace and in 774 and 775 Chinese men were murdered by Uighurs in Chang'an. The head of the Uighur community refused to allow

the murderers to be punished, and the Chinese governor did not
dare enforce the law.

In the event, to his disappointment, Kumtugh was not among
those allowed to proceed to Chang'an. But while still at the border
he heard disturbing news about Dzungaria, his homeland. Uighur
and Chinese forces had been defeated at the city of Beshbaliq in
southern Dzungaria by Tibetan-led forces. The Uighurs had
retreated north across the Gobi to Karabalghasun and the Chinese
had fled south over the Tianshan to Kocho. A joint counter-attack
was planned for the autumn and orders had been sent to all the
tutuks to call every adult man to arms. Kumtugh started back for
his homeland in northern Dzungaria immediately to prepare for
the campaign.

The problems in Beshbaliq had a long history, dating back to
Rokhshan's rebellion in China. Just as Uighur forces had gained
dominance in China after helping to suppress the rebellion, so the
Tibetans had profited from the Chinese empire's increasing weakness, although not immediately – in 755, the same year as the start
of the Chinese rebellion, the Tibetan emperor had been assassinated by two of his ministers. However, a new emperor was
installed in 756, by which time China had recalled most of the
troops stationed in its western garrisons, and the Tibetans lost no
time in advancing north. By the late eighth century they controlled most of the Silk Road. Only a few unsupported Chinese
garrisons remained. Beshbaliq, called Beiting by the Chinese, was
one of these. The direct route into China from Beshbaliq led
south-east through the Gansu corridor, but this area was also controlled by the Tibetans. Several envoys from Beshbaliq had tried to
find an alternative route, but it was a decade before the first arrived
safely in China, having travelled north to Karabalghasun and then
south-east to the Uighur–Chinese border. This was in 781, and
since then all supplies and messengers had used this very circuitous
route, for which privilege the Uighurs exacted a large transit toll.

Finding their resources drained by these constant raids, and
by combined reparations to the Uighurs for past assistance, the
Chinese had actively sought peace with the Tibetans. A treaty was
negotiated and signed in 783, freeing Chinese troops to deal with
another internal rebellion. The settlement negotiated between the

two powers promised Tibetan assistance against the rebels and Chinese agreement to cede Beshbaliq, but neither side stuck to its terms and in retaliation the Tibetans arranged the assassination of two senior Chinese generals. A third, invited to a negotiating session which was no more than an excuse for an ambush, narrowly escaped. The Tibetan attack on Beshbaliq was further revenge for the broken treaty.

This attack also marked the culmination of several years of covert operations in the area. Beshbaliq was populated largely by non-Uighur Turks, and the plains surrounding the city by tens of thousands of Shatuo Turks. The two peoples lived in peace with each other, but the Uighurs to the north made themselves very unpopular. Armed groups of young Uighurs made regular raids into the area, seizing clothes, food and livestock. With few men and no recourse to reinforcements, the Chinese forces were powerless to retaliate. Moreover, the Uighurs were supposed to be their allies.

The Tibetans had spies in the town who reported the rising level of popular discontent among the Turkic residents, and the Tibetans fomented it, secretly offering Turkic leaders their full support should the townspeople decide to rebel. Finally, in 789, the Tibetans judged the mood to be favourable and invaded across the Tianshan, capturing Beshbaliq in January 790. Uighur and Chinese forces reunited for the first time since their battles against the rebels in China in 763 and the city was briefly retaken, but in the summer the residents went over to the Tibetans, and the Uighur and Chinese armies were both forced to retreat.

Both the Uighurs and the Chinese had much to fear from the Tibetans. Tibetan raiding parties made regular incursions deep into both their territories and in 763 Tibetan soldiers had even briefly captured the Chinese capital. The new combined Uighur–Chinese army that Kumtugh was to join had been formed to face a common enemy, but it was not clear quite who was helping whom. The Uighurs had more to lose. Beshbaliq was the only buffer between them and the Tibetan empire. The Chinese regarded Beshbaliq merely as an impotent outpost, a vestige of their former control. The relative size of the two forces reflected this disparity: the Uighurs called up every adult man, and their forces numbered between fifty and sixty thousand, while the Chinese only contributed two thousand men.

Kumtugh rode his string of horses non-stop back to Dzungaria. It was late summer by the time he arrived. The tutuk of his tribe had been summoned to Karabalghasun, but the main forces of his army were training on the plains and preparing their horses and weapons for battle. The same scene was repeated throughout the Uighur empire as the ten tribal leaders called their men to arms. Kumtugh gathered his armour, weapons and best horses and joined his fellows in their manoeuvres. The northern and eastern tribes converged on the capital and marched south in early autumn. They were joined *en route*, by other forces, Kumtugh's being the last, and then they marched south as a combined force under the generalship of the Uighur chief minister, eager to avenge the earlier defeat at the hands of the Tibetans. Messengers were sent ahead to tell the Chinese soldiers of their approach and instead of entering Beshbaliq from the north, the direct route, the general took his army in a wide sweep to the south, across the Tianshan to Kocho, where the Chinese forces joined them. By now some of the Uighur forces had marched for almost a thousand miles.

The Uighurs considered themselves more than a match for the cumbersome Tibetan cavalry. Their bows were strengthened with horn and sinew, and their wooden arrows were flighted so as to produce a loud whistling sound to intimidate the enemy. The Chinese infantry were equipped with crossbows with leather-flighted arrows, and with longbows whose steel-headed arrows could pierce Tibetan armour. The Tibetan infantry were the main threat. Heavily armed and encased in armour, they were known for their bravery under attack. But the Tibetan army was also re-inforced with Turkic soldiers, rebellious former subjects of the Uighurs, who were excellent cavalrymen.

The generals wore swords with hilts and scabbards mounted with silver, gold and precious stones. Chinese alchemical theory held that the finest swords were a combination of female and male essences, *yin* and *yang*. To produce them, the bellows had to be worked by a virgin girl and boy. In ancient times, swords had been made in pairs – male and female. Legend spoke of such magical swords as dragon spirits and producers of lightning which would cut through jade. Chinese artisans producing swords without imperial authorization were subject to severe punishment, and trade in weapons across China's borders was prohibited.

From Kocho, after the Chinese contingent had joined them, Kumtugh and his fellow soldiers marched north, back across the Tianshan. The Tibetan army was waiting for them on the plain below the walled city of Beshbaliq and both sides took up their positions. The next day the standard bearers, trumpeters and drummers led their respective armies into battle. Each day the scene was one of a tangled mass of men, horses and weapons. Each evening when the armies retreated behind their lines, those who had fallen were left behind. The Uighur and Chinese forces could make no headway against the Tibetan lines and as the battle progressed they grew weak and dispirited. Then at last the Tibetan lines began to advance. Kumtugh was caught up in the tumult of horses and men trying to flee, their commanders behind the lines slashing at their own men in an attempt to frighten them back into battle as the grey mass of the iron-clad Tibetan infantry rolled relentlessly forward across the plain like a great tidal wave.

The Uighur and Chinese armies were routed. The Chinese commander escaped with only 160 men and fled back south across the mountains to Kocho. The Uighur general followed hard on his heels – his direct route north blocked by the Tibetans – and promised him temporary asylum in Karabalghasun and then safe passage back to China. Since the Kocho garrison was isolated and vulnerable to attack, and there were no reinforcements to be had, the Chinese commander eventually agreed, and the two armies started their long journey north. But he had made a bad mistake: he was assassinated shortly after entering the Uighur capital.

Uighur troops were to return to Beshbaliq the following year and retake the town but Kumtugh was not among them. His body had been left on the battlefield the previous year and now his family wore the facial scars that were part of the Uighur ritual of mourning.

The Princess's Tale

Taihe, 821–843

I have left my beautiful country, China,
And have been taken to the nomads' camp.
My clothing is of coarse felt and furs,
I must force myself to eat their rancid mutton.
How different in climate and custom are China and this land of nomads.
    Lady Weng, 'Eighteen Refrains to a Barbarian Flute', 3rd century AD

IN THE AUTUMN of 821 Taihe, an imperial princess, sister of the current emperor of China and daughter of his predecessor, rode in a howdah on a Bactrian camel. Her female attendants rode beside her on the treasured Ferghana horses from the imperial pastures, not side-saddle but with their silk pyjama'd legs straddling the high-pommelled saddles. As the sister of the Chinese emperor, the princess had been chosen as 'tribute': she was on her way to wed the Uighur kaghan to cement their countries' friendship. The emperor had already received soft cloth made of camel hair, brocades, sable furs, jade girdles, fifty camels and one thousand ponies as her bride price. Although she came from the east – from the imperial palace in China's capital, Chang'an – much of her dress, her ornaments and her aesthetic preferences came from the west, from the distant Central Asian steppe through which she was now travelling.

In her hair she wore fine pins of translucent white jade from the riverbed in Khotan, and decorations made of tortoiseshell from Vietnam and lapis lazuli, traded in Khotan but originating further west in Badakhstan. Her Buddhist rosary beads were of amber, perhaps from the shores of the Baltic or northern Burma. She

*Chinese Tang hairstyle and phoenix hair ornaments, from a
stone engraving in an imperial Tang dynasty tomb near Chang'an*

carried perfumes for her body, her bath and her clothes, some
believed to be aphrodisiacs and many originating in India, and
mixtures of aloeswood and musk to make her breath smell sweet.
Before leaving Chang'an, she had started to learn a new style of
dance, the 'whirling' dance, usually performed by Sogdian girls
dressed in crimson and green, spinning on a small, round rug. And
she was especially fond of Kuchean music, a pleasure which she
would continue to enjoy in the kaghan's palace where she would
play on a gold-inlaid zither. 'Western' music was extremely popular
among city society in China and there were several resident foreign
orchestras at the imperial palace who performed at banquets and
other functions, while the palace courtesans adapted the words of
traditional Chinese songs to fit the new tunes. The courtesans in

96

the city made up their own lyrics, often satires on political scandals or corrupt officials. Street children soon picked these up and ran around the streets singing them in return for a few coins.

As an imperial princess, Taihe had left the palace infrequently, and then only to visit her country estate. But she was not wholly inactive or confined to the domestic sphere. She played polo, another import from the western regions, and, like many of the court ladies, she was an excellent horsewoman:

The Palace ladies in the front hall with their slender waists
Are greatly afraid the first time they learn to ride.
But soon they manage to sit up in the saddle and immediately
    want to gallop.
How many times they lose the reins and clasp the pommel in
    their arms!*

The imperial palace in Chang'an had its own polo field and five stable blocks which, apart from polo ponies, provided horses for generals, for hunting and for ceremonial purposes. Many of these were horses from western Central Asia, unrelated to the small, tough steppe ponies used by the ordinary soldier, and acquired as tribute or in trade from distant Central Asian kingdoms. Such horses were the subject of many legends. The most common held that they were half-dragon, that they were born in water and could carry their riders to heaven. In fact, some were probably related to the Nisaen horse, bred in Medea for the kings of Persia and mentioned by Herodotus as sweating blood. Others may have been a breed known as the Aryan horse, common around the Caspian Sea. It stood 15 or 16 hands high and was usually grey or bay in colouring with a large head and long, slender legs.

Chinese stories told of many countries renowned for their horses, such as the land in the far north, always covered in snow and called 'The Land of the Dappled Horse', or Arabia, where it was said that the horses could understand human speech. Gifts of horses were received from numerous countries and peoples, including Kashmir, Gandhāra and Arabia, but the moist valleys of

---

* Poem by Lady Xu, consort of the ruler of Shu in south-west China, Meng Chang (r. 935–6).

Sogdiana and Ferghana to the west of the Pamirs were the main supply for China's finest mounts. During the reign of the emperor Xuanzong, before Rokhshan's rebellion, six famous 'dancing horses' from Ferghana were stabled in the palace. These horses performed their dance on the fifth day of the eighth month, the emperor's birthday, and were commemorated in stone reliefs. But that was in the past. The Tibetans had raided the imperial pastures so many times since then that it had not been possible to replenish the stock of fine horses. Now the Chinese military relied on the Uighurs for their vital supply of cavalry ponies, paying up to forty or even fifty bolts of silk per head under the implicit threat of Uighur raids should they refuse to buy. In 773 the emperor had tried to curb the Uighur's extortionate demands when the amount asked for 10,000 head exceeded the annual income of the Chinese state. Decreeing that 'the afflictions of the people should not be increased' he had bought only 6,000. But now the Uighurs regularly sent herds numbering tens of thousands, draining the Chinese exchequer. As each horse arrived at the Chinese pastures, it was branded with several marks to show its origin, agility, stamina and occupation – whether it was a post horse, a mount for a general or for use in government service.

Taihe was the fourth Chinese princess to be promised to a Uighur kaghan. The first had been her great-great-aunt, sent in 758 after the Uighurs had first helped fight the rebel Rokhshan. She was no longer young when she was sent, having been widowed twice, and when, after only a year among the Uighurs, she was widowed for a third time she returned to China. Her younger sister, who had accompanied her, remained behind and married the next kaghan. She died in Karabalghasun in 790, two years after another princess, Taihe's great-aunt, Xian'an, was sent in a hastily contrived bid to obtain Uighur military assistance against the Tibetans. Xian'an stayed there until her death in 808, marrying three other kaghans in succession. After stalling for seven years, in 820 the Chinese emperor eventually offered Princess Yong'an, Taihe's elder sister, to the present kaghan's predecessor. Fortunately for her, the kaghan died before she left Chang'an and not long afterwards

Yong'an requested permission to be ordained as a Daoist priestess, thus avoiding any threat of future marriage alliances. She was not the first Tang princess to take this course. At the very beginning of the eighth century the way had been led by Princess Gold-Immortal and Princess Jade-Perfected, who started the long ordination procedure as young girls. Their father used state funds to endow each with an abbey, until complaints were made by the people and officials, after which the princesses used their own money to complete the work. Since then fifteen imperial princesses had been ordained, including two of Taihe's nieces.

Princess Taihe's fate had been decided only a month before she embarked on her journey, when nearly six hundred Uighurs had entered Chang'an to collect Princess Yong'an. The original embassy had numbered several thousand, but the majority had been asked to wait at the border, since Chang'an was ill-equipped to quarter so many foreign envoys at one time. Now that the kaghan to whom Yong'an had been promised had died, the emperor was in a dilemma. It was expensive for the court to give away a princess: the bride had to be sent with a dowry befitting her status, and the ponies and other goods brought by the Uighur embassy as 'tribute' had to be purchased with hard currency – in this case, silk. But though the Uighurs were not as strong as they had been, they were still important allies and would want the original agreement to be honoured.

Eventually it was decided that Taihe would be sent in Yong'an's place and a minister was dispatched to inform the Uighur embassy of the emperor's decree. A Chinese embassy would accompany the princess to Karabalghasun and bestow the insignia of office on the new kaghan: China always maintained the pretence that her neighbours were vassal states. An armed escort of Uighur cavalry would join them at the border to ensure their safety. The need for this was emphasized only a week later when Tibetan raiders were repulsed just south of the princess's intended route. A few years before, Tibetan soldiers had ridden to within two stages of Karabalghasun itself. In fact both sides hoped the guard would not be necessary as a Chinese embassy was already on its way to Lhasa to sign a peace treaty. This declared that 'henceforth, on either side, there shall be no enmity, no warmongering and no seizure of territory'.

The betrothal was announced on the first day of July and Princess Taihe left at the end of August by the city's north-eastern gate. The journey of over a thousand miles would take until the new year. Post horses could cover the distance in less than two months, but such a large caravan travelled slowly and stopped frequently. Taihe's brother, the emperor, and all the officials lined up in rank to bid her a ceremonial farewell. The people of Chang'an had also come out to watch the spectacle. The procession of Uighur horsemen, the princess and her retinue, Chinese officials and camels laden with gifts for the kaghan took several hours to pass through the gate and start on its northward journey.

Princess Taihe was on her way to a palace that could rival the imperial court in its opulence, but it must have felt as if she were bound for a very alien land. The first part of her journey was through Chinese territory which extended to the northernmost reaches of the Yellow river. The river flows from its source on the Tibetan plateau far to the south-west of Chang'an, crosses the Gansu corridor and then makes a long sweep north before turning east and then south, doubling back on itself almost to the capital. The land enclosed by this great curve is called the Ordos, a region of desert and mud, and home to the Tanguts. Beyond, to the north and west, lies the Gobi desert, and to the north-east the steppe home of other peoples such as the Khitans. The Chinese sought to control the Ordos and had established garrisons on the far banks of the river. Here also were the trading-posts established at the instigation of the Uighurs. But the Chinese hold on the territory was precarious; since they had withdrawn their forces from the western garrisons during the rebellion of 763, their western flank was unprotected. The Tibetans regularly crossed the Gansu corridor into Uighur territory and made raids along the western edges of the Ordos, while the Tanguts and Khitans, two peoples who were to form powerful kingdoms in later centuries, threatened from the north-east. The eroded, stamped earth walls marking the boundaries of earlier Chinese kingdoms and bisecting the river's bend at the southern edge of the Ordos were a reminder of the long struggle between the Chinese and their northern neighbours in this land.

Though the Chinese army had powerful crossbows, sophisticated armour, steel swords, gunpowder and mechanical catapults, and Chinese soldiers could ride and shoot like nomads – indeed, many were themselves nomads – they never succeeded in dominating the many peoples pressing at their borders. For this reason, they had long used diplomacy and bribes as much as military force in defence of their territory. The princess was part of this strategy. The practice of sending princesses to cement alliances had started hundreds of years before, and during the course of the current Chinese dynasty over twenty 'princesses' were dispatched. In the seventh century a Turkic kaghan has asked for a Chinese prince to marry his daughter, provoking outrage at court: 'Never since ancient times has an imperial prince been married to a barbarian woman.' (The substitute, a cousin of the empress, was imprisoned on his arrival.) However, before the princesses sent to the Uighurs, only distant relatives of the emperor – or daughters by lesser concubines – had been chosen as the brides of foreigners.

Since the rebellion of Rokhshan the ruling Tang dynasty had become insecure and lacking in confidence. This insecurity was particularly evident in their increasing rejection of all things foreign, including people: ethnicity, then as now, was largely a matter of politics. The Tang rulers of China claimed descent from the founder of Daoism but in fact their forebears were from the very cultures they were now dismissing as 'barbaric' – those of Turkic Central Asia. The influences from outside, welcomed in the early part of the dynasty, were now so assimilated into Chinese culture that few could discern where traditional culture ended and 'foreign' influence began. But where the influence was obvious – as in the case of Buddhism – there was growing xenophobia. Buddhism had been practised in China since at least the first century AD, and had been fully assimilated by the start of the Tang dynasty in 618, but towards the end of the dynasty some ministers began to use it as a scapegoat for China's ills. In 819 a leading statesman and scholar submitted an anti-Buddhist polemic to the emperor. It was rejected, but over the next few decades it became habitual to divert blame from the government for high taxes and rising inflation on to 'foreigners' and 'foreign religions' – Uighur moneylenders and tax-exempt Buddhist monks.

★

The land Princess Taihe was going to in the autumn of 821 lay north-west of Chang'an but the caravan first headed north-east to the Yellow river valley at Hezhong, meaning 'On the River'. The heart of China was defined by the course of the Yellow river and the fertile plains nurtured by its loess-laden waters. The caravan then headed north through the province called 'East of the River' to Taiyuan, 'The Extremity of the Plains', where there was a Manichean temple, established at the behest of the Uighurs to serve the considerable community of their countrymen. This was the first large town beyond their border and had recently become a major producer of expensive wine made from the mare's teat grape from Kocho: the loess slopes of the surrounding countryside were covered with vineyards. Most of the produce was sent to Chang'an where Taihe's brother, the emperor, had declared on first tasting it: 'When I drink this, I am instantly conscious of harmony suffusing my four limbs. It is the true "Princeling of Grand Tranquillity".' A contemporary Chinese poet wrote further of the charms of both the vineyards and their produce in the Taiyuan regions (also known at this time as Qin):

> The grape vine from untrodden lands,
> Its branches gnarled in tangled bands,
> Was brought the garden to adorn
> With verdure bright; now, upward borne,
> The branches climb with rapid stride,
> In graceful curves, diverging wide;
> Here spread and twin, there languid fall,
> Now reach the summit of the wall;
> And then with verdure green and bright,
> Enchanting the beholder's sight,
> Beyond the mansion's roof they strive,
> As though with conscious will alive.
> And now the vine is planted out,
> It climbs the wooden frame about,
> The lattice shades with tender green,
> And forms a pleasant terrace screen.
> With dregs of rice well soak the roots,
> And moisten all its leafy shoots,

The flowers like silken fringe will blow,
And fruit like clustered pearls hang low.
On mare's milk grapes the hoarfrost gleams,
Shine dragon scales like morning beams.
Once hither came a travelling guest;
Amazed his host he thus addressed,
As strolling round he chanced to see
The fruit upon th'o'er-hanging tree:
We men of Qin, such grapes so fair,
Do cultivate as gems most rare;
Of these delicious wine we make,
For which men ne'er their thirst can slake.
Take but a measure of this wine,
And Liangzhou's rule is surely thine.*

The caravan stayed in the town for some time, resting, taking on provisions – including both grapes and wine for the princess on her journey – and preparing for the next stage which continued north on the eastern side of the Yellow river, thus avoiding the treacherous and dangerous Ordos country, and led to the army garrison where the Sogdian and Uighur merchants had been massacred half a century before. From here it turned west to follow the northern banks of the river. Hills rose on the northern horizon but once past these, at the river's southern bend, the road veered north-west to the Piti springs. This was the northern boundary of Chinese territory. From here there were many months of marching across the Gobi desert before the Princess would see water in any abundance, let alone another river.

The short summer was nearing its end and the ground was hardening with frost, but it was clear, dry and bright. The caravan only made short stages, stopping to camp early each day to allow the animals to graze. Later the camels would need fodder, for unlike horses they were unable to scrape away the ice and snow from the pasture with their soft pads, and the Uighurs would go out to hunt gazelle to supplement their diet of mutton and beef. When the second kaghan had declared the country Manichean,

---

* Poem by Liu Yuxi (772–842), translated by T. Sampson, 1869.

apart from ordering that 'all sculpted and painted images of demons be entirely destroyed by fire', he had also suggested that the people should 'eat vegetables'. However, Taihe saw little sign of the suggestion being heeded during her journey or thereafter. Everyone ate meat in large quantities: cattle, sheep, yak, camel, horse, gazelle, fox, hare or whatever could be raised or caught. Nor were they abstemious in drink: the caravan carried large quantities of fermented mares' milk.

As they advanced into Uighur territory there was little to remind Taihe of home. She had not visited much of her homeland but she knew it through literature and art. For her it was a land of verdant river valleys, lush and spectacular mountain scenery, rain-drops falling on plantain leaves, chrysanthemums set among the rust-coloured leaves of autumn, bamboo-covered hillsides, and distinct seasons characterized by a variety of flowers, insects and birds. The contrast with the desolate, snow-swept grey landscape she awoke to every morning was startling. The words written by a Chinese princess sent west as a bride eight hundred years before ran through her mind: 'My family married me to a lost horizon . . . I wish I were a brown goose and could fly back home.'

One long day in the seemingly featureless landscape followed another. Princess Taihe had nothing to do. In the mornings she was dressed and brought food by her attendants, and her camel was prepared. During the first couple of months when the weather was still mild and the landscape showed some variety, the stages passed quite quickly. When she arrived at each camp, her tent would already be erected and rugs, tables and small folding chairs laid out inside. She was brought water for washing, fresh tea and various dainties to eat. On many evenings she would practise her zither or try to compose poetry about the landscape and her feelings of homesickness, both perennial subjects of the Chinese poet. But after a few months the dry air was bitter with frost and she had to cover her face for protection: there was nothing to look at anyway. She grew bored with the interminable journey, as each day merged into the next, and each month into the one that followed, until she lost all sense of time.

★

The lunar new year, an important festival in China, was approaching and she thought of the celebrations she would be missing. But gradually the mood in the caravan became livelier and she realized that they were finally approaching the capital. A track became discernible which soon widened into a well-trodden road. Now there were small villages and farms scattered across the land and people lined the road to watch the caravan pass. Riders went ahead to inform the kaghan of their approach and one evening a delegation arrived from the capital, now only two stages away. After some discussion between the delegation and the Uighurs in the caravan the Chinese officials were approached. It transpired that the kaghan wished the princess to proceed with them by a slightly different route so that she would arrive at the capital unannounced and could be presented to the kaghan in private: he wanted to see her before the marriage. The request was refused, despite protests from the Uighur courtiers that a previous Chinese princess had agreed to this. The ministers accompanying Taihe assured the kaghan's envoys that it would be an unallowable breach of protocol, whatever the previous princess had decided.

The next day the walls of Karabalghasun came into view on the left bank of the Orkhon river. The river spread across the flat land in broad, shallow branches. Since it was deep winter – February 822 – the water was frozen and so easy to cross. The trees, like everything else, were grey with frost. The city itself was rectangular, enclosed by walls that stretched almost five miles from north to south and one and a half miles from east to west. The royal palace, which was also walled, lay in the north-eastern corner. Nine large iron gates led into the city. The princess could clearly see the kaghan's famous tent, erected on the flat roof of his palace and completely covered in gold. She had heard that the Tibetan emperor also had such a tent, a link with the nomadic past. The kaghan would hold court in his, which could accommodate a hundred men. There were numerous other tents erected both inside and outside the city walls, most of them to house the large Uighur army.

When they reached the city Princess Taihe was shown into a large tent. Thick wool rugs covered the walls and floors, overlaid with finer silk carpets. The large cushions laid out along the walls were covered with the finest Chinese and Sogdian woven silk and brocade in red, green, blue and gold, and the armrests were made of sanderswood decorated with gold, camphorwood and stained ivory. Furs of every description were heaped around – sable, ermine, spotted hare and purple-dyed deerskin. The princess was offered wine from a purple cup with a delicate motif of grapes and vines, made from translucent crystal, rare even in the Chinese court. Before her she saw low tables spread with fruits and nuts – apricots, grapes, melons, apples, walnuts and almonds – and she was then served fragrant tea in a delicate cup of fine porcelain, lobed in imitation of Persian silverware. There were few luxuries that the Uighurs could not afford with their plentiful supply of Chinese silk from the pony sales. Her interpreter explained that the kaghan wished her to dress in Uighur clothes and that he was sending Uighur princesses to teach her the customs of their country. An older maidservant would help her dress and prepare her hair. The Chinese ministers, in the meantime, selected a suitable day for the ceremony.

Taihe's Chinese dress consisted of an under-robe and baggy trousers made of thin silk, the trousers tied with a cord. Over this she wore a richly woven robe, like the Japanese kimono, tied loosely below the waist and cut so as to reveal considerable *décolleté*. On top she wore an apron-like garment in a contrasting colour which reached to the floor and was fastened around her chest (as in traditional Korean dress). Finally she draped a long, narrow silk shawl across her shoulders and over her arms. Her hair was elaborately styled in a high bun and the toes of her red silk embroidered slippers curled up so that they could just be seen peeping out below her robe. The silk was all woven in the imperial workshops. In the heady days of the emperor Xuanzong, a hundred imperial weavers made cloth solely for the Lady Yang, the emperor's favourite consort. Then it had been the fashion among palace ladies to wear the 'foreigner's robe', a plain, collared garment like that worn by Turkic horsemen. Now the latest fad was for impossibly wide sleeves which used as much silk as the rest of the robe.

On the chosen day Taihe first had to show herself outside the tent dressed in ordinary Uighur clothes and bow to the kaghan,

Chinese girl dressed in hufu, *from a wall painting
in a Tang dynasty imperial tomb near Chang'an*

who was sitting on the tower of the palace. She then returned
inside and the Uighur maidservant helped her to change. She was
given first an undergown of red silk with a modest, plain, round
neck, over which went a long crimson robe with wide, embroidered lapels and decorated with red and white braid down the
central opening, sleeves and skirt of the robe. The sleeves were
narrow, again in contrast to Chinese fashion. Next her hair was
styled in large loops on either side of her head and decorated with
gold and lapis pins and animal ornaments. Then a wide, red silk
scarf was wound around her head, both ends falling down her back
almost to the floor, though tied in elaborate bows at her hips.
Lastly she was given long, gold earrings and a narrow, gold crown
resembling a small boat with high points fore and aft.

Now dressed in her queen's robes she again left the tent and
bowed. Then she was helped into a sedan-chair which was led by
the nine chief ministers nine times around the court. After this she

Uighur princess holding a lotus bud, ninth-century cave mural

climbed up the tower and sat beside the kaghan, facing east. The
kaghan's silk robe was also long but had a high collar and bore a
pattern of large roundels. He was bearded and moustached and he
wore his hair long. On his head there perched a high, pointed
crown held in place by a red ribbon fastened under his chin. Broad
ribbons wound around his hair and reached down his back. His
robe was split up each side to reveal his high, leather boots and he
wore an elaborately decorated belt made of gold and jade, from
which hung his jewel-encrusted dagger. The ministers were similarly dressed, although less finely. They presented themselves in
turn to the kaghan, addressing him as 'God of the Moon and God
of the Sun', and then to Taihe, recognizing her as their new
khatun – their queen. She also noticed the Manichean clergy in
their distinctive white robes and tall white hats: unlike the
Buddhists they did not shave their heads and many had long
beards.

Taihe was not simply a symbol of the alliance between the
Uighurs and Chinese: as khatun, she had power in the Uighur

court. She was allowed to establish her own quarters and for almost a year she had the company of the Chinese ministers. When they had to return to China in the late autumn of 822 she was distraught. She arranged a great banquet and presented them with bolts of silk and all sorts of ornaments to take back to her sisters, including hairpieces made of beaten gold in the shape of the steppe deer. That summer the kaghan had received an envoy sent by the leader of the Arab forces in Transoxania, Tanim ibn Bahr. There had been Arab embassies in Chang'an so Taihe knew something of these peoples. Her husband sent relays of horses to transport the envoy from Lake Issuk-kul in the far south-west of Uighur territory. Tanim ibn Bahr covered three stages each day, travelling for twenty days across the steppe where, he reported, there was grass and water but no villages and therefore no food. The men in charge of the horses lived in tents at each post, but had no spare provisions. After this he reached the start of cultivation and travelled for another twenty days through villages and farms before reaching Karabalghasun. He also reported seeing the golden tent from afar but failed to mention the queen in his brief account of his journey.

We know nothing of Taihe's relationship with her new husband. China during the Tang dynasty was not particularly prudish and the restrictions which characterized late imperial Chinese society were not yet in force: foot-binding only started to appear in the next century, divorce by mutual consent was still part of the legal code, and widows were allowed to remarry. Uighur women were probably subject to even fewer restrictions than their Chinese counterparts – Uighur princesses accompanied several of the embassies to China, including the one sent for Taihe. Chinese authors produced explicit sex manuals and the 'Art of the Bed-chamber' was regarded as a branch of medicine. Deprivation of sex was considered by many doctors to be injurious to health, although Daoist practitioners enjoined their male patients not to ejaculate, believing that semen contained the vital energy – *qi* – necessary for health and long life. A seventh-century text by a Daoist physician, for example, states:

Until a man has reached forty he is usually full of vigorous passion. But as soon as he has passed his fortieth year he will suddenly notice that his potency is decreasing and, just at that time, countless diseases will descend on him like a swarm of bees. If this is allowed to continue then he will be beyond cure, but Pengzi has said, 'Curing one human being by another is the real cure.' Thus when a man reaches forty it is time for him to acquire a thorough knowledge of the Art of the Bedchamber.

The principle of the Art of the Bedchamber is very simple, yet few can practise it. It is simply to copulate with ten different women on one night without once emitting semen.

Erotic poetry, essays and literature also circulated, written by respected literati. Reproduction was discussed openly. The dates of menstruation of all the wives and concubines of the Chinese emperor were carefully noted along with the date and hour of each of the emperor's successful sexual encounters. We do not know if Princess Taihe was similarly monitored in the Uighur court nor if she bore the kaghan children.

The princess's husband died only two years after her arrival and a new kaghan was appointed. At the death of her husband, the first Chinese princess to marry a Uighur kaghan had been informed that she was expected to commit suicide so that she could be buried alongside her late husband. She refused to do so, but made a concession by slashing her face with a knife, a traditional Uighur sign of mourning. Taihe did not commit suicide either, but neither did she leave, though she would have had the opportunity to do so either with the Uighur embassy which was sent to inform the Chinese court of the kaghan's death, or with the Chinese embassy that was sent back to acknowledge the new kaghan in the spring of 825. This latter brought a staggering half million bolts of silk for pony purchases. A bolt, about thirty feet, is the maximum amount that can be made by a skilled silk-weaver in a day. Half a million bolts therefore represented over ten thousand days' work.

Perhaps Princess Taihe was persuaded to remain in Karabalgha-sun by her Chinese advisers for political reasons, or to avoid the expense attendant on providing a new princess; perhaps by this time she had married the new kaghan. Embassies arrived every few years from China and the city was home to a considerable Chinese population. The embassies always brought letters, news and gifts for her, and would pay her court, and in return she sent elaborate gifts of her own, among them five female archers, exceptionally skilled on horseback, and two young boys from the tribe of Shatou Turks on the Uighur empire's southern border. Another kaghan came to the throne in 832 after the assassination of his predecessor and many of his ministers. Still Taihe remained. By this time Uighur fortunes were in serious decline: there was dissent at court and frequent incursions by Kirghiz armies.

The Kirghiz were a forest-dwelling people from the north-west of the Uighur empire, some forty days' journey from the Uighur capital, a land where 'the pine trees grew so tall that an arrow could not reach their peaks'. They had been in conflict with the Uighurs for twenty years and although their language was Turkic, they were a tall people with light hair and green or blue eyes. They despised those with dark hair and dark eyes, believing them to be the descendants of a renegade Chinese general of the first century BC who had defected to the nomads. Many of their customs differed from those of the Turks: they did not lacerate their faces as a sign of mourning, and their ruler was called the aje, not the kaghan (although they later adopted the Turkic appellation).

In 839 a crisis was reached in Karabalghasun when the kaghan executed two of his ministers for treason and their supporters retaliated by assassinating him. The winter of 839 was exceptionally severe. Frost settled early into the earth, there were heavy falls of snow and by the end of the year supplies of fodder had been exhausted. Livestock died in their tens of thousands. The army defending the capital was no longer able to repel the continuing Kirghiz advances and, in 840, they seized the capital, killed the new kaghan and set fire to the city. Its residents and those who lived on the surrounding farms fled south: Princess Taihe was among them.

The Kirghiz soon moved back to their base in the forests, but owing to the lack of any serious opposition, they held control of the former Uighur lands until 924 when the Khitans, a people from the north-east of China, moved in.

★

Princess Taihe's journey in 840 was very different from the one she had made two decades before. She was travelling in haste, fleeing for her life across land which was now as familiar to her as her homeland. When she and her fellow refugees reached the bend of the Yellow river in the autumn the Chinese armies garrisoned nearby were alarmed at their numbers: some 100,000 eventually gathered and set up residence in the lee of the Yin hills. The new kaghan informed the Chinese envoys sent to ascertain his plans that he had no immediate intention of trying to recapture his kingdom but would settle on the Chinese border until the situation was more favourable. The Chinese sent food and clothing to the restless Uighurs at Taihe's behest, but in the meantime they called up their troops, repaired the border forts and issued weapons. What followed was no surprise.

In the spring of 843 a Chinese expeditionary force took the Uighur camp unawares. The Uighurs were driven back and thousands were killed at a place the Chinese later named 'Slaughtering the Uighurs Hill'. Many more surrendered and still others fled south to the Silk Road where they settled in Ganzhou, on the Gansu corridor, and Kocho, in the Tarim basin. The kaghan also fled but was hunted down and murdered a few years later in the Gobi desert. Over the next few generations those Uighurs still remaining in north China became naturalized.

Meanwhile the princess had travelled south and reached the Chinese capital in the late spring of 843. Her Uighur escort was turned back at the city gates and rumours that she had murdered the Uighur prince accompanying her were not confirmed. The emperor called his ministers together to discuss what to do with her. Some were opposed to allowing her back because of hostilities with the Uighurs but the emperor pleaded on her behalf: 'It has often made me sorrowful to think of her,' he said. 'She must have thought many times of her homeland with great longing.' In the end it was decided to welcome her back, and the imperial guards were sent to escort her to the palace from Zhangjing temple, outside the north-eastern gate of the city from whence she had departed over two decades before. Her Central Asian life was over.

The Monk's Tale

Chudda, 855–870

The Kingdom of Kashmir is about 2,000 miles in
circumference and is surrounded by mountains. The soil is
suitable for growing grain and abounds with fruit and
flowers. Here also are dragon-holes, fragrant mounds and
medicinal plants. . . . The people wear leather doublets and
clothes of white linen. They are light and frivolous, of a
weak, pusillanimous disposition . . . handsome but given to
cunning. There are both heretics and believers, the latter
numbering some 5,000.

Xuanzang, *Buddhist Records of the Western World*, AD 646

THE YOUNG MAN watched intently as the brown-robed foreign
monk dipped his brush in ink and traced out a complex
pattern on a square of rough paper. The monk waited for the ink
to dry before giving the paper to the young man with careful
instructions. He must make copies and burn them on a certain day
each month while reciting a spell. The young man handed over a
few copper coins and pushed his way out through the crowd
milling around the table. He had come to the monk because his
hair had started to fall out a few months before. He had already
paid a local herbalist for a remedy – juice from pounded water-
melon leaves that had to be rubbed into the head – and he had also
tried head massage, but neither had worked. He had come to the
temple fair that morning in the hope of finding a more effective
cure.

It was 870 and the monk was a Kashmiri called Chudda. He had
been practising medicine in the Silk Road town of Dunhuang for

The Monk's Tale

Charm for ensuring order in the house,
from a ninth-century printed almanac

nearly fifteen years, living in the monastery next to the cliffs twelve miles outside the town. On this day he erected his stall at another monastery in the centre of the town, a small establishment with only a score of monks living in the little wooden rooms lining the perimeter walls. They had reserved the best pitches by the small wooden gateway, selling scrolls, paintings, booklets and prayer sheets offering 'protection against all conceivable misfortunes'. Townspeople and visitors wandered in and out of the monastery, stopping to light incense sticks to the two guardian warrior statues protecting the gate, and then idling along looking at the many stalls which lined the main path and spilled out into the adjoining marketplace. Other monks, local and itinerant, offered various methods of divination. One of the most popular would give those who consulted him a tube containing several long, wooden spills which they shook until one of the spills worked its way loose. Each spill was inscribed with a cryptic line of characters, only intelligible to the master at the stall who would consult his manual before pronouncing its meaning. Others offered the interpretation of dreams and strange events, of hexagrams or of physiognomy. Then there were the almanac readers. Almanacs were on sale everywhere and, though the Chinese emperor had forbidden their ownership by individuals, many people possessed one. Few, however, were sufficiently skilled or literate to decipher their cryptic messages, and they willingly paid the diviner for his interpretation.

The brown-robed monk was not the only one offering medical services: there were herbalists with small piles of dried flora and fauna laid out on a cloth in front of them, acupuncturists, palmists, doctors who were expert in reading the pulses, masseurs, surgeons, children's doctors, and both Buddhist and Daoist exorcism specialists. If none of these remedies worked, the afflicted could pay a scribe to copy a Buddhist scripture, a sutra, to which was added an appeal to Buddha. Alternatively they might recite a prayer designed for the purpose or pay for it to be read during a Buddhist service, or make offerings of incense and fruit.

The drugs on sale came from far and wide, for the traditional medicines of Greece, Arabia, Persia, India, Tibet and China were all on offer in Dunhuang. Indeed, an official Chinese *materia medica* of this period listed no fewer than 850 drugs, with detailed instructions on their preparation and administration. However, medicine was not confined solely to the administration of herbal remedies. There were schools of acupuncturists, pulse readers and masseurs. In India an operation for cataracts had been developed, and Greek and Persian doctors were famed for operations on the brain. There was even a handbook that advised Chinese magistrates on the conduct of post-mortems in cases of suspicious death, instructing them, for example, on how to differentiate between someone who had died before entering the water and someone who had drowned.

Spells, charms and exorcism were an essential part of most traditions. A Chinese cure for possession by demons called for pulverized cinnabar and realgar, roasted croton seed, root of hellebore and aconite, arsenphyrite, burned for half a day in the earth, and a broiled centipede, with feet removed (this must have taken some time). The resulting mixture was passed through a sieve and combined with honey to form small pills. The patient was advised to take one pill daily, with an additional dose at midnight if the symptoms were not relieved, and to avoid 'pork, cold water, and fresh bloody meat' during the treatment.

Chudda had entered his local Buddhist monastery in the Himalayan kingdom of Kashmir as a child, many years before, taking the full precepts – the vows of abstinence – to become a fully ordained monk in his twenties. By the ninth century most of north India, home to Buddhism, had been conquered by Turkic and then Hindu dynasties, and Buddhism was in decline. The rulers of Kashmir, the Karkota dynasty, were Hindus, but were fairly tolerant of Buddhism.

Like many Buddhist monks, Chudda had only a little learning and no inclination to become a great scholar. Nor was he particularly interested in ideological or philosophical questions. Joining the monastery was not a great act of faith, but simply something one did, a way of life. Not that Chudda was without faith: he kept his vows and attended all the services. He had heard from itinerant monks who had travelled to China that there, when the mood in the chanting hall became intense, some monks mutilated themselves in the name of Buddha, searing the flesh on their arms or burning a finger until only the stump was left. Chudda was puzzled by this practice for he had been taught that Śākyamuni rejected the extreme acts of the Hindu ascetics, but there were also many stories of Buddha in his previous reincarnations mutilating his own body to help others. In one of the most famous, Buddha threw himself from a cliff in order to provide a tiger with food for her starving cubs; and a chapter of *The Lotus Sutra*, a popular text, described how a follower burned himself to death in honour of Buddha: 'Anyone who follows his example – even if he only burns a finger or toe – he shall exceed one who offers a country, a city, wife or children, or even all the lands, mountains, forests, rivers, ponds and precious objects as offerings.'

Self-mutilation in all religions is sometimes motivated by baser desires: seeking distraction from his lust, a contemporaneous European Christian monk burned each of his fingers in turn over the flames of a candle. Chudda himself had heard of a Chinese Buddhist monk severing his penis. The monk had written that he had done so to make himself undesirable to women, rather than to curb his own desires. Buddha had easily resisted the temptations sent to distract him during his final meditation under the Bo tree, but not all monks and nuns found a celibate life easy. The castrated Chinese monk later attracted crowds of thousands to his sermons, although whether it was his eloquence or their curiosity that drew them is not recorded.

Salacious stories about illicit relations between monks and nuns circulated widely. *A Poetical Essay on Supreme Joy*, an eighth-century Chinese handbook on sex, contained a chapter on monasteries in which were recounted tales of homosexual monks, and nuns who slept with 'tall, dark foreign monks with enormous cocks and closely shaved heads'. Doubtless an illustrated version was also available. A few communities of monks in Central Asia disregarded the Buddhist rule forbidding sex, and lived in the town with their wives and children.

Chudda had heard many such tales of Central Asia and China. Two centuries previously the famous Chinese pilgrim Xuanzang had stayed in Kashmir for two years on his way to India to gather Buddhist scriptures. Xuanzang was impressed by the level of debate in Kashmir and collected texts on logic to take back to China. There were now other Chinese monks in residence in the Kashmiri monastery and Chudda had learned to speak and write a little of their strange language. He had long wanted to travel and in the spring of 855 he decided to make a pilgrimage to Wutai moun-tain, north-east of the Chinese capital, Chang'an.

Wutai was the home of a famous bodhisattva, one who, although on the verge of enlightenment, delays leaving this world in order to help others. The bodhisattva of Wutai mountain, Mañjuśrī, was able to appear in whatever form he chose and, be-cause immense benefits accrued from simply seeing him, pilgrims flocked there, keen to interpret anything unusual as a sighting, be it an unusual cloud, a strange animal, a beggar encountered on a mountain path, or Buddha himself. The kingdom of Kashmir had been in conflict for several years, and Chudda had vowed to dedi-cate his pilgrimage to peace and the flourishing of Buddhism in his country. Once he had made his decision he was inundated with requests from fellow monks. Some wanted him to carry letters to their friends and fellow countrymen along the route; others wanted copies of certain sutras, jade rosary beads or silk cloth; still others asked for souvenirs from Wutai mountain.

It was more than 3,000 miles to the Chinese capital and several hundred more to Wutai mountain, and Chudda could not expect to be back for well over a year. His servant, a young novice from a poor local family, asked to accompany him. Chudda arranged horses for them both and two pack ponies for their luggage. They would seek food and lodgings in monasteries or in the homes of lay believers, but they had to carry fodder for the horses, some money for incidental expenses, and extra clothes for the mountain crossing. He also packed a medicine chest of herbs and charms.

Chudda had decided against travelling through Tibet to the north-east of Kashmir, though many former pilgrims had done so in the past. The last Tibetan emperor had been assassinated in 842 and the country was still unsettled. There were four main routes out of Kashmir, all with gates and guards. The quickest route to the Silk Road was through the north gate to the Gilgit river valley, but Chudda rejected this in favour of the western gate. This would take him through the ancient kingdoms of Gandhāra and Uḍḍiyāna to the north-west of Kashmir, countries in which Buddha himself had lived in his former reincarnations.

It was late spring when Chudda and his servant left the monastery and headed west through the orchards of apricots up the Jhelum valley. The mountain slopes were covered in new grass and flowers — edelweiss, yellow gentian, martagon lilies and cyclamen — and the pilgrims could see the capital city (present-day Srinagar) spread out below them on either bank of the river. It was only one day's stage from their monastery to the swampy Wular lake, and from here the valley narrowed to a gorge, the fruit trees giving way to forests of fir and silver birch. The stone frontier gate was placed at the gorge's narrowest part. All Chudda's papers were in order and the Kashmiri guards allowed them to pass without any delay. From the gorge gate at Baramula it was five days' journey along the Jhelum river to what is now Muzaffarabad and another couple of days across the Jhelum–Indus watershed to the Punjab, the route of today's Karakorum highway.

The road led south out of the high mountains to Takṣaśilā (called Taxila by the Greeks, the name by which it is known today). The city and the land around it were then a dependency of Hindu-ruled Kashmir but had an illustrious history of their own. In the fifth century BC Takṣaśilā had been the site of a famous university offering courses in mathematics, astronomy, medicine and other subjects. The *kharoṣṭhī* script was developed here to write the Sanskrit and Gandhāri languages and, in the fourth century, Alexander the Great passed through on his way south to India, pausing to talk philosophy with the locals. But it was in the third century that Takṣaśilā's importance as a Buddhist site began, with the succession of Aśoka in 272 BC as king of the Mauryan dynasty whose lands included both Takṣaśilā and Kashmir. After his conversion to Buddhism following a particularly bloody battle, Aśoka had spent his reign proselytizing and had erected stone inscriptions throughout his country in the local languages, urging religious tolerance, the foundation of hospitals for both humans and animals, and the cultivation of medicinal plants. Aśoka also disinterred the ashes of Buddha who had been cremated and buried in eight stupas, or shrines, in the Ganges valley and, so tradition says, redistributed them to the main cities in his country. In Takṣaśilā the Dharamarajika stupa was built to house one portion.

After this Takṣaśilā had many rulers, all of them tolerant of Buddhism, until the city was invaded and destroyed twice, in the third and fifth centuries AD, by nomads from the north. The monasteries and stupas were burned, the monks were killed or fled, and the country did not recover its former glory. Chudda had heard from travelling monks of the decline of Buddhism in the countries west of Kashmir but he was still surprised at the number of ruins in and around the city. Of the fifty monasteries and stupas that had surrounded Takṣaśilā in its heyday, only a couple were still occupied.

In the second century AD the original small stupa at Takṣaśilā holding the Buddha's ashes had been enclosed within a much larger stupa that was plastered and covered in gold. Surrounding it were numerous other votive stupas and monastery buildings, but most were in ruins. The gold leaf from the main stupa had flaked away and the decorative statues of Buddha and bodhisattvas had been decapitated and mutilated. The friezes around the stupa narrated episodes from Buddha's life, and Chudda walked round it clockwise (so as to keep his right, or clean, hand next to the stupa) in silent worship. He made an offering of fruit and incense, and draped a silk banner on the stupa itself, gestures he would repeat thousands of times at thousands of sites before his return from China.

The monk and his servant visited several other sites at Takṣaśilā before continuing their journey. The road now led north-westwards into the Indus valley at Hund and thence back into the mountains, passing the rock inscriptions left by Aśoka on the banks of the Makam river, and over the Malakand pass to the Swat river. This valley country was now ruled by Turkic Hindu kings from the north who had built great forts on promontories overlooking the river. Monsoon rains fed the vines and fruit trees which grew in abundance in the lower part of this valley and, in autumn, it was carpeted with purple saffron crocuses.

A large community of Buddhist monks still lived in the valley but their number was insignificant in comparison with earlier times: a seventh-century Chinese pilgrim monk had written of 1,400 monasteries and 18,000 clergy. In the eighth century Padmasambhava, a monk born in the valley, had been invited to Tibet by the emperor and had founded a new sect of Buddhism, known as the Red Hat sect because of their distinctive clothing. Padmasambhava had passed through Kashmir and some of the monks there still followed his Tantric teachings: Tantrism, a later development of Buddhism, concentrated on attaining enlightenment through ritual and meditative practices.

By the time Chudda reached Swat the active monasteries numbered hundreds rather than thousands. Chudda and his servant, therefore, did not always find lodgings in Buddhist monasteries or Buddhist households, but they had the consolation of visiting many sites related to Buddha's lives. In fact, there were so many sites that sometimes the pilgrims' whole day would be spent in circumambulation and worship. As they travelled on north through the Swat valley they made frequent deviations into the mountains to visit special sites, such as that commemorating the place where Buddha turned himself into a serpent to feed the starving populace, or where he used his skin as paper and his bone as a pen in order to write the Buddhist law. Chudda had heard of manuscripts in Chinese monastery libraries which had been written in emulation of Buddha, using a bone as a pen and with blood for ink.

As the road continued to the upper reaches of the river the forests of pine and fir gave way to barren, rocky slopes. Often the pilgrims would see carvings of Buddha, made by earlier pilgrims, on the bare rock of the mountainside far above them. It was now only a few days' journey to the confluence of the two rivers which combined to form the Swat. Here the mountains opened out into a small plateau, 2,000 feet above sea level and delightfully fertile and cool. Nearby lay two sites which the pilgrims were eager to visit: the rock where Buddha dried his clothes and another rock showing Buddha's footprints. They continued up the eastern river to the headwaters of the Swat, a spring-fed lake. The spring was home to the tutelary god of Uḍḍiyāna, Naga Apalala, a semi-human serpent. Before his conversion to Buddhism, the Naga would send great white waters down the river every summer to take the crops. After he accepted the true faith he only took the crops once every twelve years, leaving them to the people for the other eleven.

The story was familiar to Chudda. Kashmiri legends told of many other nagas, including one called Suśravas. The man appointed to guard the farmers' fields in Suśravas's homeland was an ascetic who had previously made a vow never to eat any of the fields' produce. This made things difficult for the Naga, as he was not allowed to take the produce until after the field watcher had himself partaken of the crop. Consequently Naga and his two beautiful daughters were reduced to eating grass seeds to avoid starvation.

One day a young nobleman went to Suśravas's pond to rest and happened upon the Naga's two daughters. The sound of their ankle bracelets alerted him to their presence, but it was their eyes which drew his attention. They were highlighted with a line of antimony which, the storytellers said, 'appeared to play the part of a stem to the ruby lotuses of their ear ornaments'. The young man was smitten. He shared his porridge with them and they invited him to meet their father. The Naga explained his problem to the young man, who promised to help. While the field watcher was diverted from his cooking, the young man clandestinely dropped fresh corn from the fields into his bowl of food. The field watcher ate it unsuspectingly. The Naga was then free to steal the crops, which he did by sending down a great hailstorm to crush them.

As a token of gratitude, the young man was offered one of the Naga's daughters in marriage. They lived in great happiness until the local king, on seeing the young woman, was overcome with passion 'like an elephant in rut'. After several failed attempts to win her by persuasion he sent soldiers to carry her away by force. While the soldiers attacked the front of their house, the young man and his wife fled through the back door to her father's palace. The Naga was so furious at the king's behaviour that he sent down a rain of fearful thunderbolts which burned the king, his palace and most of his subjects. The Naga's sister, Ramaṇyā, even came out from her mountain retreat with great piles of stones to assist her brother in his destruction. Hearing of his success before she arrived she dumped her stones on the villages where she stood. The place is still called the forest of Ramaṇyā.

Remorseful at what he had done and weary of the reproaches of the people, the Naga left the scene of his carnage at dawn the following day. For his new home, he created a lake of dazzling whiteness resembling milk on a distant mountain, and his daughter and son-in-law lived in a neighbouring lake.

Chudda and his servant had been travelling since spring and now it was almost summer. In fact, the whole journey from Kashmir to Kashgar through the northern gate into the Gilgit and Hunza valleys could be achieved in less than a month with the right weather and fit ponies, but Chudda had chosen a slower route and had made numerous excursions to holy sites. Now that they had left the Buddhist pilgrimage sites behind, Chudda was eager to cross into the Tarim basin before the onset of winter.

As the pilgrims continued to follow the river, the road became more precipitous, winding its way through lowering grey-brown peaks of jagged rock and across scree slopes. They were told by the locals that it was six days across the passes to the Yarkhun valley on the other side, and that no supplies were available on the route. The Yarkhun valley led north-east to its headwaters in the mountains between the Baroghil and the Darkhot passes, near the site of Seg Lhaton's battle in the Pamirs. From here, the pilgrims intended to turn north, taking the road over the Baroghil pass to Sarhad and thence across the Oxus river and over the Pamirs to the Silk Road, thus retracing one of the routes taken by General Gao's army from China when he marched to attack the Tibetans in 747.

The pilgrims hired another horse to carry extra fodder and provisions. In places the path hung above great chasms, its surface composed only of twigs and brushwood laid on a foundation of wooden posts fixed into holes in the rock face. The bridges were also made of twigs, twisted together and slung across the narrow gorges, held by posts sunk into the rock. After a day they left the river gorge behind and began to cross the great glacier and boulder-strewn slopes that led to the pass. At 15,800 feet it was covered in snow even in summer.

Once over the pass, it was a relief to descend to the fertile Yarkhun valley where grain, vines and fruit trees grew and a patch of flat land was marked out as a polo field next to every village. But the dried fruits from the previous year's crop were small and sour compared with those in the monsoon-fed Swat, and above the green ribbon running along the valley floor were only bare, brown slopes. The villagers lived in houses dug into the ground to protect them against the bitter winter winds blowing down the valley, their only entrance a hole through the roof.

The road was busier and the pilgrims met travellers with news from the Tarim basin that Khotan was newly taken from the Tibetans by local forces offering allegiance to the Chinese emperor, and that the road into China had been reopened, although it was not always safe: the Tibetans still controlled some of the towns in the east and Uighur soldiers were abroad. The Uighurs had been driven out of their land by the Kirghiz a decade before and many had fled south, establishing communities in several of the oasis towns, most especially Kocho to the north, and Ganzhou in the east. Their relations with the Chinese had deteriorated since the Sino-Uighur war of 843 and the subsequent persecution of their countrymen in Chang'an, and recently they had attacked the Chinese envoy sent to Khotan to buy jade for the emperor, stealing his precious stone and killing many of his entourage in the process.

The pilgrims pressed on. Some parts of the Yarkhun valley were impassable during summer when the river flooded the road, and even now the upper reaches were particularly treacherous. The pilgrims and their horses suffered from the cold and altitude and in those places where the road had been flooded they were forced to negotiate the almost sheer mountainside to find an alternative route. The gorges were dark, damp and cold, hardly penetrated by the sun. It was only fifty miles to the start of the Baroghil pass road, but it took them five days to reach it. To cross the pass itself took another two, but then they descended to Sarhad in the Oxus valley and saw the Pamirs rising ahead of them. These were the last obstacle before the descent into the Tarim basin and the desert road to China.

Even though it was now summer, the mountain landscape was desolate. The green flush that arrived with the spring and cloaked the mountain slopes had faded, and the mulberries and poplars that grew in the high valleys had not yet acquired their brilliant orange and red autumnal colours. The pale green of their leaves was lost among the unrelenting brown-grey earth of the valleys. The pilgrims' only companions on their stages over the high passes were marmots and mountain goats, but as they descended below the snow line to the summer grazing grounds, they met Turkic sheep and yak herders. The pilgrims were always treated hospitably and were invited into the herders' tents and offered sheep and yak offal, but since the monks were vegetarians they had to resort to their own provisions. Further down the valley there were terraced fields, some only a few feet wide, perched on the steep slopes, but the villages and towns on the valley floors were poor places, with little food to offer travellers.

The pilgrims had one more pass to negotiate before reaching the valley leading down into the desert. The summer grazing grounds on the southern side of the Karlik pass were called the Milky Plain because they were seldom completely free of snow. The pilgrims made their last camp here and then, as usual, set off at dawn before the sun rose and melted the top crust of ice. The ground widened up to the snow-covered, flat saddle of the pass where a jagged peak to the east cast a shadow on the snow. It took another two hours down through softening snow to reach flat ground suitable for a camp, but when they got there, still at an altitude of nearly 14,000 feet, the temperature was so low that they decided instead to press on. After three more hours they descended into a grassy valley, dotted with the tents of Turkic nomads.

After this the valley turned north and broadened out in its

approach to Tashkurgan, the capital of the Pamir kingdom of Sarikol, on the south-west borders of the Tarim basin. The snowy peaks to either side receded slightly. It was a pleasure after so many days among the rocky defiles of the high Pamirs to be in this warm, fertile valley, its gentle slopes covered in flowers and herbs. Chudda saw several plants he did not recognize and tried to discover from the herders what they were. With no language in common, the herders managed with elaborate sign-language to explain various uses of the plants. These seemed to be medicinal and Chudda took specimens so that he could find out more about them later.

Tashkurgan now lay only two days' march away, but first they had to ford a river. It was in spate and it proved difficult to find a place to cross; by the time the monks and their ponies reached the opposite bank they were thoroughly drenched. Tashkurgan was built on a square, rocky crag about a third of a mile in length. It contained a Chinese fort on the side nearest the river and there were soldiers at a checkpoint questioning all arrivals. Chudda showed them letters from his monastery and his official travel documents from Kashmir and was told that he would have to request permission to travel in China. The soldier directed the pilgrims to a monastery in the town where they could stay while the necessary papers were being prepared.

The town stood 10,000 feet above sea level and only grain and pulses grew in the surrounding fields. Other provisions were brought in by army suppliers and by traders. The monastery had its own small area of sheltered ground where various herbs and the few vegetables that could endure the high altitude and short summer were grown.

After several days the monks received permission to continue their journey. Their next destination, Khotan, lay to their east, but first they had to head northwards to emerge from the mountains at Yangi-hissar on the road from Kashgar to Khotan. They had followed the river for a day when the valley opened on to a great slope of gravel, several miles across. To the north-west they could see the snowy peak of the Mustagh-ata among the continuation of the Pamirs northwards. The Chinese called these the 'Onion Mountains'. But when Chudda awoke the next morning and

looked for the mountains to the south and west, they had disappeared in a haze.

From Yangi-hissar it was a two-week journey to Khotan along a
well-travelled road, but once they left the oasis the first stage was
through a landscape completely alien to these mountain-bred pilgrims. The sands were the same grey-yellow as the mountains they
had just left, but there was an almost total absence of vegetation and
no sight of the familiar snowy peaks that had accompanied them
from Kashmir. Their bodies had grown acclimatized to the high
mountain air and the bitter winds, but here the heat was searing,
without any hint of a breeze. The sands stretched into the distance,
punctuated only by great mounds of tamarisk and sarakaul. Both
Chudda and his servant were silent, praying to Buddha and
fingering their rosary beads beneath their robes. In the mountains
the scenery had changed with each bend in the road, but on some
desert stages there was nothing new to see for hour after hour.

The road seemed endless, but in the mid-afternoon they finally
arrived at a small oasis. The sight of a man sitting by the side of the
road in the shade of the first tree they had seen since the morning,
surrounded by melons and large pots of water, was an immense
relief. The next day the road to Yarkhand straggled along through
similar small oases and both pilgrims felt more sanguine about
their ability to survive the desert stages. But they had yet to
encounter the worst.

At Yarkhand they found a caravan of Sodgian merchants on
their way to Khotan to buy jade and they decided to join it. They
would have to travel more slowly because the caravan's pace was
dictated by its camels, but at least the merchants were familiar with
the desert. The pilgrims soon settled into the desert routine,
though travelling at night to avoid the summer heat of the desert
meant they saw little of the road or landscape. Immediately after
sunset the cameleers would don their heavy sheepskin coats as the
temperature fell suddenly, 'like an icy breath stealing along the
earth's surface'. However, a merchant would occasionally point
out a Buddhist shrine and the pilgrims would light incense and
make a small offering, and they usually found a community of
monks in the hamlets where the caravan rested during the day.

The last stage to the city of Khotan was through a series of oases.

The road was lined with willow and poplar, and though it was dark the pilgrims could see the shadows of fruit trees in the orchards to either side. Several hours from the city they crossed the Kara-kash river on a small ferry. The river was swollen with summer flood water and it took a long time to negotiate all the animals and their cargo on to the ferry and safely across. The caravan approached the city as dawn was breaking: the haze that usually hung in the air had not yet formed and the morning was clear, so that the tall brick and mud walls of Khotan were visible from a considerable distance.

Khotan was situated between two rivers, the Kara-kash and the Yurung-kash, which flowed northwards from the Kunlun mountains. Beyond it the rivers merged and their combined waters, known as the Khotan river, continued for some time into the desert sands before disappearing underground. During the spring and summer floods, when the ice melted on the Kunlun peaks, the waters briefly filled the dry river bed, but they vanished as quickly as they had come, their passage recorded only by the shrubs and low trees which grew in their wake.

Apart from irrigating a considerable area and providing water for the local paper-making industry, the two rivers washed lumps of precious jade down from the mountains: hence their names, which mean black jade (Kara-kash) and white jade (Yurung-kash). Much of the jade went to China where it was carved by highly skilled artisans into trinkets for the imperial family and the aristocracy. Jade, nephrite, is an extremely hard material, and to shape it takes hours of grinding with fine sand, water and drills made with diamond points. Intricately carved pieces, such as hair ornaments and belt buckles, were therefore particularly prized. Khotanese jade varied in colour from deep green to snowy white, the latter described as 'crystallized moonlight'. Chudda knew that jade was considered an important aid to prolonging life in Chinese medicine and was ingested to purify the inner organs. He had seen Daoist healers offer what was purported to be liquid jade for sale, but he doubted whether it was genuine.

The pilgrims rested for several weeks in Khotan. The city was a lively centre of Buddhism, and it was a relief to be back among such a large community of monks. There were numerous lectures to attend and Chudda also wanted to meet some of the local monk–physicians. The pilgrims ate well in the monastery refectory, thanks to the cereals and fruit which grew in abundance in the locality, and soon they had recovered from the privations of their long journey.

The monastery was a large, walled institution with buildings arranged symetrically around a north-south axis. The larger buildings – the lecture hall and main hall – were built of wood, with wooden pillars supporting the deeply raked roof with its upturned, overhanging eaves. The smaller buildings and the walls were made of the ubiquitous yellow baked brick and tamped earth reinforced with tamarisk stalks. The monks' cells were all arranged against the walls, and were small, square rooms with earth floors and a window to the front. Chudda and his servant were accommodated in one of these.

There were many sites to see in Khotan. A large statue of the Heavenly King, Vaiśravaṇa, stood to the side of the main gate through the city walls. The four Heavenly Kings, one for each point of the compass, are important figures in the Buddhist pantheon who fight against the forces of evil and are distinguishable by the weapons they carry. Virūḍhaka, King of the South, carries a club; Dhṛtarāṣṭra, of the East, a bow and arrow; Virūpākṣa, of the West, a sword; and Vaiśravaṇa, of the North, a lance and a stupa. The storytellers in the marketplace recounted how, many centuries before, the founder of Khotan had gone to the Vaiśravaṇa temple to pray for a son and heir. During his devotions the head of the statue opened to reveal a baby boy. The king thanked the god and took the baby back to his palace. The baby, however, refused to eat and became weak, so the king took him back to the temple to ask advice of the Heavenly King. The ground in front of the statue split open to reveal a breast from which the baby suckled milk. From this time on, the story continued, Vaiśravaṇa had been the Guardian King of Khotan. He even became popular in China after the Khotanese king had sent an emissary to the Chinese emperor in 725 to paint him an image of Vaiśravaṇa.

Many of the statues in the kingdom of Khotan were from other countries. There was even a Buddha figure with a jewelled crown

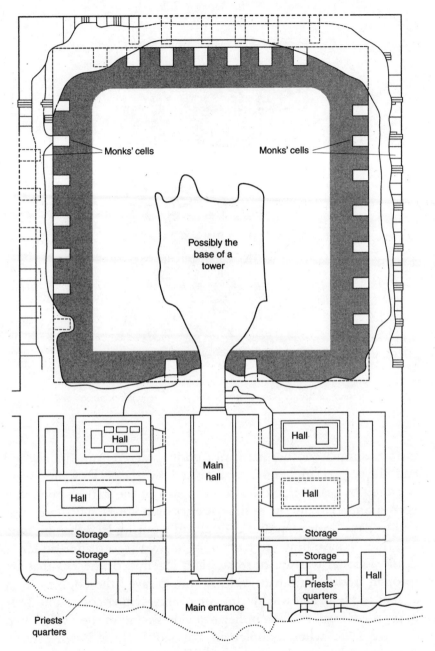

Buddhist temple in Chinese Central Asia, late ninth – early tenth century

Vaiśravaṇa, Heavenly King of the North, from a woodblock print dated 947

from Kashmir. Another statue of Buddha, carved from sandalwood and thirty feet in height, was visited by the sick. Cures were obtained by placing gold leaf on the area of the statue's body that corresponded to the site of the patient's own illness. The statue was said to have been carved in central India during Buddha's lifetime and then to have flown to Khotan of its own accord after Buddha's death. Khotan was full of stories and legends: of the rats that ate through invading nomads' bridles and so saved the country from attack; of the princess who smuggled silkworm cocoons and mulberry seeds out of China in her head-dress; and of the dying town that was saved when a nobleman married the local Naga, causing the river waters to flow again. All these stories were commemorated by monuments and paintings.

★

But now it was time for Chudda and his servant to move on. Once again they attached themselves to a caravan for the journey from Khotan to Dunhuang, this time travelling by day as the worst of the summer heat had passed. The caravan was large, composed of several groups of merchants, and Chudda and his servant were not the only independent travellers who sought its protection. Among their companions were a Khotanese dance troop headed for a festival in Dunhuang, families travelling only a few stages to visit relatives, and several other monks. The camels were loaded with Khotanese products: rugs, fine felt, silk and, of course, jade.

Chudda was pleased to be with the caravan, for the road east from Khotan soon left the comfort of the oasis and entered a great desert of drifting sands whose landscape changed with every turn of the wind. The road was rarely visible under the sand, and there was no sign of water or grazing. Two stages beyond Charklick they passed the deserted fort at Miran, abandoned only a decade before by Tibetans retreating south from their desert bases as locally raised armies loyal to the Chinese regime successfully challenged Tibetan rule. Already the scouring sand had all but obliterated the small rooms hugging the inside of the eastern wall. Miran had never been a Chinese garrison: its only advantage over Charklick lay in the fact that it stood at a point where the road from Tibet over the Kunlun mountains to the south reached the desert. There were still some monks and a small farming community in the town but they could barely maintain the irrigation system now that the soldiers had left. Already the branch canals were choked and the desert had reclaimed the fields on their fringes, underlining the precarious-ness of life in such places. Further to the east Chudda would encounter the ruins of many abandoned villages in the Lop desert. It could not be long before Miran was reduced to the same state.

On the third day beyond Miran the camels suddenly stopped and knelt down, pressing their noses into the sand. The cameleer shouted to the travellers to take cover and not to move: a hot wind was approaching. Chudda and his servant were a little way behind the rest of the party, having stopped to pray at a small shrine, so they did not hear the cameleer's cries and were unaware of the wind until it was upon them. They had encountered hot desert winds before, but never such a ferocious one. They knew that they should cover their faces and mouths and stay where they were until the wind blew over, but there was no shelter and they were isolated and frightened. They both panicked and tried to gallop ahead to join the others, but they could see nothing in the whirling sand: it was like a scene from hell depicted on their temple wall. At last they were forced to stop and bury themselves behind their horses, hardly able to breathe for the sand clogging their noses and throats.

After several hours the swirling hot wind disappeared as quickly as it had arisen. It took them some time to regain their senses and then they realized that in their panic they had let go of their pack horses and these were now nowhere to be seen. The caravan had disappeared and the landscape had changed. They took it in turns to search but night was falling. The great dunes of sand, several hundred feet high, took an age to climb and from the top all they could see were more dunes. Eventually they found one of their horses, but by then it was dark and they could only set up camp and stay where they were. Luckily, they both still had their water containers and some provisions.

The next day and for several days after, they had little choice but to follow the sun to the east. Struggling across range upon range of dunes, without sign of water or life, they came across plenty of reminders of their own mortality in the form of bleached bones littering the sand. Chudda could not tell whether the bones were one or one hundred years old, or from man or beast, but he tried not to think about them. He felt responsible for their own predicament and he calmed the fears of his servant with prayers. After three days they ran out of water and then their horse became too weak to continue and they had to leave it to die. The servant became delirious and kept trying to run off in response to calls from the desert spirits. Chudda had been warned about these and their baleful influence, and he held the man back, until both of them were so weak that there was no need. Chudda called constantly upon Avalokiteśvara – the bodhisattva who hears the cries of the world – to save them. Finally, they could go no further. The servant collapsed into a fitful sleep. From his remaining possessions Chudda set up a small shrine with a statue of Buddha and a prayer sheet. For two days he prayed, fingering his rosary and falling in and out of consciousness.

When he saw figures approaching he thought they must be mirages, but then they spoke and offered him water. He pointed to his servant, but it was too late: the man had died. Chudda was helped on to a new horse, the body of his servant and what remained of their belongings were loaded on to a camel, and the caravan continued. He did not remember much of the next few days but when he was fully conscious again, the caravaneers told him that he had been barely two hundred feet from the main path, but hidden in the lee of a sand dune. They had come across him by chance when one of the party spotted the remains of a bundle of incense he had left on top of a dune.

Chudda was extremely relieved to reach the city of Dunhuang. He had lost almost everything, but he was most distraught about the death of his servant, for the young man had been his responsibility and in travelling together for several months they had become very close. Now, before continuing his journey, he wanted to spend his time in prayer. He arranged a cremation and gave what little money he had left to the abbot for prayers to be said for the dead man and for the horse that had died in his charge. He also decided to have a sutra copied to dedicate to him and was fortunate enough to meet a scribe who was suffering from stomach pains and agreed to do the work in exchange for a charm. The sutra was dedicated not only to his dead friend but to all sentient beings in the universe. Finally he wrote a letter explaining his servant's death and gave it to a monk travelling to Khotan. Monks regularly communicated by sending letters with pilgrims, and Chudda had little doubt that his missive would be passed from pilgrim to pilgrim until eventually it reached the monastery in Kashmir.

A few months later Chudda set out to complete his pilgrimage. He had had doubts about the wisdom of continuing. The monks at Dunhuang had told him of the terrible persecution of Buddhism in China a decade before, when in 845 hundreds of thousands of monks and nuns were forced to return to lay life, and thousands of Buddhist establishments were closed. The persecution was as much for economic as for ideological reasons: the Chinese exchequer needed money and Buddhist monasteries were tax-exempt. The return to lay life of large numbers of clergy greatly increased subsequent tax revenues, and many thousands of copper Buddhist statues were melted down and minted into coins. However, the persecution was also part of a turning inward of the Chinese state, a process which had been developing since the rebellion of Rokhshan a century before. Fortunately the emperor responsible for the desecration died in the following year and his successor proved more tolerant. Some of the monks and nuns had now returned to their monasteries, but many more monasteries remained deserted and were falling into disrepair.

Chudda's renewed enthusiasm for his pilgrimage had been kindled by the sight of paintings of Wutai mountain in the cave temples outside Dunhuang. Before setting out he dedicated the visit to his servant and offered prayers on his behalf, his original vow to pray for his country's peace forgotten.

He noticed little of the landscape on his journey into China, but took care to stay with the main party at all times as they passed through the narrow strip of land between the mountains and desert, and thence across the low pass into the great plain of central China. Reaching the great city of Chang'an, Chudda stayed only as long as it took to get permission to visit Wutai mountain and then joined a party of pilgrims. They left by the city's northwestern gate, the same through which Princess Taihe had passed on her journey north fifty years before, and by which she had returned just before the Buddhist persecution. His fellow pilgrims were Chinese monks, several of whom were not very strict in their observances, regularly eating after midday and being none too fussy about what they ate either. Chudda had met many monks and nuns in Dunhuang who lived in the town with their families and still worked in the fields. Moreover, the monks at the monastery where he had stayed did not eat together, nor did the monastery provide their food, except for special feasts.

Chudda did not enjoy his travels through China: there was a mood of depression in the countryside, engendered by the increasing tax burden imposed by a weak government. Chudda and his fellow pilgrims often found it difficult to find lodgings on their journey north. They were even turned away from monasteries whose rooms were already all occupied by rent-paying merchants and military men. At once place the monks ran inside at their approach and no amount of knocking would get them to open the gate. At another they were chased away with brooms. Often they had to rely on the hospitality of local lay believers, and even this was not always forthcoming. At one village, after trying twenty houses, Chudda finally had to force his way in and even then the host refused to feed him.

The land through which he now travelled was of loess, heavily eroded by rain and river water, and divided by great chasms. The towns and villages along the way were poor, and he heard many complaints about the double tax levied to pay for the soldiers sent to quell the frequent rebellions in the south. When they reached Taiyuan, the nearest large town to Wutai mountain, Chudda realized that Buddhism had not been the only faith to suffer under the previous emperor. The Manichean temple was in ruins, and the few remaining Uighurs in the town spoke of the terrible persecution of their countrymen in the Chinese capital. Two years after the Uighurs had been driven from their lands, their remaining armies were massacred in a battle against the Chinese at the border north-east of Taiyuan. The Chinese chief minister had then ordered the round up of Manichean clergy in Chang'an. The monks and nuns were forced to dress in dark Buddhist robes and had their heads shaved as a sign of humiliation: Manichean clergy traditionally dressed in white and did not cut their hair. Rumours told of more than seventy nuns being killed and of the rest of the monks and nuns being sent into exile; and Manichean texts were burned on the streets. The persecution against Buddhists started only two years later.

When the emperor died, a rebuilding programme had been started, but the new emperor insisted that the monasteries be renamed to symbolize his secular authority. Even now, a decade later, Buddhism had still not regained the confidence of former years.

Wutai, or Five Terraces, mountain is so called because of its five flattened peaks that lie some 9,000 feet above sea level. Monastery complexes had been built on the peaks and in the surrounding depressions since at least the third century AD and by the fifth century there were over two hundred establishments. In the seventh and eighth centuries the monasteries flourished, attracting considerable state support and tens of thousands of pilgrims. Monks from India, Korea and Japan were regular visitors, some staying for several years to study and leaving behind inscriptions recording their presence. In 824 the Tibetan emperor had successfully requested a plan of Wutai mountain from the Chinese emperor and Tibetan monks now also started to make pilgrimages. The Tibetan ruling family had officially adopted Buddhism in the previous century and, although Buddhist belief was not to become widespread in Tibet until later, the emperor initiated a monastery building programme at the time that the Swat valley monk, Padmasambhava, was resident there. The main central temple of bSam yas monastery (Samye) in the Zangpo river valley in southern Tibet was built as a symbolic world mountain, flanked by temples of the sun and moon and enclosed by a circular wall symbolizing the Iron mountains which surround the universe. Many Tibetan ideas for this and subsequent Buddhist buildings were based on existing temples in China, including those at Wutai mountain.

Chudda stayed at Wutai mountain for several months, visiting all the different temples, shrines and other sites, including a famous hexagonal revolving bookcase. There were always sutra lectures to attend and he was often invited to vegetarian feasts, arranged by patrons for the monks or in commemoration of special events. He also saw an ordination ceremony where young novices took the full set of vows. Neither had he forgotten his own vow. He 'moistened the brush' of several local artists and scribes, and the resultant paintings and sutras were all dedicated to his lost companion. It was deep winter when he left. The monastery buildings were covered with snow and the countryside around seemed to reflect the desolation that filled Chudda's heart.

His pilgrimage over, Chudda applied in Chang'an for papers to return home. In Dunhuang he halted for a while intending to commission more works, including copies of some of the wall paintings. While he was there, news arrived of the fall of the ruling

Karkota dynasty in Kashmir. Though the new king was well spoken of, Chudda decided to wait for further reports before continuing.

Over a decade had now passed. Chudda sat at his stall outside the monastery awaiting his next patient. His skills as a doctor had been in great demand in Dunhuang and, like many before and after him, he had been seduced by the Silk Road into staying.

The Courtesan's Tale

Larishka, 839–890

Outside my door the dog barks,
I know what it is, my lover's here.
Off with my stockings, down the perfumed stairs,
My good-for-nothing lover is drunk tonight.
I help him into my silk-curtained bed.
Will he take off his silk gown? oh no, not he.
My lord is drunk tonight, and drunk let him be.
Better that than sleeping alone.
                              Lyrics by anonymous poetess to the tune 'The
                              Drunken Young Lord', 10th century

LARISHKA'S MAIDSERVANT FOUND her sitting in front of the mirror, her hand raised but arrested in action, a small pekinese dog at her feet. The girl chided her mistress: her guests had already arrived and were expecting her. Larishka dipped a brush into a tiny pot of yellow orpiment pigment and carefully painted a crescent moon on her forehead to cover a scar. She was no longer young, but her thick make-up made it difficult to tell her age. The maidservant checked her mistress's hair ornaments and helped her finish dressing. Then Larishka took her lute from its case and carefully removed the silk wrapping. She fingered the strings and warmed her hands at a brazier before leaving the room to entertain her guests.

It was a domestic scene but in fact there was little in Larishka's life that could be called domestic. She had no husband or children; she knew little of housework or cooking; and only twice in her life had she had a place she considered her home. The first was her grandmother's house, and the second the place in which, in 890, she now lived. Both were in the city of Kucha on the northern Silk Road.

Like her grandmother and mother before her, Larishka had been trained as an entertainer. From late childhood, she had attended music, singing and dancing classes but, having shown great early promise, she was trained to specialize in the Kuchean lute, a four-stringed instrument with a bent neck. She could perform solo pieces but more often played in an orchestra. This had three sections: percussion, strings, and woodwind, including flute and oboe. Most compositions were in three parts, with the mode of the piece established by the pitch of the woodwind in the prelude and developed in the second and third parts.

Kuchean music was famed along the Silk Road, from Samarkand to Chang'an. Chinese music at this time comprised twenty-eight modes, based largely on the tuning of the Kuchean lute. Skill on the small Kuchean drum, which rested on a stand, became *de rigueur* among emperors and noblemen in China. One of its practitioners was the eighth-century Chinese Tang dynasty emperor Xuanzong who, in addition to his six famous dancing horses, housed thirty thousand musicians and dancers in the imperial palace, many of them from Kucha or playing in a Kuchean style. Kuchean orchestras also accompanied singers in musical dramas. The titles of the songs they played reveal the wide geographical and cultural milieu from which they were drawn: 'The Three Platforms of the Turks', 'South India', 'Music of Kucha', 'Music for Releasing Goshawks' and 'Watching the Moon in Brahman Land'. Kuchean singers could sing in many languages, including Sanskrit, although scholars mocked their pronunciation.

Many of the musical dramas had originated in India, but as they were passed along the Silk Road they absorbed new elements and were adapted to suit local culture. From China they were passed on to Korea and Japan, where some are still performed today. They varied from traditional Indian legends and stories of the gods – the Hindu god Śiva featured in several -- to depictions of everyday life, such as preparation for a polo game. Many were little more than burlesques: 'Sprinkling the Barbarians with Water' was accompanied by drums, lutes and harp, and was performed outside during the winter solstice by youths dressed only in masks. In it, the

Sogdian dancer, from a mural in a Chinese Tang dynasty tomb near Chang'an

dancers splashed cold water on each other and on unwary members of the audience.

Kuchean dancers were as renowned as their fellow musicians for their skill and were sent by the Kuchean court to Samarkand and Chang'an as representatives of the best of its culture. Kuchean dance was not unlike Indian dance, with its emphasis on hip movements, changes of gesture and expressive eyes, but it also adapted dance forms from other places, such as the famous Sodgian 'whirling' dance, performed by both men and women. Music, song and dance were Silk Road commodities, bought and sold like silver and jade. Itinerant dance troops from India, Burma, Cambodia and Sogdiana performed at both the royal court and the public marketplace in every Silk Road town, and their 'wares' were absorbed into the Silk Road repertoire.

★

The walled city of Kucha lay on the northern Silk Road about half-way between Kashgar and Kocho, with the mighty peaks of the Tianshan rising to its north. Its circumference was about six miles, but its king ruled territory which extended 300 miles from east to west and 200 miles north to south and included rich mineral deposits of gold, copper, iron, lead and tin. Kucha itself was something of a maverick kingdom. Its people and language were Indo-European, and it maintained a loyalty to Hīnayāna Buddhism, even though Mahāyāna Buddhism was ubiquitous elsewhere in the Tarim basin. Kucha had many famous sons, among them one of the most prolific and respected translators of Buddhist sutras from Sanskrit into Chinese, the fourth-century monk Kumārajīva, and one of the most successful Chinese generals of the mid-eighth century, Koso Khan. He was actually Turkic rather than Kuchean but, like all Silk Road towns, Kucha had a cosmopolitan population.

Ever since Larishka could remember, Kucha had been under the jurisdiction of the Kocho Uighurs. The first Uighur refugees had arrived in Kocho to the east of Kucha when she was a baby, fleeing their capital, Karabalghasun, on the Orkhon river beyond the Tianshan as the Kirghiz armies approached. That was in the winter of 839–40. Over the following years many more Uighur refugees and soldiers fled from the Orkhon river south-east into China where they massed on the northern borders and decided to settle, much to the consternation of the Chinese government, who had long experience of the Uighurs' skill in warfare. Regarding the Uighurs as a threat to their security, the Chinese secretly prepared for war and, in 843, annihilated most of the Uighur army. Following this, at first hundreds and then thousands of Uighur refugee families crossed the Tianshan to join the existing refugee community in Kocho. Their numbers ensured their supremacy, although there were skirmishes with Tibetans and local soldiers loyal to China. Within a few years, they started to move westwards from Kocho, and the Uighur population in Kucha multiplied. By this time Larishka was a young girl and she remembered their arrival clearly. They travelled in huge convoys, with their traditional felt tents piled on camels and carriages, and everyone, young and old, riding small, shaggy ponies, their progress marked by a great cloud of dust. The

Uighur soldiers were eager to carve out a new kingdom for them-selves after losing their former lands to the Kirghiz, and they soon asserted control over a large area around Kocho and Kucha.

Kucha was used to garrisons of foreign soldiers. The Tibetans had been the most recent, and before that the city had been one of China's four western garrisons. The Kuchean royal family, who lived in a splendid palace faced with gold and jade, continued to rule even while offering allegiance to these foreign empires, and both Tibetan and Chinese families had made their homes in the city. A century before, it had been besieged by troops of the Abbasid Caliphate and Kuchean storytellers still recounted how the king sent an urgent request to China for military aid to save the city. The Chinese emperor, it was said, asked the advice of a famous Zen Buddhist monk: 'It is 4,000 miles from the capital. The troops will have to travel for eight months. How can I help them?' The monk replied that he should request the aid of the troops of Vaiśravaṇa, Heavenly King of the North, through the intercession of a foreign monk then resident in the capital. The foreign monk was duly sum-moned and he and the emperor prayed together. At the very same moment, or so it was said, enormous demons descended in a great fog on Kucha and the Arabs were driven away.

The story symbolized the traditional twin reliance of Kucha on Buddhism and foreign troops. Great statues of the Buddha, 90 feet high, flanking the western gate, and the numerous monasteries and stupas in the city itself, were a reminder of its debt to Buddhism. And while Chinese forces were stationed in the city, the Kuchean king was diligent in paying tribute to the emperor. He sent fabulous presents such as dragon horses, the offspring of mares and dragons who lived in one of the city's pools, and a stone dream-making pillow – all those sleeping on it would dream of incredible journeys over land and sea. Kucha was also a major supplier of sal ammoniac, an ingredient in many Chinese prescriptions for relieving conges-tion and used by metal smiths as a flux for soldering the gold mined in the Tianshan. Among the gifts of good were fresh fruits which grew profusely in Kucha's temperate climate – grapes, pomegran-ates, pears, peaches, plums and apricots. Kuchean almonds, too, were highly prized.

★

Soldiers had been responsible for most of Larishka's travels and much of her livelihood in one way or another. They were the cause of her departure from Kucha, when she was little more than a girl. It was the start of the lunar new year which was marked by a great festival. Larishka and her troupe were to perform at a banquet that evening, but in the morning they went out on to the streets to be entertained themselves. The performers were as various as the goods traded on the Silk Road. Apart from watching musicians, dancers and singers – in whom Larishka had a professional interest – she could choose to be diverted in any number of ways. Child acrobats somersaulted between camels. Ex-soldiers made a living as strongmen. Monks performed illusions of self-disembowelment. There were puppet shows, storytellers, conjurers, tightrope walkers, performing midgets, jugglers, contortionists, and fire-eaters. But the big event of the day was held outside the city walls. It was traditional at the new year festival to select stallions, oxen and bull camels to fight one another, and the outcome of each encounter was thought to indicate the state of the respective herds over the following year. That evening, performing at court to assembled chiefs and local nobles, Larishka was noticed by a general from the Uighur headquarters in Kocho, several hundred miles to the east. Much taken with the girl, he demanded that she accompany him on his return to Kocho to entertain his guests. She had no choice but to go.

Larishka's journey to Kocho marked the beginning of her itinerant life. She now joined hundreds of other men and women, many of them captured in war and enslaved, who travelled in the soldiers' wake and carried out a variety of services for them. Inevitably, a large number of the women fell or were forced into prostitution. Larishka was recognized as a professional musician and joined the large band of entertainers who were called upon to perform at various celebrations, festivals and private events, but the general soon made it clear that he expected other services from her. He was the first of several such 'patrons'. In return for her services, musical and sexual, Larishka was kept in some comfort. She had a maidservant and ample supplies of fine cosmetics, silks and jewellery, and she rode about the town of Kocho on a richly caparisoned horse.

Only months after her arrival at Kocho she was on the move
again. The general's division had been ordered east as reinforcements. Uighur troops quartered at Lapchuk, east of Kocho, were
wont to raid the nearby city of Hami, seizing the inhabitants, their
belongings and livestock. Hami was not the only city to suffer
from such depredations. Farms around Dunhuang, further south,
were frequently beset by Aza nomads from Koko-nor, who were
allies of the Uighurs. Now Zhang Yizhao, a Chinese general, was
preparing to retaliate. In 848, after raising a local army, General
Zhang had driven the Tibetans from the city of Dunhuang and
then from other towns to the west. Since their last emperor had
been murdered by a Buddhist hermit in 842, Tibet had been in
disarray and its soldiers retreated from the Silk Road garrisons into
the safety of the Kunlun, there to fight on behalf of the various
contenders for the Tibetan throne. Following his victories,
General Zhang sent an envoy to the Chinese Tang emperor declaring his loyalty and in return he was honoured with the title of military governor to the 'Returning to Allegiance Army District'. It
was now 856, and Uighur and Aza spies reported that General
Zhang was preparing to march north to confront the Uighurs of
Lapchuk.

Lapchuck lay three hundred and fifty miles north of Dunhuang
but the Chinese loyalists under General Zhang made the journey
in only a few days, surprising the combined Uighur and Aza forces
outside the city, driving them back into the walled town and capturing vast herds of livestock. Larishka's patron was killed in the
battle, but she did not have to fend for herself for long before she
was claimed by an Aza chief. A few months later, when the
Chinese troops had withdrawn south, Larishka started out for
Koko-nor with the Aza, but near Dunhuang they were surprised
by an armed posse of soldiers and men from the town. In the
confusion that followed, Larishka was separated from the Aza and
forced to return with the Chinese to Dunhuang.

In Dunhuang her music was greatly appreciated and she soon
found a new patron among the Chinese general's commanders.
She also often played her lute for other officers and one among
them transcribed several of her works. She did not want for luxuries and was free to attend Buddhist services with her maidservant.

Chinese women's hairstyles, Tang dynasty (618–907)

She had always suffered from bad period pains but found a Kashmiri monk named Chudda in the town who was able to prescribe an effective herbal remedy, obtained on his recent pilgrimage to Wutai mountain. Both were strangers to Dunhuang, and they often exchanged stories about their homelands when her patron was away on one of General Zhang's many campaigns against the Tibetan forces still holding eastern Silk Road towns. She also heard that a local artist had used her as a model for his commissions at the cave temples outside the city where many murals depicted orchestras and dancers. At this time she wore her hair in the Chinese style then fashionable in Dunhuang, gathered into a long bun which fell in a lopsided fashion on the top of her head.

Her patron had quite a collection of textbooks on sex and erotic prints and often read her passages or showed her pictures describing new techniques and positions. One of his favourite books, *The Poetical Essay on Supreme Joy*, was written by the brother of a famous Chinese poet of the time and described how the newly married couple would choose a romantic setting – a pagoda in the moonlight or the library window in early spring – and sit together to examine the illustrations in a sexual handbook. A couch was prepared for them, surrounded by screens, and there follows a lengthy and explicit description of their foreplay, until 'the woman's expression changes, her voice falters, her hairpins fall out and her chignon is in disorder, tresses falling down at the side over her languid eyes. Her hair comb loosens and hangs down over her shoulder like a sickle moon.' The section ends: 'The joys of such moments shall not be forgotten until the end of their days.'

Despite her prayers to the bodhisattva Avalokiteśvara, who was supposed to help all those who cried out to him, Larishka was not fated to have a settled life. In 867 General Zhang, having finally driven the Tibetans from the city of Liangzhou, east of Dunhuang, decided to abdicate in favour of his nephew and retire home to China. He was accompanied by a retinue of hundreds, including Larishka, with a division of soldiers to guard them against raiders on the long journey east. In China Larishka's patron announced that he no longer required her services. Women were often passed on as gifts from one man to another, but Larishka's patron decided instead to sell her as a courtesan to a 'stepmother'. He had papers confirming that she was a prisoner-of-war, so there were no problems with the authorities. Larishka was still young and her skills as a musician ensured a good price. Thus her life changed yet again.

The city of Chang'an covered thirty square miles and had a population of nearly two million, but it was several years before Larishka saw much beyond the courtesan quarter, which lay just south-east of the imperial city, abutting on the Eastern Market. On the other side of the market lay an exclusive district containing the villas of high officials, luxurious hotels, Daoist and Confucian temples, and the palaces of provincial representatives. The stepmothers who ran the courtesan houses were themselves mostly former courtesans. Both the houses and the women in them were registered with the local authorities and paid taxes, receiving government protection in return. They were graded according to the services they offered and by the accomplishments of their girls.

1. Statue of Maitreya Bodhisattva, Gandhara: 'This would take him through the ancient kingdoms of Gandhara and Uddiyana to the north-west of Kashmir, countries in which Buddha himself had lived in his former reincarnations' (p. 118)

2. 'The cameleers wore shoes made of felt or thick wool stitched with a scale design' (p. 45)

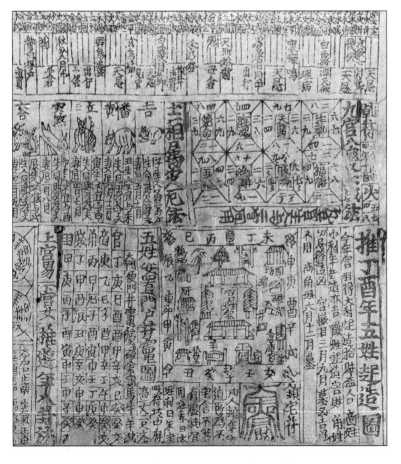

3. 'The central register of the almanac for 877 which Fengda studied so intently was devoted to the animals of the twelve-year cycle ... the lower register contained a charm and geomantic information' (p. 197)

4. 'Once Islam Akhun realized he had been discovered, he confessed to Stein that the documents had all been forgeries, manufactured by himself and various colleagues from locally made paper prematurely aged over fire' (p. 4)

5. 'She felt for her rosary beads and started to recite the *Guanshiyin Sutra*. This had always been one of her favourite texts and she had carried around a small, illustrated booklet' (p. 171)

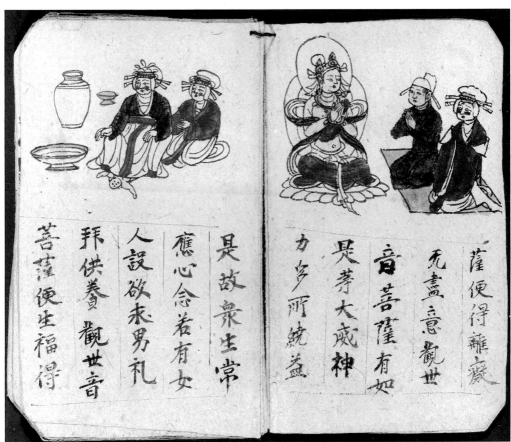

6. Bundle of manuscripts inside wrapper: 'She was clever with her hands and embroidered sutra wrappers from old silk which she presented to Miaofu, the abbess of a local nunnery' (p.183)

7. Tomb-guarding monsters: 'She arranged his funeral and spent long hours praying to Avalokitesvara to save her son from rebirth as an animal, a hungry ghost, or a demon in hell' (p.185)

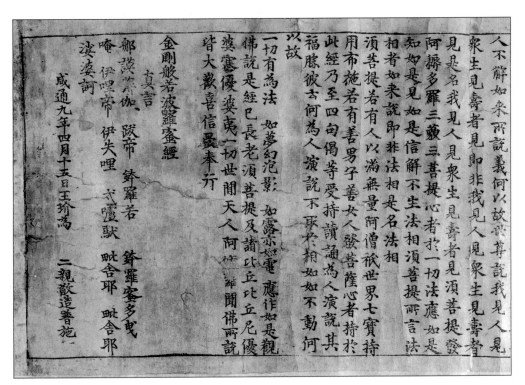

人不解如來所說義何以故說我見人見
眾生見壽者見即非我見人見眾生見壽者
見是名我見人見眾生見壽者須菩提發
阿耨多羅三藐三菩提心者於一切法應
知如是見如是信解不生法相須菩提發
相者如來說即非法相是名法相
須菩提若有人以滿無量阿僧祇世界七寶持
用布施若有善男子善女人發菩薩心者持於
此經乃至四句偈等受持讀誦為人演說其
福勝彼云何為人演說不取於相如如不動何
以故

一切有為法　如夢幻泡影
如露亦如電　應作如是觀
佛說是經已長老須菩提及諸比丘比丘尼優
婆塞優婆夷一切世間天人阿修羅聞佛所說
皆大歡喜信受奉行

金剛般若波羅蜜經

真言

那謨婆伽　跋帝　鉢羅若
波羅蜜多曳
唵　伊利帝　伊室唎　戍嚧馱　毗舍耶
毗舍耶　莎婆訶

咸通九年四月十五日王玠為
二親敬造普施

8. A printed copy of *The Diamond Sutra*: 'Printing, using carved wooden blocks, had been invented in China by at least the eighth century and was used by Buddhists to propagate their teachings' (p. 196)

9. Sketches for sutra illustrations: 'They had heard that he had grown used to the nomadic lifestyle and could not bear the monotony and toil of "the bitter land", as he called it' (p. 187)

10. 'Clubs made up of wealthier townswomen could afford to sponsor paintings on silk or a mural at the temple caves, thus gaining more merit for their members' (p. 186)

11. Dunhuang caves: 'Then they set off to tour the cave temples. There were several hundred of them honeycombing the cliff' (p. 191)

12. 'Mahayana [Buddhism] holds that the Sakyamuni is only one of many manifestations of Buddha, and its iconography therefore contains many different Buddhas' (p. 17)

13. 'Before their fate was decided, the dead had to appear successively before ten judges
... in the third year after death, the final audience [was] before "The King Who Turns
the Wheel of Rebirth in the Five Paths"' (pp. 203-4)

At the lowest end of the scale were government-run brothels where the girls were prisoners-of-war, convicted criminals, or the wives and daughters of criminals. Clients visited them for sex and nothing more, although they sometimes came away with gonorrhoea or other sexually transmitted diseases (syphilis was not to appear in China for several centuries).

At the other end of the scale were houses offering the services of girls trained for several years to be 'mistresses of the table'. Apart from musical skills, they were well-versed in drinking songs and games, and were excellent conversationalists. They were hired as companions for banquets, and were expected to drink along with their patrons, although they had been taught ploys to avoid getting drunk themselves. Chewing cloves was supposed to be particularly effective. The girls came from all backgrounds, but most had been sold by impoverished parents or kidnapped as children. After entering the house they went through several years of rigorous training. The best were adept at composing poetry and were paid for their cultural rather than their sexual skills: the going rate was 16,000 cash per evening.

Stories abounded about legendary girls. One was so proficient in the art of perfuming herself, it was said, that when she went out of doors, 'bees and butterflies followed her, in love with her fragrance'. Another girl had been fed with perfumes as a child and by the time she was grown her body was saturated with a natural fragrance. This story reminded Larishka of the gecko lizards, so-called 'palace warders'. Her stepmother told her of the geckoes that were bred at the imperial palace and fed on cinnabar until its redness permeated their bodies. They were then killed, and their bodies were pounded into a paste which was used to mark the emperor's concubines. The marks of the gecko, tradition said, only disappeared when the concubine had sex.

Larishka was no more free than the palace concubines. Her stepmother was her warden, without whom she was not initially allowed out unless accompanied by a servant. She was too old to be trained in the refined and subtle arts of the hostess and drinking companion, and started to be sold almost immediately on the basis of her musical skills. But it was impossible to refuse the advances of the most assiduous and generous patrons: this would have displeased her stepmother and made her position in the house uncomfortable. Larishka had no money of her own and relied on her stepmother for everything: food, clothes, cosmetics, perfumes and musical instruments. Some women found men to redeem them and set them up as concubines, but hardly any achieved a position as principal wife and most were discarded when they grew old.

While she was in Chang'an, Larishka heard the other girls talk of one of the most famous Chang'an courtesans. Originally from a poor family she was able to support herself, without a stepmother, on what her clients gave her for composing poetry. Then she moved out of the city to a lover's home, but his principal wife was jealous and there were frequent rows between the women. During their many subsequent separations, the courtesan composed sad and passionate poems for her lover:

> The mountain road is steep, the stone path dangerous,
> But it is not the road that pains me, but my love for you.
> Hearing the tinkling of the breaking ice, I think of your lovely
>   voice,
> The snow on the far mountain peaks reminds me of your pale
>   face.
> Don't listen to vulgar songs, don't drink the spring wine.
> Don't invite leisurely guests for long nights of chess.
> Remember our sworn bond of love that should last for ever,
> Even if our living together tarries to be restored.
> Although I hate this lonely trek, alone on a winter's day,
> My hope is at last to see you again when the full moon is in the
>   sky.
> Separated from you, what can I offer?
> Only this one poem, stained with bright tears.

Eventually she had to leave her lover for good, and took up residence in a Daoist nunnery, although this did little to cramp her style. Her parties were renowned and all the most elegant young scholars and officials were invited, with the religious authorities, it was rumoured, getting rich on the profits of sales of wine and food to the guests. But when she was arrested on charges of beating her maidservant to death, none came to her aid. Larishka never knew whether the charge was true. Some people said that the courtesan had been framed by resentful creditors. In any case, she was tried and convicted of murder, for which the penalty was execution. The sentence was carried out in 871.

Although Larishka stayed in Chang'an for nearly two decades, she never considered it her home, despite having her own suite of rooms, a maidservant and a pet lapdog. The house she lived in was the stepmother's: she was an employee. She tried to find a patron who would take her as his concubine and establish her in a separate residence, but such men were few. There were some who continued to appreciate her for her skill on the lute, but many more rejected her and she grew old in this house. Each year she had to spend longer over her make-up to hide the signs of age, for her green eyes and light hair alone were no longer sufficient to assure her attention. Larishka powdered her face, taking care to cover the fine wrinkles around her eyes and mouth. It was the fashion among high-class women to apply massicot, yellow lead, to the forehead, and courtesans followed their example. She used an indigo stick to paint her eyelids and make a small beauty mark on her cheek. Her eyebrows were plucked and she drew two marks, like the wings of a butterfly, high on her forehead with the indigo stick. Her lipstick was made from onycha, blended with wax and the ashes of fragrant fruits and flowers. Her nails were painted with an extract of balsam mixed with alum. Finally, she applied various scents to her body. Her clothes were perfumed with sweet basil, and a small, delicately embroidered silk-gauze bag which hung from her waist contained other fragrant herbs and flowers. Only after this was she ready to meet a client.

As her earning powers decreased, Larishka spent more and more time in the house training the younger girls and chatting to her stepmother, with the aim of being appointed as her successor. She was extremely fond of her pupils and one girl in particular showed unusual aptitude at the lute. Kuchean music was no longer so popular in China: like so much else imported from the Silk Road, it had become unfashionable as the Chinese sought to rediscover and promote home-grown traditions in a time of political disintegration. Nevertheless, the taverns and restaurants were full of western girls:

The western courtesan with features like a flower
Stands by the wine warmer and laughs with the breath of spring.
Dancing in a dress of sheer silk gauze, she asks
'You won't be going anywhere, sir, surely not before you are
    drunk?'

In the autumn of 880 rumours circulated in the city that a group of rebels were advancing towards the capital from the south. There had been periodic rebellions there for many years. All had either petered out or had eventually been suppressed by government troops, but each campaign had further drained the already depleted exchequer, and each subsequent increase in taxes compounded popular discontent. Farmers forced into bankruptcy had nothing to lose by joining rebel bands. However, the government had not been seriously threatened by a rebellion since that of Rokhshan a hundred years earlier.

The residents of Chang'an were used to stories about rebellions – this particular one had been rumbling on since 874 – but they believed that the army would not allow the rebels to enter the imperial city and so remained sanguine even when it was reported that they were just beyond the final pass leading to the city. Unfortunately, the army sent to halt their advance was of little use. The troops stationed in the capital were drawn from the sons of the wealthy, but more often than not their fathers bought their sons out of military service, paying anyone, including the sick, willing to take their place. Consequently, this motley army was routed by the rebels who then marched on the city.

It was late afternoon when the advance guard arrived. The emperor and several of his wives had secretly fled the night before. Soldiers and residents alike now took the opportunity to loot the imperial treasuries and offered no resistance to the rebels. One of the generals even went out of the city gates to greet the rebel commander: he knew that this man might well become the next emperor and it was therefore important to impress him. The rebel commander was magnanimous in victory, declaring that his objective in taking up arms had been to benefit the common people, and the inhabitants of Chang'an welcomed him and his soldiers. Nevertheless, many people stayed barricaded indoors. Their fears were not unfounded. Discipline could not be maintained and the rebel soldiers, jubilant at their victory, sacked the city. Larishka and her fellow courtesans escaped lightly, since the rebels were chiefly interested in the wealthy and the influential, but they did not dare go out on the streets. Three days later the rebel leader declared himself emperor of a new dynasty.

The rebel soldiers soon grew tried of plunder and their generals reasserted control. By May 881 things were almost back to normal, the courtesans being kept especially busy with all the soldiers in town. But just as they were starting to get used to the new regime, the soldiers withdrew. Imperial forces had regrouped and were advancing from the west. Once more the city was invaded by soldiers, and these were no more disciplined than their rebel counterparts. Again the residents barricaded themselves in their homes and waited for the worst.

Larishka would always remember the day the rebels marched back into the city to confront the imperial troops. When soldiers broke into the house she did not know which side they were on, such was the confusion. Only later did she learn that they were rebels. To her it made no difference. Having forced the imperial army out of the city, the rebels now declared war on the city's residents for having welcomed the imperial troops in the first place. The rebel commander ordered his forces to 'wash out the city', but it was washed with blood rather than water.

Larishka was with the other girls and servants in an upstairs room. The sound of metal drums, galloping hooves, shouts and screams grew louder. The women held each other, none daring to speak of what was happening. Men came bursting into the room, swords drawn and blood on their faces. The stepmother and older servants were killed immediately, while the soldiers dragged the girls from each other's grasp and raped them in turn on the matted floor. Larishka had told the youngest to hide in a cupboard, but one of the soldiers heard her screaming. When Larishka saw him open the cupboard, she bit the man on top of her and, as he withdrew his hand in pain, she wriggled free and threw herself in front of the young girl. Enraged, the soldier raised his sword and struck her. When she regained consciousness, she saw the young girl lying beside her, her clothes torn off, her body slashed and her head severed. The soldiers had gone. The rest of her companions and her dog were also dead.

Larishka did not stop for anything. Even her lute was left behind. She ran from alley to alley, cowering in doorways when she heard the approach of soldiers, until she reached the western gate of the city. Her only concern was to get as far away as possible from the scene of carnage. She was in open countryside before she stopped. It was night, and when she looked back she could see only the flames of the burning city in the distance. It was her last view of Chang'an.

Larishka fled west, towards her old home in Kucha. There were many other refugees on the move and the guards at the Chinese border post on the edge of the desert did not try to stop them: their loyalty to the emperor was wearing thin. Most of them had in any case been recalled to help fight the rebels, leaving only a small force behind, but even so the emperor did not succeed in retaking Chang'an until he enlisted the help of the Shatou Turks. That was in 883, but the rebel leader was not cornered until the summer of the following year, far to the east, where he cut his own throat to evade capture. The Chinese emperor returned only briefly to Chang'an before fleeing again from another group of rebels, and during this time many of China's military governors took advantage of the lack of control at the centre to establish *de facto* autonomous fiefdoms. When some semblance of order was finally restored in 886, the capital lay in ruins. The emperor installed himself in a town to its west where he died, aged only twenty-seven, in 888. It was now only a matter of time before the Tang dynasty fell: what is surprising is that it survived until 907, after which the empire was once again divided into a number of kingdoms. It was only reunited in 960 with the advent of the Song dynasty.

Beyond the border Larishka joined a group of merchants who, hearing of the troubles, had decided not to proceed to China and

Musicians on a bullock cart, detail of a painting on silk from Dunhuang

were on their way back along the Silk Road. She had to beg for food and take whatever transport was offered, but after several months she reached Kucha safely. There she found family and friends to help her, and she established a house of her own. Larishka had left Kucha as a young woman in 855, twenty-six years before, and when she returned at the end of the century, it was to see even more signs of Uighur influence: in dress, art, religion, and culture, as well as in administration. By now the Uighur kaghan had established his summer capital at Kocho and a winter residence at Beshbaliq, north of the Tianshan. His jurisdiction extended even beyond Kucha. Previously Kuchean orchestras had always performed at regal and official ceremonies, but now Uighur military bands played loud, raucous music on their horns, drums and gongs.

Larishka's girls were popular with the Uighur soldiers, but Larishka herself was often called upon to play Kuchean songs by the older residents who preferred the traditional music. She never spoke of the rebels, but she could not forget that night in Chang'an. Unlike the scar on her forehead, her memories did not fade. Her maidservant often found her sitting lost in thought, tears rolling down her cheeks.

The Nun's Tale

Miaofu, 880–961

> This fleeting world is like
> A star at dawn, a bubble in a stream,
> A flash of lightning in a summer cloud,
> A flickering lamp, a phantom, and a dream.
> > Prayer from the end of *The Diamond Sutra*.

MIAOFU'S ROOM WAS dark and thick with smoke. Offerings of flowers, fruit and incense had been placed in front of an image of the Amitābha Buddha which hung on the wall above a small shrine. In accordance with death-bed ritual, the abbot asked Miaofu in which Buddha-land she wished to be reborn, and he then described the joys she would encounter there, intoning the Buddhas of the Ten Directions and comforting her by explaining how each in turn would welcome her after her death. Then he led the clergy in chanting *The Sutra of Impermanence*.

Miaofu was the former abbess of a large nunnery in Dunhuang. It was 961 and word had recently reached the city that after half a century of division China had been reunited under the Song dynasty. Miaofu's father, an official in the military governorship of Dunhuang, had been Chinese, while her mother was Tibetan. The Tibetan empire had ruled Dunhuang since 781 and, even after its soldiers were driven out by a local force in 848, many Tibetans remained in the town. Their empire, too, had been subject to years of division and civil war but, unlike China, there was no sign of a new emperor to reunite the country.

Miaofu had always been eager to learn about the world outside

Dunhuang, her curiosity aroused as a child by the stories her father and grandmother told. Her father spoke with great nostalgia of his youth in China during the Tang dynasty. Her maternal grandmother spoke with equal feeling of the heyday of Tibet and the great Buddhist temples that surpassed anything found in Dunhuang. As Miaofu lay dying, surrounded by the sound of the monks and nuns chanting, she drifted in and out of consciousness, reliving memories of her youth.

She was a girl again, preparing for her ordination which was to take place in a roped-off area within the main monastery building. The ceremony to purify the building and its precincts was over, and only those who were to be ordained and the officiating clergy remained inside the incense-filled hall. Banners of coloured silk with depictions of the Buddha and bodhisattvas hung from the wooden columns and rafters. Miaofu was one of several local girls receiving the initial ordination. When her turn came she stepped forward and prostrated herself in front of the great statue of the Buddha and then saluted the abbess. One of the nuns took a knife and cut off her long hair near the roots, placing it in a small tray held by another nun. Again Miaofu prostrated herself, three times. Her head was washed and shaved smooth while she closed her eyes and recited the name of the Buddha. She then had to recite the ten vows, prostrate herself once more in front of the Buddha and thank the ordaining nuns and monks. She was presented with monastic robes and a begging bowl. The day after the ceremony, she was given a certificate stamped with images of the Buddha and a government seal for which her father had paid two donkeys. Miaofu was now a novice nun in the eyes of both the church and the state.

Miaofu's parents were devout lay Buddhists and had not objected to her entering monastic life. Her father sometimes said that it was fated that she should do so, since she had been born on the same day as the rebels had taken the Chinese capital, Chang'an, and killed his mother and sister. That was in the winter of 880. In the months that followed, refugees fleeing from the rebels brought stories of the violent destruction of Chang'an and reported that few women left there had escaped rape and death. Miaofu's father heard more from a courtesan called Larishka who passed through Dunhuang on her way back to Kucha in 881. She had a livid, red scar across her forehead, and she told of how all her fellow courtesans had been raped then murdered by the rebels, and that she had been wounded while trying to protect the youngest girl. Miaofu's father had been awarded three years' leave to mourn his mother, the traditional period for a parent in China, but he was unable to return to Chang'an to arrange a proper burial in the family plot until 884, when the rebels were finally defeated. He went alone, for China was still unsettled, though under nominal control of the Tang dynasty. He found the capital in near anarchy and the emperor still absent.

He returned to Dunhuang several months later with his own stories of the sack of Chang'an, bringing back a poem composed by an examination candidate who had been in the capital in 880. In the poem a young woman, caught by the rebels when they entered Chang'an, recounted what had followed. Miaofu was not allowed to read it but on several evenings she was woken by the sound of her father weeping. After this she found an opportunity to look at the poem without her parents' knowledge. It was difficult for her to read, and when she had struggled through two stanzas she wished she had not. The words conjured up images that she would have preferred to forget, images far worse than any of the scenes from hell depicted on the local temple walls:

Every home now runs with bubbling fountains of blood,
Every place rings with a victim's shrieks that cause the very earth
    to quake,
Dancers and courtesans must undergo secret outrage;
Infants and tender maidens are torn living from their parents'
    arms.

It was at this time that Miaofu learned that she had been born on the day her grandmother and aunt had died. Perhaps this was also when she decided to become a nun. There were certain advantages attached to entering a nunnery for not all nuns did so as a vocation. A nun could study, even though many monks and more nuns remained illiterate, and she was able to avoid an arranged marriage: several Chinese princesses entered the Daoist order seemingly for this reason. Other girls were persuaded by their parents, who saw it as a means to avoid paying a dowry and an opportunity to gain influence in the monastic community. A contemporary contract records the loan of 18 pecks of beans by a monk to the father of a novice. The loan carried no interest, which was unusual at this time, for monks were the main usurers in the community and regularly charged interest above the legal rate of 6 per cent. The debtor was to repay the loan at the end of the eighth month, after the harvest, and if he defaulted, his goods would be seized.

Miaofu was only eleven when she was ordained in 891, though the minimum age stipulated by Buddhist law for ordination was twelve. Her father therefore had to apply on her behalf to the military governor for permission for her to enter the nunnery early. The permit was prepared and the governor made his mark after his surname and added three impressions of his large, square seal in red ink. Some parents were less willing to hand over their children. A contemporary collection of stories about famous nuns recounted the argument used by a monk to persuade a reluctant father: 'If you consent to her plan she will indeed raise her family to glory and bring you blessings and honour. She will guide you across the great ocean of suffering to nirvāna.' Another story told of the Abbess Miaoyin outside whose house hundreds of carriages bearing visitors with gifts would line up, and who was reputed to be richer than many members of the imperial family. The blessings offered by monastic life could be both spiritual and material, the stories implied.

After Miaofu's ordination, a local monk complained to the military governor about violations of the Buddhist law, citing Miaofu and forty other nuns. 'Their parents', the monk wrote, 'all gave permission for these girls to become nuns and the girls were all happy to receive the precepts. However, some of them are too young and some have not followed Buddha's teachings and have contravened secular statutes. They must be controlled and disciplined.' We do not know what their particular crimes were, but there was considerable prejudice against the institution of female clergy, especially among more doctrinaire monks. Women were held to be further down the chain of rebirth than men, and Buddhist texts made it clear that Buddha had only accepted women as part of the monastic order after considerable persuasion from his own mother. Some monks even refused to ordain women and others would not allow them into the monasteries or let them attend their lectures. Nevertheless, there were five nunneries in the Dunhuang area, the largest housing almost two hundred nuns.

The process of ordination was more demanding for women than for men. At twelve both boys and girls took the first set of precepts – vows to abstain from drink, sex, murder and others sins – but boys could undergo full ordination at eighteen, taking between 215 and 263 precepts dictated by the monastic code. Girls at eighteen took only an intermediate stage of ordination and were then supposed to undergo another two years' study before being fully received into the order. This additional requirement had been instituted, so tradition said, after a nun ordained by Buddha at the age of eighteen had turned out to be in the early stages of pregnancy. At twenty, nuns were required to take between 290 and 380 precepts for full ordination. However, Miaofu had heard from Tibetan and Indian monks of the female deity Tārā, worshipped by many in their countries as an equal to the bodhisattva Avalokiteśvara. When it was suggested that she change sex in order to attain enlightenment more quickly, Tārā replied: 'There are many who desire enlightenment in a man's body, but none who work for the benefit of sentient beings in the body of a woman. Therefore, until the world of suffering is empty, I shall work for the benefit of sentient beings in a woman's body.'

Miaofu received her temple name, which means 'Wonderful Blessings', when she took her first set of vows. The ordination took place in the Pure Land monastery in Dunhuang which she had entered several months before to study the precepts. Some of her classmates had already spent many years in the monastery and were only now considered ready to take their vows. Others were, like her, from outside. Their classes were led by experienced monks and nuns in a large hall. Miaofu was taught all the practical aspects of life as a nun: how to sweep floors, how to eat, how to walk (this depended on whether she was wearing the wide-sleeved outer robe or the narrow-sleeved under-robe), how to salute a

Tārā, Tantric Buddhist deity

superior, how to speak, to dress, to make a bed and to make her clothes into a bundle for travelling. In addition, she was taught how to receive guests and how to hand these duties over to another nun the following day. She was expected to learn extracts from the sutras and to recite them throughout the day. In addition, there were many times during her daily activities when she had to recite an appropriate prayer:

> On first awaking from my sleep,
> I pray that every living thing
> May wake to saving wisdom, vast
> As the wide and boundless universe.

The boys and girls lived in segregated dormitories on either side of a central courtyard within the crowded buildings of the monastery complex. The privies stood in a corner that backed on to the vegetable garden, making transport of the night-soil to the garden an easy affair. In addition to this small plot inside the walls, the monastery owned much of the surrounding farmland which was cultivated by serf labourers and tenant farmers. The produce was stored in granaries inside the monastery, to be lent out at advantageous rates of interest, or used as currency for the purchase of various necessities such as the hemp seed needed to produce oil for cooking and light.

The income earned from such transactions was considerable, and it was supplemented by donations and by the sale of ordinations, sutras and services. But the monastery gained most of its income from its mills and oil-presses and was easily the richest institution in the community. For many of the local residents, it was also the most important since it offered services, whereas the secular authorities always seemed to want to take something. Government was associated with military service, the collection of taxes and law enforcement. No one paid their taxes willingly: many of the local landowners pledged their land to a monastery, thus making it tax-exempt, while they carried on working and profiting from it as before. Others exploited the tax-exempt status of the clergy and purchased ordination certificates so that they were registered as monks and nuns, but they continued to live ordinary lives with their families in the towns and villages. The law was an uncertain ally. Although some found it useful in civil cases, such as broken contracts or the incorrect allocation of land, criminal justice was feared. Many of those arrested did not return from prison. Some were tortured to extract a confession – the mainstay of most prosecution cases – and died as a result, while others died of disease in the noisome prison cells while still awaiting trial. Once a case came to trial the luckiest would receive a comparatively light sentence, a beating with the light or heavy stick, but for more serious crimes men were sent to undergo military service in a distant province and women were assigned to government-owned brothels. For the most serious crimes, capital punishment was meted out, although since the emperor usually announced a general amnesty at the beginning of each new year many of those condemned to death were reprieved. In contrast, the monastery had no prison, and it could help when people were in trouble – with loans of seed-grain for the next harvest, a cooking pot for winter, or a small plot of land. It offered the poor employment, the rich redemption, and a tax haven to both.

*

Detail from the frontispiece of The Diamond Sutra,
showing the monk Subūthi flanked by lions

Miaofu drifted back into consciousness. She was aware of the small group of monks and nuns on their prayer mats around her bed. She tried to concentrate but the rhythmic drone of their chanting soon set her thinking once more of her past. She was sitting on the rush mat floor of the lecture hall with ten other nuns, reciting *The Diamond Sutra*. The hall was dim, but the smell of a hot, dry summer's day filtered in, making her restless. It was 900. She had been a novice for almost ten years at one of the several nunneries in the city and was preparing for full ordination.

For several years after her initiation as a novice Miaofu had been expected to runs errands and help the other nuns. She also had to attend sutra lectures and classes with the Master of the Law and the Master of the Teaching: monks who were her guides in the monastic rules and Buddhist teachings. Because she was literate, Miaofu was given sutras to read, memorize and chant during her work. She was instructed in meditation techniques and also started to learn Sanskrit sounds so that she could chant sutras and prayers in their original language.

The Buddhist canon consisted of three parts, known by their Sanskrit name Tripiṭaka (literally 'Three Baskets'): the sutras (the lectures of Buddha); monastic rules (the vinaya); and commentaries on sutras written by monks after the time of Buddha. Works which were considered apocryphal, such as *The Sutra of the Ten Kings*, were not incorporated into the canon. Certainly not written at the time of Buddha and almost certainly composed in Chinese, these sutras were nevertheless often popular among both clergy and lay believers.

The taking of the full vows was a much longer and more complex ceremony than the initial ordination. The ordinands were of all ages. A special platform was erected for the occasion in the neighbouring monastery and its construction took over a week. Cartloads of earth were brought into the courtyard in front of the lecture hall and emptied into an area marked out by a square wooden frame. When the frame was full and the earth piled in a high mound, labourers stamped it down with heavy wooden posts until it was completely flat and flush with the top of the frame. Several layers were created by the same method, and then a smaller platform was built on top. Stairs were then cut from the earth, and the posts erected around the perimeter were festooned with banners and streamers made from colourful silk. Many ordination platforms in monasteries elsewhere were similarly temporary, but at Wutai mountain there was a permanent structure made of great blocks of stone, its sides faced with jade with lotus designs, on which was laid a green silk carpet. There, at the height of Chinese Buddhism, hundreds of monks and nuns were ordained each year.

Miaofu's ordination coincided with the annual spring vegetarian banquet. Like a similar banquet held in the autumn, this was paid for by the military governor of Dunhuang, General Zhang, a descendant of the famous general who had driven out the Tibetans. After the ceremony was over the twenty newly ordained monks and nuns were given 'The Three Sets of Clothing' by the military governor's office: an assembly robe (the kāṣāya), an over-garment (the uttarāsaṅga), and a shirt (the antaravāsaka). They then entered the banquet hall and recited a prayer before the meal started. The ordination had finished early, for the banquet had to be arranged in the morning – no eating was allowed after midday.

An exception was made only when monks had to carry out manual work in the afternoon: they were then allowed 'night food'. More than fifteen hundred local people attended the banquet – officials, soldiers, rich and influential lay believers and members of the Dunhuang monastic community. The monastery kitchens had been busy for days, preparing the food.

After the banquet many of the monks and nuns left the monastery to return to their family houses in the city and neighbouring villages. Some of them were needed at home to look after aged parents or to help on the land. Miaofu had a sister-in-law who could carry out these tasks and so there was no need for her to return home. Moreover, she wanted to make her life in the monastery. She had read several texts concerning rules for the monastic community and was struck by the disparity between their injunctions and the actions of many of her fellow monks and nuns. She was keen to become an abbess of one of the local nunneries so that she could enforce the rules more strictly.

Miaofu woke again, startled by this recollection. For a moment she could not remember whether she had made a confession. When she had first realized the seriousness of her illness a few months before, she had arranged for seven copies of *The Sutra of the Ten Kings* to be made as an act of repentence. At the end of each she

Demon supporting one of the Heavenly Kings, ninth-century silk painting from Dunhuang

wrote: 'The disciple Miaofu, a troubled nun, with the thought of enlightenment in her mind, reverently had this scripture written on seven separate scrolls, and offers them with a concentrated mind.' In addition, in her will she left cloth to pay for offerings and the recitation of prayers at set intervals after her death. These prayers would be said on the days on which she would be brought before each of the ten kings of the underworld, when he would mete out the punishment for her evil deeds. The wall paintings in the cave temples outside Dunhuang showed the kings in the garb of Chinese magistrates sitting behind desks while the dead were brought before them. Those who protested when their sins were recounted were made to look into a mirror which reflected their past deeds. Others, their fates already decreed, were put in cangues, great wooden collars, and herded away by axe-wielding demons to the fiery city of hell.

The opening of *The Sutra of the Ten Kings* pronounced that 'if

Demon guarding the gate to Hell, tenth-century illustrated manuscript of The Sutra of the Ten Kings

any person commissions this scripture or receives and reads or recites it, then after giving up his life he will not be reborn as an animal, a hungry ghost or a being in hell, nor will he enter any of the great underground prisons'. Offerings given on each of the appropriate days – the seventh day after the death, and every seventh day after up to the forty-ninth day, and thereafter on the hundredth day after death, a day during the first year, and another during the third year – also protected the deceased from rebirth as a lesser being.

Miaofu's conscience troubled her because her early intentions of living according to the monastic rules had soon been overtaken by the realities of life in the nunnery to which she moved after her first ordination. The nunnery itself was far less well endowed than the large monastery where she had been trained for her ordination. There monks in need had 'borrowed' food and goods from the monastic holdings and Miaofu had soon realized that these 'loans' were not always paid back. In addition, her Master of Teaching had often used monastic goods to make loans to others, at a high rate of interest, repaying the capital to the monastery but keeping the interest for himself. Often his debtors had defaulted on their loans, and had repaid him by allowing him free use of their land for a set number of years. She remembered how, when his will became public after his death, everyone was amazed at the extent of his wealth. The will had distinguished between those items considered to be monastic property and those originating from family property. The former were left to the monastery and the community. They included 'seven pieces of silk and felt, two suits of fine silk, blankets, fur-lined cloaks, cloth and leather shoes, a belt made from fifteen ounces of silk and gold, silver dishes, copper dishes, oil containers made of wood with lids and handles, a she-ass of five years, and an ass of five years'. His family property, which included items and land obtained as a result of his speculations on monastic holdings, was left to his various nephews, cousins and fellow monks. To one of the novices he bequeathed 'a piece of fine white silk, a square saucepan with handles, the body of a lamp worth seven ounces of silver, a small ivory dish, other sundry items and a four-year-old ox'.

But commerce and usury were the province of men: there were

few opportunities for nuns to accumulate wealth. Many were orphans or daughters of local peasants whose families had nothing to give them. All the nuns and monks begged in the town, but for some it was their only source of income. Miaofu's family was not poor and they had provided her with a considerable sum on her ordination. Nevertheless she was determined to augment her income. There were fees to be had for the recitation of sutras on behalf of the sick and the dying, and copying sutras was similarly rewarded, although professional scribes were usually men and rarely clergy. Thus, over the years Miaofu gradually increased her wealth, investing in some land which provided a small annuity in grain and gaining patrons from among the local elite who, valuing her education, often presented her with gifts. Her father had taught her to read the Chinese classical texts as a child, and as a novice she had started to learn Sanskrit. Her grandmother had also taught her Tibetan. She enjoyed chatting with the wives of local dignitaries and learning the latest news from China and Tibet, as well as the local gossip of the town.

Ten years after her full ordination, in 910, the Zhang family who had ruled Dunhuang since 848 were supplanted by the Cao family. Cao Yijun, the first ruler, continued to offer allegiance to China and to call Dunhuang the 'Returning to Allegiance Army District'. The Chinese Tang dynasty had just fallen after many years of weak and ineffectual government, and during most of the Cao family's reign China was split into several regions, none powerful enough to reunite the country let alone to re-establish control in Dunhuang, over a thousand miles away. Nevertheless, the city's rulers continued to send envoys to the successive dynasties that claimed Central China, and in turn they continued to be awarded the title of military governor.

It was now 960 and the Cao family still ruled Dunhuang. Cao Yuanzhong, the current king and a keen patron of Buddhism, had been awarded the title of military governor by a succession of Chinese dynasties, and had even visited China in 955, only six years before. At Miaofu's bedside the monks and nuns, sustained by strong green tea to keep them awake during their long vigil, continued to chant. Miaofu was a senior member of the monastic community, respected as much for her actions as for her age. Not everyone had agreed with her appointment as abbess of the largest nunnery in Dunhuang when she was barely forty. But Miaofu had ruled strictly and well and, most important, she had directed the nunnery's affairs extremely shrewdly. During her tenure, the nunnery gained possession of more land, two mill-wheels and an oil-press.

Monks and nuns were not supposed to involve themselves directly with 'impure' things, which included gold, silver, slaves, agriculture, animal husbandry, blankets and saucepans, as well as mill-wheels and oil-presses. Instead, each monastic institution had families bound to it in perpetuity – effectively serf households – who carried out the work on their behalf. Such families worked the mill-wheels and oil-press that belonged to Miaofu's nunnery, though they were not permitted to carry out work on their own initiative but had to apply for permission to the nunnery. A fixed percentage of the produce – flour and oil – was paid in kind to the nunnery as rent, and the nunnery in turn paid professional mill-wrights in kind to maintain and repair their property. After major repair work was completed, Miaofu had always ordered that a banquet be arranged for the nuns and artisans. The nunnery also provided the miller with the material necessary for his work – gauze to make sieves and an ox to carry flour to the nunnery's storehouse. A nun was appointed as steward to keep a careful written inventory of all goods entering and leaving the storehouse.

The mill-wheels were driven by water, and since this reduced the water available for irrigation, the local government forbade their use during the growing season. The sluice gates to the diversion canals were padlocked, and a local official was in charge of the key. If during spring or summer there was more than enough water for irrigation then an exception was made and the gates opened: this was an occasion for another banquet, held at night at the mill-race by lamplight. The local government also levied a tax on the mills and presses in spring and autumn.

The mills provided millet and wheat-flour for the nuns. The coarser flour which remained behind in the sieve was used to feed the serf households, and the bran was fed to the horses. Hemp-seed for the oil-press had to be purchased but the resulting oil was used both for cooking and to supply the lamps which burned perpetually in the Buddha Hall. Some of the nunnery's land was specifically allocated to defray this expense. Oilseed cakes were also used to fatten livestock.

The sounds of the nunnery filtered through into Miaofu's room. It seemed unusually noisy. But then she remembered: it was the end of the summer retreat and everyone was preparing for the Ghost Festival. The summer retreat was a practice inherited from India where the monsoon rains curtailed the monks' activities. There was no monsoon in the desert, but the clergy still went into retreat from the fourth lunar month to the seventh, the height of summer. They were supposed to spend their time in confession and meditation, but tempers often became frayed as clergy usually resident in the city moved into the monastic buildings, and their permanent residents were forced to share rooms and facilities. This summer one of the nuns complained about another who, she said, made too much noise when walking past her room to get water from the well. Miaofu was asked to speak to the offender, the daughter of one of Miaofu's friends, a wealthy local landowner. The nunnery did not want to lose the patronage of her mother, especially so near to the Ghost Festival, a time when the laity traditionally made generous offerings to the church.

Miaofu's thoughts turned to the central story of the Ghost Festival, that of a disciple of Buddha who rescued his mother from hell. The disciple was named Mahāmaudgalyāyana, but was known in Chinese as Mulian. She imagined the storyteller in the marketplace unfurling the scroll depicting Mulian's mother falling into the deepest hell of all, Avīci Hell, and the audience gasping in horror. He would then go on to explain why Mulian's mother deserved her fate.

When Mulian goes abroad on a trading mission, he leaves his mother money to feed beggars and to pay for vegetarian feasts for the Buddhist clergy. His mother hides the money, and when Mulian returns she lies, saying that she has used it as he directed. After his parents' deaths, Mulian becomes a monk and, when he realizes that his mother is not in paradise, he goes in search of her. The king of the underworld, Yama, summons his karma-watcher, fate-investigator and book-keeper. Mulian sets off and crosses the

Wathellwedo river where those bound for hell stand wailing on the river's banks, about to be herded across by ox-headed demons. One tells Mulian:

> Please inform those sons and grandsons of ours who are still at
>   home
> That it is pointless to make coffins and caskets of white jade.
> Gold is spent in vain when it is buried in the grave.
> Endless sorrow and signs of mourning are ultimately of no
>   avail . . .
>
> If they wish to obliterate the suffering of the dead
> They can do no better than cultivate blessedness to save our souls
>   from darkness.

Mulian enters the realm of the General of the Five Ways, whose voice 'rumbles like thunder and whose flashing eyes are like lightning'. Here he sees men and women whose bellies are being ripped open and others whose faces are being skinned. 'Even Mulian', the storyteller relates as he unfurls the scroll showing these horrors in gory detail, 'is frightened out of his wits.' The General tells him that his mother had been sent to Avīci Hell because of the weight of her sins. Mulian goes from one hell to another, his story related in further scrolls that depicted these intermediate hells:

> Irons discs from the air constantly plunge into their bodies,
> Fierce fires burn continuously beneath their feet,
> All parts of their skin have been stripped into shreds,
> Every inch of their bones and flesh has been charred.
> Bronze-coloured crows peck incessantly at their hearts,
> While molten iron pours constantly over their heads.

The storyteller continues in a similar vein for some time, enjoying the effect on his audience. Mulian's mother is in an even worse place, the storyteller informs them, 'a place where, though your heart be made of iron or stone, you too will lose your wits and tremble with fear'. This is Avīci Hell. Here Mulian finds his mother nailed to a steel bed with forty-nine long spikes through her body. When she is released to see her son, 'she clanks and clatters like the sound of five hundred broken-down chariots' because of the metal thorns in her body. She explains how, though her body is broken a thousand times, yet, at a cry from her gaolers, it renews itself to be tortured once more.

Mulian has to leave his mother for she is not allowed out of hell even though she claims she has repented. He therefore goes to plead with Buddha who agrees to go in person to save her. Because Buddha is impartial, he rescues all those in hell at the same time. Mulian's mother still has karmic debt to repay and so she is reborn as a hungry ghost, fated never to be able to satisfy her hunger and thirst. When her son brings her rice and water, they turn to fire. Buddha then tells Mulian to organize a large, purgatorial feast on the fifteenth day of the seventh month, the end of the summer retreat and the only day on which hungry ghosts can eat their fill. After attending this feast, Mulian's mother disappears. Buddha explains that she has been reborn as a black dog – a step up from a hungry ghost. He finds her and together they pray for seven days and seven nights, after which she is again transformed into a woman and thereafter allowed into heaven, her karmic debt now repaid in full.

Miaofu shuddered in her sleep at this vision of hell, and her hand was squeezed by one of the attending nuns. She did not believe her sins to be as bad as those of Mulian's mother, but she hoped she had done enough to be reborn in heaven, or at least to be reincarnated as a human. She felt for her rosary beads and started to recite the *Guanshiyin sutra*. This had always been one of her favourite sutras and she had carried around a small, illustrated booklet of the text. Guanshiyin, or Guanyin, is the Chinese name for bodhisattva Avalokiteśvara, the manifestation of compassion.

When she was first bed-ridden Miaofu had asked a scribe to come and transcribe her will. Several monks and nuns were called as witnesses and the completed will was handed over to the abbot. Miaofu had her own substantial house and grounds in the nunnery with quarters for her servant girl. Her will was primarily concerned with the disposal of this girl and of some of her moveable goods. She bequeathed the girl to her niece. As for the goods, it was not uncommon for such property to be auctioned after their owner had died if an heir had not been specified. The monastic rules laid down certain regulations about the conduct of these auctions. A bid could be raised so long as the previous bid had not been called out three times, but after that it was unlawful to raise it again. 'Unseemly language' was also prohibited, although this did not stop auctions becoming boisterous affairs. Miaofu had witnessed several where wealthy monks from neighbouring monasteries had vied with one another for the finest silks.

Miaofu also owned silk robes, though it was against monastic law to do so since the production of silk resulted in the death of the silkworms that had spun it. Some of the monks had their assembly robes, or kāṣāya, made for them out of the most luxurious silk from Central China. The kāṣāya was little more than a large patchwork rectangle, draped over one shoulder and across the chest like a shawl. The patches were meant to be old or discarded remnants of cotton or hemp and thus to symbolize the monks' state of poverty. The deep, lustrous colours of the silk kāṣāya made a mockery of the robe's significance and the monks' vows. Miaofu left her silk robes to the local community of monks and nuns, along with several thousand feet of cotton cloth. They would be added to the goods received from other monks and nuns, rich individuals and those who had paid for religious services, and distributed at a general meeting of the community.

One such meeting, held in Dunhuang in 936, listed silk brocades, quilted materials, gauze, felt, cotton and other cloth as well as furniture and household items as the property of the local Buddhist community. Over 70,000 feet of cotton cloth had been donated to the monasteries in the previous three years, and after subtracting various expenses – which included a gift of fine silk to the queen of Khotan and a saddle to local officials, as well as smaller gifts to the organizers of the ceremony – each monk and nun received 60 feet and each novice 30 feet for their personal use. There was a surplus of over 4,000 feet, presumably retained by the monastery for future disbursements. Though Chinese copper cash and silver ingots had long been in use, and a system of paper money was just starting to be established among merchants, cloth and grain were the usual currency in tenth-century Dunhuang.

The Chinese state dealt only in multiples of 1,000 cash, strung together through a square central hole in each coin. A thousand cash, equivalent to about an ounze of silver, weighed more than 1.5lb. In loan transactions among the local people at Dunhuang, however, the capital and any accrued interest were usually paid in kind – in grain or cloth – as were state taxes.

The day of the Ghost Festival dawned. This was one of the busiest times of the year for the nunnery, especially important since the Ghost Festival was the main festival of giving, so the nuns rose early. Bowls were placed all round the nunnery for the offerings which people would make to prevent their ancestors suffering the same fate as Mulian's mother. After the morning banquet, the streets of the city filled with people who had come to watch the Buddhist procession that always took place on religious festivals. The monks and nuns set up stalls in the marketplace and on the roads leading to the monasteries and nunneries, selling sutras, divination and medicine. The streets were full of music and laughter and entertainers. The storyteller, as Miaofu had imagined, unfurled his scrolls and began his tale of Mulian's journey.

But Miaofu was not there to watch the festivities. She had died during the night.

The Widow's Tale

Ah-Long, 888–947

I offer this incense to announce the misfortunes that rain
down upon me as fast as the lightning sent by the god
Luling. I beg that my prayers will reach the ears of the Star
God Rahu, and that he will force the hundred demons that
beset me to go far away, that he will strengthen the power of
the good spirits, let my illnesses fade away day after day, year
after year. I entreat him for happiness and blessing, for the
end of my misfortunes and to pardon my sins.

Prayer of a 64-year-old Dunhuang woman,
probably 10th century

WIDOW AH-LONG carefully unwrapped the small bundle she
had bought at the pharmacist's. It was a special order and
the pharmacist's boy had come to tell her of its arrival that
morning while she was still struggling to get dressed. Rare medicines such as this were expensive and Widow Ah-long gave thanks
to Buddha for her recent victory in the courts. Now she was
assured some income from her land to pay for such purchases.
Whether it would be sufficient to discharge all her gambling debts
too remained to be seen, but at least she had something to leave
to her grandson. She finished the unwrapping and the bundle
revealed its treasure – several small, shrivelled, white worms.

It was 947 and Widow Ah-long, who was in her sixtieth year,
suffered badly from rheumatoid arthritis. During the dry, desert
summer it was bearable, but in the cold, winter nights she was
often in great pain. She had tried everything, from the usual herbal
remedies, acupuncture and massage to exorcism and prayer, but

The Star God, Rahu

every winter the pain grew worse. She could no longer use her hands and found it difficult to dress. Fortunately, she still had her servant girl to help her around the house. A friend had told her of a special medicine – a worm found only on snowy mountain peaks – that was said to be especially efficacious in the treatment of rheumatoid fevers. She had asked the pharmacist to procure some. That had been almost a year ago and he had not been able to obtain them until a few days before, when a Tibetan trading party, regular suppliers of drugs from the Tibetan plateau, had passed through town after a long absence.

Widow Ah-long was one of the most senior members of the community. She had outlived her husband, her son and numerous cousins and most of her friends were also dead. Yet her own life had been punctuated by illness. Her first memory was of lying in bed doubled up with stomach ache. She could not remember how old she had been, but she did recall her father departing for town to buy medicine. He had come back the next evening with turmeric root, which her mother ground into powder and forced her to swallow. Colic was to plague her throughout her childhood and she had soon got used to the yellow medicine. As an adult she kept a supply of turmeric in the house, and took it as a prophylactic before heavy meals.

Her parents ran a public hostel two stages north-east of the city of Dunhuang, half-way to the next town. There were no villages on this stretch of road, just inns with mud and tamarisk-stalk walls, sheltering under a few poplar trees next to a well or a spring. The Dunhuang government provided the innkeepers with supplies – grain, fodder and firewood – but it was a meagre living. The surrounding land was covered with a soggy crust of salt and nothing could be grown on it. Even the camels hated it, and their drivers were often in bad humour when they reached the inn after a day spent dealing with the recalcitrant, spitting beasts.

The next major event in Ah-long's childhood was also associated with illness, although this time she was one of the few people who was not stricken. It was the start of summer and there was an epidemic in Dunhuang. The military governor sent an urgent letter to the chief abbot in charge of the monasteries and nunneries of the town, in which he attributed the plague to the spiritual shortcomings of the monks and nuns. The abbot replied at once, promising that the institutions under his control would immediately begin a continuous service of confession and prayer, and all-night sutra recitations. Ah-long's parents heard of the plague from travellers, perhaps those same travellers who brought the infection. In a few days both her parents had fallen ill. Ah-long's uncle and aunt in Dunhuang were informed, but by the time they arrived, her parents were dead.

Ah-long's uncle and aunt lived in Dunhuang itself but they farmed land outside the city walls. Several years before, they had lived in a hamlet closer to their land, but then Aza bandits came over the mountains from Koko-nor in a raiding party and abducted their young son. Ah-long's uncle and a posse of local men, all of whom had lost children, animals or property to the raiders, rode after them. They were gone several weeks but returned empty-handed. Unable to find the raiders they had not dared to travel too far into nomad territory. After this, from time to time Ah-long's uncle would join all local posses or any group of travellers heading south, hoping that he would recognize his son among the herdsmen on the pastures of the Tsaidam basin or near Koko-nor, for although he and his wife had other children, all were girls.

The family was not rich, but they could afford to employ seasonal labourers to help work the fields. In addition to their labourers' wages – usually paid in the form of grain and a suit of

Ploughing scene from a Dunhuang cave temple, seventh century

clothes for the summer's work – they had to pay taxes to the local government. As head of the household, Ah-long's uncle was also liable to corvée duty – a period of unpaid labour for the government – but he usually paid someone to do that for him as well. The local government taxes consisted of payment both in grain and cloth, more common currencies at this time than copper cash or silver ingots. For each *mu* of land (roughly one-seventh of an acre) a householder paid 4 *sheng* of wheat (one *sheng* was approximately 3 pints), 3.5 *sheng* of millet, and 0.5 *sheng* of hemp. In addition, one bolt of cloth (about 30 feet) was levied for every 250–300 *mu* of land, and since most farmers did not own this much, the tax was shared between neighbours. The cloth tax was paid at the start of summer and the grain tax after the harvest. Each household was also responsible for maintaining the network of irrigation channels that threaded between the small fields and for supplying the local authorities with firewood. The firewood, tamarisk and poplar wood gathered from the surrounding area, was used in military beacon towers.

Ah-long was a striking girl. Her parents had spoken Chinese but they were both the result of several mixed marriages between the different peoples of the Silk Road. Ah-long did not know it, but she had Chinese, Tibetan and Turkic ancestors. Her combination of black hair and green eyes was not an uncommon sight in

Dunhuang, but nevertheless people commented on her beauty. She was married at seventeen. She and her future husband had encountered each other several times at festivals, and Ah-long's aunt had soon contacted his parents to ask whether they were interested in a match. A go-between was then employed to make the necessary arrangements. The groom's family owned a small parcel of land north of the city, near the military beacons and ruined Chinese fortifications, but most of their income came from property: they owned several houses in the city which were rented out. Labourers were employed to work their land. It was not very productive, for it was hard to till and irrigate, but they kept it because the geomancers had said that it was ideally situated for burials, and on it stood the family graves. The family consulted a diviner to establish an auspicious day for the wedding, and he in turn consulted an almanac. Ah-long had been born in the year of the rat and her husband in the year of the ox. The almanac advised that those born in the year of the rat should only marry between the fifth and the eleventh month, and those in that of the ox between the third and the sixth month. That left only two possible months in which, as the almanac showed, only three days were noted as being suitable for weddings. Having looked at the birthdays of the bride and groom the diviner selected the most propitious of the three days.

Marriage among aristocratic Chinese families was a complex affair. First the day was chosen for an exchange of cards which contained information about each family, the bride's dowry and the groom's property. If all was satisfactory to both sides, the 'ceremony of the cups' followed on another lucky day, during which promises and cups of wine were exchanged between bride and groom. Then both families exchanged presents. The bride's family's gifts traditionally included two sticks and two bowls with four red fish swimming in them, fish being symbolic of abundance. The wealthiest families sent sticks and fish made of gold. More gifts were exchanged before the day arranged for the wedding itself, and the bride's dowry was displayed on the eve of the wedding. On the wedding day itself the groom would come to the bride's house to claim her. She would be dressed entirely in red and carried in a sedan-chair or carriage back to his house in a colourful and noisy procession, complete with musicians and singers. There the bride and groom would drink more rice wine to seal their vows and everyone would sit down to a great banquet in celebration.

Poorer families only performed some of these ceremonies, although the banquet was obligatory, and in some cases the groom lived with the bride. But Ah-long's family followed the tradition, exchanging gifts, and, on the chosen day, Ah-long was carried in a sedan-chair to the groom's house, where she and he exchanged cups of wine to symbolize their vows. Everyone they knew was invited to the banquet and all of them remarked on how well Ah-long was treated by her uncle and aunt, who had provided an impressive dowry. Ah-long did not remember her wedding day with any great joy. Her period pains had started on the morning of the wedding, which her aunt declared a very bad omen. Ah-long had taken an infusion of herbs and her aunt had heated a stone and wrapped it in a silk cloth which Ah-long held against her stomach during the rather uncomfortable journey to her future husband's house.

The wedding procession did not have far to go but the groom's family wanted to display their wealth and had employed a large band for the occasion. The beating of the drums and the shrill horns reverberated off the mud walls of the houses crowded along the narrow streets. Shopkeepers and stallholders all stopped their trade and stood watching from the side of the road while the children ran along in the bright sunshine beside the men, adding to the noise and clamour.

A sexual handbook circulating in Dunhuang at the time but written in Central China described the events of the wedding night:

The groom takes out his Crimson Bird and loosens the bride's red trousers, his white stalk rises and she strokes it and delights it . . . the man's tongue seeks the woman's and their minds are joined together. . . . Then he moistens his penis with his saliva and offers it to her vagina like making an offering to an altar . . . the 'boy' then ejects his abundant semen into her. Afterwards they wipe their private parts with special cloths which are placed in a basket. From this moment on they are wedded and their journey of yin and yang will continue without interruption.

After the wedding, Ah-long lived with her husband and in-laws. A popular poem circulating locally at the time provided an ironic comment on the effect of marriage and in-laws on a headstrong young woman. 'The Shrewish Young Wife' describes a young woman who hits her husband and screams abuse, seemingly for no reason other than that it is her nature. When her parents-in-law try to reprimand her she refuses to listen, upsetting all the pots and pans in the kitchen in her rage. Her anger, the poem says, 'is like fighting water buffaloes, and her laugh like the creaking of a rusty winch'.

After more arguments with her mother-in-law the young woman takes to her bed, feigning illness, and refuses to get up. When her husband enters the room, tears come to her eyes and she tells him that his parents treat her like a servant or a slave. Her husband does nothing and she asks for a divorce. The in-laws are jubilant: 'We'll give you back your clothes and those items which originally came from your home, and we've even made a new cover for your bed, but go quickly and promise that we'll never see or meet you again.' The young woman leaves with the remark: 'I may have neither wealth nor achievements, but at least I'm leaving the home of these old devils.'

Divorce was allowed under Chinese law in cases of mutual incompatibility or where a wife disobeyed her parents-in-law. Divorce certificates in such cases began with an account of what marriage should be: 'mutual affection like that between water and fish'. But the text continued: 'The union of cream and milk will eventually separate into two streams. How can a cat and a mouse live for long in the same home? Having consulted with our fathers and their children, with our elder and younger brothers, with their wives and children, we are no longer to be called husband and wife.' The certificate did not mention the problems attendant upon moving into someone else's home as a junior member.

In the poem the young woman resettles in a village where she is 'free and at ease'. The poem notes that she ignored convention. Because she did not like 'women's work', she went to the fields with a bamboo basket on her arm to collect vegetables and managed to look after herself. 'Dear mother-in-law,' she says, 'it is in my nature to be wayward. If you had wanted me to perform the proper duties of a wife, then you needed to peel away many layers of my skin.'

The poem ends with the moral that it is essential to know all about the woman you choose as a daughter-in-law, and that it is no good relying on the information given by matchmakers. Unlike Shakespeare's Kate, the shrew in this case was saved by divorce rather than by marriage. However, the young wife's quarrel was always with her in-laws and not with her husband. In refusing to defy his parents he behaved like a filial son, but doing so lost him his wife.

Ah-long did not get divorced – it does not seem to have been that common at the time – but she did get pregnant. This was the next defining moment of her life and, as usual, it was an uncomfortable one. Her labour was protracted and extremely painful. To ease the birth she was given medicine containing the powdered seeds of the balsam flower and her mother-in-law burned charms under the bed. Everyone was surprised when both she and the baby survived. Moreover, it was a boy.

After the birth she was very weak from loss of blood. The monk-doctor prescribed an Indian drug called citragandha which was mixed with wine and contained tamarisk manna, pine resin, liquorice, rehmannia root and something called 'hot blood'. A sample of the drug had been sent to China in the eighth century by an Indian king and a Chinese *materia medica* noted that 'foreigners test the efficacy of the drug by taking a small child and cutting off its foot. They put the drug in its mouth then make it stand up. If the child is able to walk, then the drug is of good quality.' Needless to say, tall stories about the barbaric practices of foreigners were as endemic then along the Silk Road as they were to be later elsewhere.

Ah-long tried to breastfeed the baby herself, but without much success. Her mother-in-law made an aubergine poultice for her cracked nipples and offered advice, but eventually they resorted to a wet nurse. After the birth of her first child Ah-long suffered a succession of miscarriages and, when she did not miscarry, she gave birth to weak, sickly babies who died within hours or days. After each failed pregnancy she and her husband went to the local Buddhist temple and paid the monks to say prayers for the dead child. But at least they had a son to continue the family line, unlike the poor women whom they saw at the temple praying for a son in front of the image of the bodhisattva Avalokiteśvara.

Ah-long and her husband grew prosperous. A few years after their wedding, her husband's parents died and left him all their property – he was the only surviving child. Ah-long also received a share of her uncle and aunt's land: the rest was divided between her cousins and sister. All the land needed careful management and their tenants sometimes defaulted on the rent, but each year they had a surplus after their taxes and debts had been paid. They could even afford to make occasional loans themselves at interest. They were able to avoid having to borrow grain for each year's sowing and to buy a servant girl to help Ah-long, who enjoyed having someone to fetch and carry for her. They had received the young girl as payment for a debt of three pieces of raw silk and two pieces of spun silk owed them by a local petty official. She was an Aza girl, captured during one of the skirmishes between the local army and marauding families, and so was considered a prisoner-of-war slave, able to be bought and sold. It seemed as if the traditional prayer that Ah-long's bridegroom had recited on their wedding day was being fulfilled:

> Gold and silver to fill my coffers year after year,
> Wheat and rice to fill my barns at every harvest.
> Chinese slaves to look after these treasures,
> Foreign slaves to tend my livestock,
> Fleet-footed slaves to attend me when I ride,
> Strong slaves to till the fields,
> Beautiful slaves to strum the harp and fill my wine cup,
> Slender-waisted slaves to sing and dance,
> Midgets to hold the candle by my dining couch.

When Ah-long looked back on her life, memories of her marriage were crowded out by earlier and later events. But for a while life had been good. She could afford to make offerings to the monastery, to gamble with her friends and to have fine new clothes made from time to time. She was clever with her hands and embroidered sutra wrappers from old silk which she presented to Miaofu, the abbess of the local nunnery and a particular friend. The remnants were made into scent bags for other friends. She also made incense using her paternal grandmother's recipe, which called for aloeswood, sandalwood, storax, onycha, Borneo camphor and musk to be ground together, strained through gauze and mixed with honey. She found gambling more enjoyable, however, though this was not something that she admitted to the abbess. She and her female friends played several games, including mah-jong and cards, but their favourite was double-sixes. Akin to backgammon, this was played with black and white counters moved by two players according to the throw of the dice. The women sat in the dappled shade of the courtyard on wooden stools with painted legs and padded silk cushions, hunched intently over the delicately carved double-six table. They gambled for small amounts, only a few cash, but in the tea-houses and wine shops of Dunhuang men gambled for larger stakes, and everyone placed bets at the polo games and horse races held outside the city.

Two tragedies then struck which changed Ah-long's life. First, her husband died at the age of fifty. He fell ill without warning and, despite the efforts of doctors, monks and exorcists, he had died within three days. She was still in mourning when her son was arrested. He had been called to civil defence duty, his task to guard the large statue of the Buddha at the cave temples south-east of the town during reconstruction work. The civil defence team, able-bodied men of the neighbourhood, were issued with weapons – bows and arrows, shields and spears – which they were obliged to return at the end of their duty. Any delay in returning the arms warranted seven strokes of the wooden cane, but Ah-long's son did not return the weapons at all. This was a far more serious offence. Trade in weapons was forbidden without official sanction, for the authorities were worried that they might fall into the hands of bandits and foreign armies. The case had to be reported and investigated. Ah-long's son had fled, but he was soon tracked down and arrested.

Ah-long's son had married several years before but his wife had died while giving birth to their son. Ah-long, her son and grandson continued to live together, supported by the produce of their land. After her son was arrested, Ah-long found it difficult to manage affairs. She was not like the young wife in the poem: she had depended on her husband and son to deal with matters outside the home. It was they who had made the decisions as to what crops to grow, whether extra labourers were needed and when to harvest.

When it was decided that the son should be confined in prison in a neighbouring town to await trial, the court drew up a document that gave Ah-long's brother-in-law the right to work the land for the duration of the son's absence. He was to be responsible for buying grain, sowing, and harvesting. He was also to pay the tax due on the land and undertake corvée duty. Before the son was taken away, he and his uncle were brought before the judge and the contract was read out to them. The land was to be handed back to the son when he returned, and if either side broke the agreement, they were to pay a penalty of one sheep. Having made sure that both parties understood the terms, the judge, who was also the scribe, wrote their names at the end of the contract, along with that of a witness, and all four men signed the document. Only the judge was literate and could write his name. The rest made various marks: it was common to place the forefinger on the contract under their name and to make three horizontal marks at the position of the finger joints. Sometimes the contractees drew an outline around their finger or even their whole hand.

Immediately after this, Ah-long sold over a third of the land to the witness, a distant relative, to raise money to try to help her son's case. A few bribes to the right people, she thought, would do no harm. She also gave money to her friend Miaofu for prayers to be said in the local nunnery. Her brother-in-law was happy to manage the rest of the land and to give her part of its produce. This was not considered rent by either party: after all, they were family, and had an obligation to help one another.

Later that year there came news that Ah-long's son had died in custody. She had not managed to make any headway in securing her son's release and she decided not to make too many enquiries about the cause of death: this was an area of the law that was best avoided. But she arranged his funeral and memorial services, and spent long hours praying to Avalokiteśvara to save her son from rebirth as an animal, a hungry ghost, or a demon in hell. After this, she was to be found at the temple almost every day.

Like many women in Dunhuang, Ah-long belonged to a women's club which met regularly in a small building in the grounds of the nunnery. Sometimes a nun or monk would speak to them about Buddhism; at other times they would read sutras and say prayers together. Details of each meeting were sent round on a circular, giving the time and place and a list of all the members. Most were illiterate, but they could get a local monk to read the text and point out their names on the list. Each made her own mark after her name and passed the circular on to the next person. Often, however, news of the meeting was simply passed around verbally, but the club president still wrote the circular as a record.

The aims and objectives of the club were set down on paper after they had been agreed at the founding meeting. 'Our parents gave us life,' the document read,

> but friends enhance its value. They sustain us in time of danger and rescue us from calamity. In dealing with friends, a single word may serve as a bond of faith. On feast days the members of the mutual benefit society are each to contribute 1 cup of oil, 1 pound of white flour and 10 *sheng* of wine, and on the day in the first month set apart for the establishment of merit, they are to contribute 10 *sheng* of wine and one bowl of lamp-oil. If any member disregards procedure in either great or small matters or creates a disturbance at a feast and refuses to obey the orders of her superior, then all the members will repair to the gateway and fine her enough wine-syrup for an entire feast. . . . Any person wishing to leave the club shall be sentenced to three strokes with the bamboo.

The fifteen members of the club, including the four officers, had all signed with their marks to indicate that 'they swear by the hills and streams, with the sun and moon as witnesses' to its terms. The document concluded with an explanation as to its purpose: 'as a precaution against bad faith, these rules have been written down to serve as a memorandum for those who come after'.

Members made regular contributions to the club, usually of grain. The last to arrive at each meeting and those who did not turn up at all also had to pay a forfeit. Sometimes this was paid in grain wine, sometimes in the more expensive wine made from locally grown grapes. Club members were each guaranteed funeral expenses from the club's assets. This was very important to the women, for many of them were old and poor. The club also arranged memorial services so that, unlike Mulian's mother in the famous story, its members would not end up in hell. Most of them also tried to influence their fate by giving donations to the nunnery itself and by taking the five vows: not to kill, steal, lie, drink or have illicit sex. The donations of wine and the frequent mention of wine at Buddhist banquets suggest that at least one of these prohibitions was not strictly observed. Clubs made up of wealthier townswomen could afford to sponsor paintings on silk or a mural at the temple caves, thus gaining more merit for their members.

Immediately after the death of Ah-long's son, her brother-in-law was recruited to the militia to fight armed bandits who were making frequent raids on outlying villages. He was gone for several months and the land was left to lie fallow. Ah-long remembered how her cousin had been snatched by bandits over four decades earlier. His parents, who had been dead for several years, had never found him and had assumed he was dead. As if in response to her thoughts, a man rode into town while her brother-in-law was away, claiming to be the very same boy, and he went straight to the local government office and told his story. He said he had been part of the recent raiding party but had managed to escape with two horses when the party was close to Dunhuang. He had been only a small boy when he was seized and taken to Koko-nor with his Aza captors, but he always remembered that Dunhuang was his home town. While he could not recall the location of either his parents' house or their land, he knew his Chinese name. He wanted, he said, to make a claim on any land that was his: he had no other means of livelihood.

The officials believed his story and, when their preliminary enquiries showed that his family had originally owned land, part of which now appeared to be uncultivated, they awarded it to him without further investigation, giving him a certificate of rightful ownership as head of the household. This was Ah-long's land. The officials also bought his horses, paying him in grain and cloth. The young man moved on to the land and set up home. Widow Ah-long was amazed when she heard of this, but she did not want to get into trouble with the local authorities and decided to wait until her brother-in-law returned before challenging the squatter's rights. In any case, she was still quite comfortably off, not yet having spent all of the money from the earlier sale of part of the land.

Her brother-in-law returned after only a few months and was as taken aback as she at the turn of affairs. He went to question the man to see if he was indeed who he claimed to be. The man was quite rude, refusing to answer questions or to relinquish possession of the land. He showed Ah-long's brother-in-law the document issued by the officials that identified him as head of the household. Since there was no one left alive who could remember the young boy and so dispute this claim, the widow and her brother-in-law decided to let things be.

They never did find out whether the man was who he said he was. Almost as suddenly as he had come he disappeared again. They heard that he had grown used to a nomadic lifestyle and could not bear the monotony and toil of 'the bitter land', as he called it. He bought a horse, packed a saddle-bag, and rode back south-east over the Nanshan to rejoin his adopted family at Koko-nor. But their troubles were not over. During his brief stay, the man had become friendly with one of Ah-long's many relatives, a young man she hardly knew who came from a poor family and was only distantly related. He had been brought up in a monastery and had no land or other wealth of his own. When the stranger left town, the young man himself moved on to the land, claiming a right to it as the man's nephew.

For the next decade, the young man refused to surrender the land and, worse still, refused to give Ah-long any of its produce. Widow Ah-long's fortunes declined. She found herself gambling more and more, and her debts mounted. She had to sell or pawn many of her possessions and, one winter, even had to borrow a cooking pot from a local monk. She could no longer afford to give generous gifts to the monastery and was simply glad that her funeral at least was assured by her regular donations to the club. She tried to make more embroidered pot-pourri bags and other items to sell, but rheumatoid arthritis soon made her joints too painful and stiff for sewing.

By the time her grandson was near maturity, she and her brother-in-law decided they had to do something to regain the land, otherwise there would be nothing for the grandson. How would he find a decent wife without some property to his name? Despite the costs and the risk that they might lose, they took their case to court. Widow Ah-long still had a copy of the agreement made after her son's arrest between him and his uncle but this was the only piece of written evidence, the land registers being too out of date. A clerk took depositions from Ah-long, her brother-in-law and the young man which he copied out, along with the original contract, and presented to the official appointed to try the case.

The judge's decision was appended to the document containing the depositions. He noted that the squatter, although claiming distant kinship with Ah-long, gave her nothing from the land, 'not a needle nor a blade of grass'. He also noted that the widow had no other means of support in her old age. He therefore found in her favour, awarding her the land and its water.

Widow Ah-long was able to live out the rest of her life in reasonable security. Her grandson was soon old enough to work the land himself. Every year at the Confucian festival to honour their ancestors, held 105 days after the winter solstice, they went together to his father's grave taking various offerings and food for a picnic, once they had weeded and swept the grave and made their offerings. Ah-long continued to gamble, but now she could also afford to pay for prayers to relieve her arthritis and all the other misfortunes which she perceived as 'raining down upon her as quick as lightning'. In fact, her life was no better nor worse than those of the tens of thousands of farmers who tilled the 'bitter land' of the Silk Road.

The Official's Tale

Zhai Fengda, 883–966

> The duty of officials is to be the people's servants, not to
> make the people serve them. Those working on the land pay
> one tenth of their income in tax towards employing local
> officials and they therefore want the officials to work for
> justice on their behalf. Officials who take their stipends yet
> do nothing are to be found everywhere. There are even
> those who neglect their jobs and also steal from the people.
> Suppose you hire a servant in your home and he receives his
> salary yet neglects his job and steals your property, you would
> certainly be extremely angry and punish and fire him
> . . . with this kind of official the principle is the same.
>
> Liu Zongyuan, 'Essay in Praise of Official Xie',
> early 9th century

ZHAI FENGDA HAD just started school. He sat with several other
boys in a side hall in the monastery while their teacher, a
young clerk in the army, gave each a brush and a piece of paper,
already written on one side, and helped them grind ink. Then he
sat down next to Fengda and showed him how to compose the
first five characters of the *Thousand-Character Classic*, writing them
from left to right along the top of the paper. Fengda took the
brush himself and tried to copy the characters in the space below.
The first word, 'thousand', comprised only three strokes and so
was quite easy. Once satisfied that Fengda was writing the strokes
in the correct order the teacher passed to the next boy.

Fengda's father had already taught him the start of the *Thousand-
Character Classic* and so he knew how to pronounce the words he
was transcribing. The work, written in the mid-sixth century, was

still used as a primer in all Chinese schools. Each character occurred only once, and the text's tetrasyllabic structure and rhyme pattern made it easy to memorize. The children in the classroom were of various ages and ability: some were already copying more advanced primers, such as *Essential Teachings for the Instruction of Young People*, *The Family Teaching of Taigong*, or *The Poems of the Brahmācārin Wang*. Wang's advice and tone bear a striking resemblance to those of Polonius towards his son in Shakespeare's *Hamlet*. Wang advises the young on their filial duties, on how to deal with money and how to act in society at large: 'If you are told a secret, do not blurt it out. If you hear gossip, do not repeat it. If you see trouble, act as if you saw it not; always beware of taking too much upon yourself. Do not stand security for those who are not relations; do not act as a go-between where you have no business.' Following study of these primers, students moved on to the works of Confucius and other more advanced texts.

It was 890 and Fengda was just seven. His father could only read and write poorly, although he was a clerk, and his mother not at all, but they could afford to employ labourers to work their fields and servants to do the household chores, and so Fengda and his elder brother were free to attend school. His father hoped that his sons would pass the Chinese state examinations and become officials in the central government, to add honour to the family name and to ensure him and his wife a comfortable old age and the possibility of retiring back to their ancestral home in the central plains of China. But the news from the capital was not encouraging. When Fengda was born in 883, rebels still held Chang'an. They had only been ousted in the following year and, although the Tang emperor was now reinstalled, no one knew how much longer he could hold on to power.

Fengda's family lived in Dunhuang, a thousand miles from Chang'an. The town had been under the *de facto* rule of the Zhang family since 848 when General Zhang had driven out the Tibetans. Fengda's father had taken him to see a painting of the general with his victorious army on the wall of one of the caves at a Buddhist site outside Dunhuang. Fengda remembered it very clearly because it was the day of the Dragon Festival. His mother had hung a bundle of willow leaves above their door to protect against epidemics and had made him and his brother wear small wooden carvings hung from their belts. When Fengda had asked her what they were for, she had explained that they were amulets that would protect them against all the demons and malevolent animals that came out on this day: toads, scorpions, spiders, centipedes and snakes. When he had asked her why they came out on this day, she had explained that it was the fifth day of the fifth month. But when he asked why it was the fifth day of the fifth month, she lost patience and sent him off to play with his caged cricket while she prepared a picnic.

They were going on an outing to the cave temples, and then to Moon Lake and Rumbling Dune. The family rode on horses, Fengda sitting in front of his mother, and their servant followed on a donkey. The track which led to the cave temples, twelve miles south-east of Dunhuang, wound its way through the town and the surrounding farms and then crossed several miles of stony desert before reaching the half-mile stretch of cliff in which the caves had been excavated. Though they had set off early with many other townsfolk the sun was already high in the sky when they sighted the temple of the Heavenly King which marked the northern end of the cave valley. Soon they were at the foot of the cliff. While they rested in the shade of the poplars growing next to a small stream, their servant prepared lunch.

The valley was crowded with sightseers. Monks from the monastery in the valley had erected stalls outside its gate, and there Fengda and his parents had their fortunes told and bought incense. Then they set off to tour the cave temples. There were several hundred of them honeycombing the cliff, far too many to see in one day, but his parents had often visited them and had their favourites. At the Great Buddha Temple they knelt at the foot of the enormous, 100-foot-high painted statue and lit their incense. Fengda was fascinated and he ran up and down the rickety wooden stairs leading up and behind the statue. Even its toe, worn clean of paint from the many thousands of hands reaching out to touch it for luck, towered over him. Then they moved on to a newly excavated cave and then to another that contained a statue of the bodhisattva Avalokiteśvara. There his parents circumambu-

蟋蟀圖

Cricket, from a Chinese printed encyclopaedia

lated the statue, giving the monk in attendance their offering of
fruit which he purified with a prayer before placing it at the bodhisattva's feet. They lit incense sticks and stuck them into a large,
bronze urn filled with sand, and draped the statue with a cotton
scarf, also blessed by the monk. Finally they moved on. Fengda was
bored by this time and his parents led him along the wooden walkways and up some steps to the cave containing the painting of
General Zhang after his victory over the Tibetans.

The mural was painted along the lower register of the left-hand
wall of the cave. General Zhang, dressed in a red silk gown, sat
astride an impressive white charger led by two grooms. The way
ahead was being cleared by four of his attendants, two of whom
held substantial, blue umbrellas to shade him when he arrived.
The road itself was lined with mounted soldiers: first two pairs of
drummers, each holding a large barrel drum under his left arm;
then two pairs of trumpet players, heralding the general's approach
with their long, blue-painted instruments. Next to them were two
standard-bearers, their large, red flags with a blue circle motif and
black fringes blowing in the breeze. The standard-bearers and four
pairs of soldiers holding regimental pennants were all clad from
head to toe in chain-mail armour, and behind them stood officers
and more standard-bearers in blue and red gowns. A group of professional musicians and dancers were performing a ceremonial
dance in the middle of the road, and behind the general came rank
upon rank of cavalry. Fengda stared for a long time at the picture,
fascinated by its colour and movement.

It was already mid-afternoon when they set off again for Moon
Lake and Rumbling Dune, heading back towards the town for
eight miles before taking the road directly west for another mile.
Worn out by the excitement of seeing the caves, Fengda slept.
When he awoke he found they had already reached the great sand
dunes that surrounded the crescent moon-shaped lake. The lake
was perfectly blue and the air was filled with the scent of sand
jujube flowers. Crowds of sightseers milled around the water's
edge and on the terraces of a small temple on its southern shore.
There were more stalls and Fengda soon noticed a pedlar selling
children's toys which hung in a jumble of shapes and colours from
the wooden-framed pack on his back: ribbons, tops, hats, rattles,

dolls, puppets, wheeled animals, cricket cages, and many more. Fengda chose a narrow-waisted, small double drum.

The whole family then joined a crowd climbing one of the largest dunes. It was hard work clambering up the slope, and his mother kept slipping, but everyone was laughing and joking. When they reached the top, they sat in rows with their feet stuck out in front of them and then, at a shout from one of the party, set themselves downwards, taking the sand with them in a great shower. After a few seconds a deep rumbling came from the very centre of the dune and echoed around the lake. Fengda felt the dune resonating beneath him like an enormous drum. He held on to his mother as their bodies cascaded downwards in a flurry of arms and legs. In a few seconds they were at the bottom.

Fengda enjoyed school but he did not possess enough aptitude to sit the state examinations, although his father continued to dream. Fengda's fellow pupils ranged from the children of the town's elite to postulants awaiting ordination. One pupil was an orphan. Since he had no relatives to care for him, the local authorities had decreed that he be admitted to the monastery. Most of the time he was expected to run errands for the monks or carry out menial tasks – he was nicknamed 'crow-chaser' because one of his jobs was to scare the birds away from the crops – but in his spare time he was allowed to attend classes, and eventually he hoped to be ordained as a monk.

Fengda himself was interested in Buddhism and regularly read sutras, but he also found the texts on the movement of the seasons and the heavenly bodies fascinating. In the evening he would go and lie on his back in the courtyard of his house and stare at the night sky. The monastery library had several treatises on astronomy and divination, and when he had mastered the Confucian classics, he was allowed to study them. Among them was a star chart, showing the constellations identified long ago by three great Chinese astronomers, and Fengda could soon name most of what he could see in the sky. He then started to learn the lore of the stars and the planets, the twenty-eight lodgings of the moon and the implications of an eclipse, a comet or a nova. He was taught, for example, how the death of the rebel Rokhshan had been foretold two centuries before by the passage of a planet through a group of stars called 'The Mane' (the Pleiades) and associated with nomadic foreigners, wars and executions. One of the monks also showed him copies of various almanacs held in the monastery library, including several printed editions, one of which came from the Chinese capital. But the most interesting to Fengda was an almanac printed in tiny characters on a piece of paper barely three and a half feet long. It was for the year 877, six years before Fengda's birth, and contained a mass of detail. Fengda pored over it for hours at a time, determined to master its secrets.

Calendrical knowledge was, like everything else on the Silk Road, an amalgam of influences from many countries. In Dunhuang they used the Chinese calendar but by this time elements of Indian and Arabic astronomy had been assimilated by Chinese calendar makers and incorporated with their own considerable expertise. They added the theory of numbers, colours and elements, *yin-yang* and constellations. Chinese astronomers used a solar calendar for their calculations and then converted it into a mixed lunar and solar calendar. Because the lunar year is only 354 days it was necessary to make periodic adjustments – by adding intercalary months – to conform to the solar cycle of just over 365 days. The start of the year would therefore vary and it was thus not possible to assign a fixed date for sowing or harvesting crops or other farming tasks. The calendar's primary role, however, was as a significant regulator of official, rather than agricultural, life.

This was because the concept of 'Heaven's Mandate', propounded by a classical Chinese philosopher, gave people the right to rebel if the current ruler was perceived to possess insufficient virtue to retain his mandate. The emperor, man, earth, the sky, stars, sun and moon were all part of one seamless, natural order composed of *yin* and *yang*. If the emperor did not rule in accordance with the morality attendant upon his role in the natural order, then the whole universe was thrown into disharmony. This might manifest itself as an eclipse or a comet. Thus, it was in the emperor's interest to ensure that his own astronomers would predict any unusual movement in the heavenly bodies and present a harmless interpretation. Otherwise, rebels might seize upon the event and declare it to be a sign of the emperor's unfitness to rule, in order to legitimize their rebellion. At the start of every Chinese dynasty, the imperial astronomers were instructed to calculate a new calendar to show the emperor's understanding of, and harmony with, the natural order. If, however, portents appeared, then it could be taken as a sign that the astronomers themselves had made a mistake and that their calculations did not accord with the situation prevailing in the cosmic sphere.

Accordingly, the activities of astronomers and the production of calendars were carefully monitored at the highest levels. Only imperially appointed astronomers were allowed to produce calendars which were then distributed to the provinces. Nevertheless, unofficial calendars, called almanacs, continued to be produced, as a memorial of 835 noted: 'In the provinces of Sichuan and Huainan, printed almanacs are on sale in the markets. Every year, before the Imperial Observatory has submitted the new calendar for approval and had it officially promulgated, these printed almanacs flood the empire. This violates the principle that the calendar is a gift of His Imperial Majesty.'

Printing, using carved wooden blocks, had been invented in China by at least the eighth century and was used by Buddhists to propagate their teachings. Some of the earliest printed texts were short prayers accompanying pictures of popular deities such as the Heavenly Kings or the bodhisattva Avalokiteśvara, and they were sold on monastery stalls. However, almanac publishers also realized the potential of this new technology and soon privately printed almanacs were on sale, particularly in the south-east and south-west, where the central government's powers of supervision were less easily enforced. The Tang dynasty's attempt to monopolize production of the official calendar stemmed from economic as much as political motives: the calendar was essential for all officials and popular among the rest of the population, and the production of pirate copies denied the state considerable income from sales. After the memorial of 835 it was stipulated, in what is almost certainly the oldest publication ordinance in the world, that the private printing of calendars by local administrations and their private possession was forbidden. But the law was flouted, as the almanac from the Chinese capital held in the monastery library at Dunhuang clearly shows. It was produced by a family firm of printers in the Eastern Market of Chang'an, right under the noses of the emperor and his high officials whose palaces and villas abutted on the market. In Dunhuang the private production of almanacs was probably not even considered seditious.

Despite the imperial prohibition, which was reiterated at intervals, almanacs were produced everywhere and sold cheaply throughout China. Apart from giving the days and their names, according to the Chinese system of the heavenly stems and earthly branches and the five elements (water, earth, metal, wood and fire), they indicated on which days it was safe to carry out certain activities. These ranged from cutting hair to marriage, funerals and embarking on a journey. The system had a long pedigree in China, 'day books' being produced independently long before the information was incorporated into almanacs.

The central register of the almanac for 877 which Fengda studied so intently was devoted to the animals of the twelve-year cycle, a system brought from India. The almanac included tiny illustrations of the animals and nuptial advice for those born in each year. The lower register contained a charm and geomantic information. Charms were used to ward off evil: the almanac itself might be hung from a bed or doorpost for this purpose, or the charm might be copied on to a separate piece of paper which was pasted on a wall. The charm in the 877 almanac was intended to 'bring order to the household'. The geomantic, or 'fengshui', diagrams offered guidance on the placing of houses and tombs ('fengshui' literally means 'wind and water', the traditional Chinese term for landscape). Just as the emperor's actions affected the harmonious balance of *yin* and *yang*, so the wrong placement of a house or tomb might bring misfortune to the resident. Most people in Dunhuang, from the top officials to the poorest slave, held a wide range of superstitious beliefs which they believed gave them some control over their daily lives. The majority of those who bought the almanacs did not trust their own ability to interpret the mass of cryptic information – indeed, many of them could not even read – and so if they wanted something explained they would pay a specialist diviner. In the meantime, the almanac itself acted as a talisman.

★

It would be many years before Fengda mastered all the theories needed to produce his own almanac, but he had other interests. He had moved from the Buddhist school, which only taught young children, to the local government-run, prefectural school and, at the age of twenty, when he was still copying texts at this school, he started, in the style of a Chinese gentleman, to compose poetry. His handwriting was now much improved and the texts he studied were far more advanced: the one he was working on was a divination text. After he had signed and dated the copy, 2 June 902, he wrote his poems in the space left at the end of the scroll. Laden with phrases from the classics, they expressed the ambitions of a Confucian gentleman, one couplet reading: 'The youth who fails to study poems and rhapsodies is like the withered roots of a flowering tree.'

A couple of Fengda's fellow pupils had moved from the prefectural school to a specialist college attached to the government-run Rites Academy. Here they trained in ceremonial etiquette. Several manuals existed in Dunhuang on the conduct of ceremonies and social occasions associated with government office, giving guidance, for example, on how to bow properly before a polo match and the choice of appropriate music for official banquets. Others were devoted to letter-writing, providing models of letters for all situations. These letters generally started with greetings and stock phrases about the weather – 'twenty-fourth of first month, still cold', 'sixth month, unseasonably hot'. Some were for specific purposes – 'A manual on letter-writing between friends', 'Sample letters of condolence', and 'Congratulatory forms', for example – but others contained a broader selection of letters arranged in chapters: 'Communications of a complementary nature between fellow officials'; 'Letters of kind enquiry etc. to members of the general public'; 'Layman's letters to Buddhist and Daoist monks with their replies'; and 'Letters between kinsfolk'. They covered every conceivable situation, including a morning-after letter to apologize to the host for getting drunk at a dinner party the evening before:

> Yesterday, having drunk too much, I was so intoxicated as to pass all bounds; but none of the rude and coarse language I used

was uttered in a conscious state. The next morning, after hearing others speak on the subject, I realized what had happened, whereupon I was overwhelmed with confusion and ready to sink into the earth with shame. It was due to a vessel of my small capacity being filled for the nonce too full. I humbly trust that you in your wise benevolence will not condemn me for my transgression. Soon I will come to apologize in person, but meanwhile I beg to send this written communication for your kind inspection. Leaving much unsaid, I am yours respectfully . . .

The students at the Academy were destined for government appointment and were expected to be able to write the appropriate letter at the appropriate time on behalf of other officials. Documents such as the letter-writing manuals were kept in an official repository, separate from the monastery library and with its own Keeper of the Official Archives.

In 907, five years after Fengda's initial attempts at poetry, rumours reached Dunhuang of the fall of the Tang dynasty. Fengda's father's hopes that his sons might become central government officials were dashed. Though a new dynasty declared itself in the heartland of China, much of the rest of the country split into independent kingdoms and at Dunhuang the local authorities continued to use the Tang calendar and the deposed emperor's reign title for another three years until the ruling Zhang family were usurped in a bloodless coup by the Cao family, led by Cao Yijun. By this time Fengda had left school and married. Like his father he now worked as a clerk in local government, but he continued to study and copy texts and had started to produce more substantial works of his own, including a collection of miracle tales on the merits accruing from upholding, chanting or simply owning *The Diamond Sutra*.

The diamond is a Buddhist symbol of indestructability and power over illusion. *The Diamond Sutra* had first been translated from the Sanskrit in about AD 402 by the famous Kuchean monk-translator, Kumārajīva, and by the tenth century it had become very popular among Chinese Buddhists. All sutras are traditionally held to be sermons delivered by Buddha during his lifetime and transcribed after the Third Buddhist Council of the Mauryan king Aśoka. They begin with the phrase, 'Thus I have heard', and then describe the place where the sermon was first given. *The Diamond Sutra*, the text records, was originally preached in a park in northern India. The text also reports that there was a large crowd present, including over a thousand monks. The sutra itself consists of a dialogue between Buddha and his elderly disciple, Subhūti, and is a distillation in one scroll of another extremely long sutra, *The Perfection of Wisdom Sutra*, which fills dozens of scrolls. Both are central Mahāyāna texts and, like many other sutras of this school, they emphasize the merits of copying, reading, reciting and expounding sutras, so ensuring their transmission to later generations.

Fengda's composition expanded on the text of the sutra itself, in which Buddha asks Subhūti questions in order to elucidate a central doctrine of Buddhism: that the material world is an illusion and therefore there are neither individual people nor objects. This is called the principle of non-duality. One of the questions concerns the number of grains of sand in the River Ganges. 'Suppose', says Buddha, 'there were as many River Ganges as there are sand grains. Surely the total number of sand grains in all these rivers would be immense?' But this is a trick question. Sand grains are part of the material world and, as Buddha has explained before, the material world is an illusion. There are no sand grains, just as there is no River Ganges and no Subhūti.

Buddha also explains the importance of the sutra itself in the process of salvation. He again questions Subhūti: 'If a good man or woman filled more than three thousand million worlds with the seven treasures of gold, silver, lapis lazuli, crystal, agate, rubies and cornelian, or the seven royal treasuries with pearls, elephants and dark, swift horses, would he or she gain great merit?' Subhūti agrees that the merit would be considerable, but Buddha explains that if that same person were to understand only four sentences of *The Diamond Sutra* and explain them to others, the merit would be far greater.

After Fengda's own composition on this theme, he copied a text ascribed to an earlier Chinese emperor which consisted of a series of hymns extolling the merits of *The Diamond Sutra*. His dedication expressed his hope that 'for ever after, for believers as well as departed and deceased spirits, including my parents and all the people of the region, blessings will be like the grass in spring, and sins like shoots in autumn'. He signed himself as a lay Buddhist believer.

Although Fengda's education was not sufficient for him to be able to sit the state examination, it did help him get a job in the local regime. He became a military aide. His tasks were administrative rather than military, but since General Zhang's defeat of the Tibetans the Dunhuang area had been called 'Returning to Allegiance Army District' by the Chinese emperor and treated as a military garrison, with military titles for many of its staff. This was an echo of China's former glory on the Silk Road, when it controlled the whole of the desert area as far as the Pamirs. Those days were long gone.

After many years of study Fengda accrued sufficient knowledge to try his hand at calculating a calendar. It was 924 and he prepared the manuscript himself, complete with drawings of the Plough constellation. In subsequent years he employed scribes to copy his calendars, but they had to reuse old paper. Fine paper made in central China was rare and expensive, and even local paper was sometimes hard to find. As a result, paper was rarely thrown away, particularly not if it was inscribed with scriptural texts, for these made the piece of paper a sacred object worthy of reverence in itself. When a monk discovered that inscribed paper was being used in the privies of the Chinese imperial palace, he was mortified and wrote a poem to vent his feelings:

> Confucian scholars study the Five Classics, Buddhist scholars
>   the Three Baskets,
> Confucians are considered to observe the proper ritual and
>   to be filial and loyal, and so they are chosen as officials.
> Yet in their examinations they use the same characters as
>   those used to write the Buddhist sutras.

> Some of them do not think of this and they disparage the
>   sacred texts of Buddhism, using them as paper for the
>   privy.
> Their sins are as numerous as the grains of sand in the River
>   Ganges, and many lives of repentance will not be sufficient
>   to erase them.
> Their bodies will sink for five hundred ages; they will forever
>   be condemned to the life of insects in the night-soil pit.

We do not know whether Fengda used paper for such purposes, but in 928 while looking for a suitable sheet for one of his compositions, he came across his youthful poem and appended a short note: 'This was written in my youth, when I could hardly manage the way. . . . I was but twenty years when I composed it. This year, happening upon the poem again, I am overcome with shame.'

Fengda's calendar-making did not pass unnoticed. He was promoted, first becoming Chancellor of the Directorate of Education in Dunhuang and then an Erudite of his old school. In China the post of Erudite was reserved mainly for professors in the prestigious state academies, or for those attached to court bureaux with specialist medical or astronomical knowledge: the post was ranked among the top nine grades of government service. (Though China had tens of thousands of clerks and bureaucrats to run its huge empire, only the elite reached this exalted level.) With his new position, Fengda received the honorary Chinese title 'Grand Master of Imperial Entertainments with Silver Seal and Blue Ribbon', but Dunhuang was no longer really Chinese. Though such titles continued to be bestowed on the city's officials, these were vestiges of a previous age, and Fengda's title would have meant little in Central China.

Fengda's wife died in 958. He was now seventy-five but in good health and still working. He had a pupil to whom he was teaching his calendrical skills and he had recently been promoted to the position of Vice-Director of the Ministry of Public Affairs, responsible for local building projects, the maintenance of roads and irrigation channels, and the standardization of weights and measures. Some years before he had completed a work on the geography and legends of the Dunhuang area, and he used this, along with geographical treatises written by others, as guides in his new post.

Although he had not chosen a celibate life, Fengda retained his Buddhist faith, especially after the death of his brothers and grandson. He and his wife had given frequent donations to the Buddhist monastery. In one year, after a particularly good harvest, they offered five cartloads of grain for the poor of the town. Though the monasteries performed some charitable functions – in some places monastic pharmacies handed out free medicine to the poor – such activities were never co-ordinated or widespread. The poor relied on local government aid and private charity. When neither was forthcoming, and all their own assets had been sold or pawned, many were forced into a life of crime, becoming members of bandit gangs who preyed on the countryside.

Fengda was never in danger of being reduced to such a state. He had income from land, a salary and all the extra perks of an official, as well as the proceeds from his calendar-making. As he grew wealthier, he was able to make more donations, even commissioning a painting in a newly excavated cave. Since the military governor and all the local dignitaries also made contributions to the cave, it is likely that Fengda's donation brought him to the attention of influential men and gave him status in the community. The main statue group was paid for by a local guild of merchants, similarly concerned to gain both worldly and other-worldly merit.

On the death of his wife Fengda commissioned copies of ten sutras, intended for her benefit rather than his own. According to Fengda's belief in purgatory, an amalgam of Indian, Buddhist and Chinese ideas, Fengda's wife might spend almost three years in the underworld before being reborn in another bodily form. What form depended on her behaviour during her past lives, her karma. But before their fate was decided, the dead had to appear successively before ten judges – the ten kings of the underworld. The first seven audiences took place on every seventh day after death. Fengda's wife died on 23 March 958. On 29 March Fengda dedicated the first sutra to his wife, to coincide with her appearance before King Guang. He also commissioned a painting of Buddha and organized a memorial feast. Over the next seven weeks, he dedicated another six sutras, each on the appropriate day, and held six more memorial feasts. His wife's fifth audience was with King Yama, and for this event he dedicated *The Sutra on the Prophecy Received by King Yama*, also known as *The Sutra on the Ten Kings*. This described the ten audiences and the fate of those who had sinned.

After the seven weekly audiences, Fengda's deceased wife had to wait until the hundredth day following her death for the next audience. Fengda's devotions did not flag and for this day he commissioned the sutra concerning Mulian's journey to the underworld to save his mother. This story ends with Buddha instructing the bereaved to make donations to Buddhist monks and nuns on the fifteenth day of the seventh lunar month, and promising that the benefits from these acts of piety will accrue to their ancestors and the recently dead. This was the legitimization for the Ghost Festival.

Thereafter there were only two more audiences to endure, the penultimate one, which took place a year after death and, in the third year after death, the final audience before 'The King Who Turns the Wheel of Rebirth in the Five Paths'. The tenth sutra, copied on Fengda's order to coincide with his wife's last appearance, was a discussion on karmic retribution. At the end Fengda listed the whole series of memorial feasts and sutra-copyings on behalf of his wife, in case the king had forgotten them, ending with the note:

> The merit from copying the sutras listed above is dedicated as a posthumous blessing to my departed wife. I respectfully invite gods, dragons and other members of the eight classes of beings, the bodhisattva Avalokiteśvara, the bodhisattva Kṣitigarbha, the four great Heavenly Kings, and the eight Guardian Spirits to verify it. May she receive all the blessings of the field, be reborn in a happy place, and encounter good people. Offered with a concentrated mind.

Whether or not Fengda's efforts helped his wife, his own mundane fortunes continued to rise. He was awarded yet more titles, including the 'Honour of the Crimson Fish Pouch', and also named as an 'Erudite of the Classics in Dunhuang Prefecture', and he continued to make calendars and to train his pupil. Fengda lived to hear of the reunification of the Chinese empire by the Song dynasty in 960, but never made the journey to the land of his ancestors. His honours and offficial posts, although employing the nomenclature of the Chinese civil service, marked him as a citizen of the Silk Road rather than of China. He died a few years later, in about 966.

The Artist's Tale

Dong Baode, 965

While common artists concentrate on the outline, Master
Wu's strokes are split and scattered. While others try carefully
to emulate the exact shape of the subject, Master Wu was
above such vulgar techniques. In painting curves, absolutely
straight lines, upright pillars or connecting roof beams,
Master Wu did not make any use of a ruler or foot measure.
He painted curly beards and long tufts of hair waving and
fluttering from the temples of his subjects with such an
abundance of strength that the hairs seem to be detaching
themselves from the flesh. He must have been possessor of a
great secret which no one understands now. He could start a
picture eight foot high from either the arms or the legs and
make a strange and marvellous subject which was so alive
that it seemed to have blood circulating under the skin.
On the artist Wu Daozi, *Lidai minghua ji* (Record of Famous
Painters through the Ages), AD 847

D ONG BAODE WAS the Manager of the local Painting Guild and
a Master Painter, a member of the government Painting
Academy in the town of Dunhuang. It was 965 and Dunhuang,
although offering nominal allegiance to the new Song dynasty in
China, had been ruled by the local Cao family since 920. Cao
Yuanzhong, who called himself king, was the current ruler and
Baode's patron.

In addition to the Painting Academy, Cao had established a
government printing bureau. There Lan Yanmei was employed as
an official woodblock printer. Like Baode, much of his work was
commissioned by the king, and the two men often met in a local

tea–house to discuss what they were doing over a game of double-sixes. Yanmei's work involved carving both text and illustrations, but he was neither a scribe nor a painter. When the king commissioned a printed prayer sheet with a picture of bodhisattva Avalokiteśvara at the top and a prayer beneath, a scribe wrote the text and an artist drew the picture on separate, thin sheets. Yanmei then pasted the paper ink-side down on a block of wood which had been cut and smoothed for the purpose. He often used local pearwood or jujube, both smooth and evenly textured, or, if he could get hold of it, wood from the Catalpa tree, although this had to be imported and was expensive. The ink was clearly visible through the paper and Yanmei deftly chiselled out the wood in the spaces between, leaving the characters standing proud. He then carved a separate block for the picture. Next, the two woodblocks were inked and coarse, locally made paper was laid on top and rubbed with a dry brush. The printed sheets were then distributed to local monasteries. The woodblock of the illustration was also later reused separately to make multiple images of the bodhisattva. This was not the first of Cao Yuanzhong's commissions. In 947, a year after he came to the throne, he had requested that prayers be printed to mark the Ghost Festival:

> The disciple Cao Yuanzhong, Military Governor of the Returning to Allegiance Army District, Inspector for Guazhou and Shazhou, Commissioner for the distribution of military land allotments in the sphere of his jurisdiction and for the suppression of the Tibetan tribes, specially promoted Grand Preceptor, and Inaugural Marquis of Qiaojun, ordered this block to be carved for printing so that the City of God may enjoy peace and prosperity, that the whole prefecture may be tranquil, that the roads east and westwards may remain open, that evil-doers north and south may be reformed, that diseases may disappear, that the sound of the war gong may no longer be heard, that pleasure may attend both eye and ear, and that all may be steeped in happiness and good fortune.

Copies of this and the printed prayer were among Aurel Stein's purchases of documents and paintings when he visited Dunhuang in 1907.

King Cao and his wife Lady Zhai were assiduous patrons of Buddhism throughout their reign. In the years after the commissioning of the prayer, they donated numerous items to local monasteries, all of which were carefully recorded. For New Year 984, another traditional time of celebration and giving, Lady Zhai presented a sutra wrapper 'embroidered in a great variety of colours'. Sutra scrolls were stored in bundles of ten on the library shelves inside rectangular wrappers faced with cloth and often lined with old paper. A catalogue tag was inscribed with details of the contents of the bundle, for example, 'rolls 1–10 of *The Perfection of Wisdom Sutra*'. The tag was attached to the edge of the wrapper so that it was visible once the bundle was placed on a shelf.

Among the items donated by her husband during this period was a roll of fine paper that had been made in workshops in China with paper pulp from hemp (*Cannabis sativa*) and the bark of the paper mulberry tree (*Broussonetia papyrifera*). The paper was produced in a mould, a rectangular wooden frame with narrow bars across which was laid a screen made of fine bamboo strips, held in place by hemp or horsehair threads. Paper pulp was poured in the mould and evenly distributed, and the resulting sheet was turned out to dry. By this time, in a further refinement, the paper makers were also placing a fine silk sheet on the screen to prevent the impression of lines from the bamboo screen on the finished paper. Once dry, the paper sheets were brushed with size and dyed with *huangbo*, a yellow pigment extracted from the bark of the Amur cork tree (*Phellodendron amurense*). The pigment had insecticidal and water-repellent properties. Such fine paper was used to make library copies of sutras but it had been rare in Dunhuang even before the Tibetans had occupied the city in 787, and printers and scribes generally had to make do with much rougher, locally made paper. They also rummaged through old stores of documents, mainly contracts and other administrative works dating from the Tibetan period, some of which were only written on one side and could be reused. Most were undyed. Scraps were given to the school teacher for his pupils' writing exercises.

King Cao also commissioned paintings, both portable works on silk and murals on the walls of local cave temples. Many followed the king's example, and professional painters such as Dong Baode were kept busy. Dong Baode had reason to be pleased with life. He had reached the top of his profession several years before and he now made a comfortable living. He had an official title which, although it was not especially exalted, still gave him additional status in the local community. He also held the honorary titles of 'Acting Adviser to the Heir Apparent' and 'Grand Master of Imperial Entertainments with Silver Seal and Blue Ribbon'. There must have been drawbacks to his job – dealing with officious bureaucrats and lazy workmen – but his was skilled and relatively well-paid work, and there was also plenty of it. There were more than fifteen monasteries and nunneries situated in and around Dunhuang and, most important of all, there were the cave temples some twelve miles south-east of the town, known as the Mogao caves.

There an east-facing cliff rises irregularly above a small stream to a height of over a hundred feet and extends in each direction for about a mile. Poplars and elms grow next to the stream, which carries little water except during the summer floods. Since the fourth century, monks and lay Buddhists travelling the Silk Road had excavated caves in several tiers along the cliff face first as meditation cells and later as places of worship, paying for elaborate murals and painted stucco statues to adorn them. Much of Baode's work consisted in renovating paintings in existing caves and in decorating newly commissioned caves.

Three years earlier, in 962, Baode had supervised the decoration of one such newly excavated cave sponsored by King Cao. The excavation itself had been carried out by unskilled labourers. A space was chosen at the foot of the cliff to erect scaffolding which was then built to the height of the proposed cave's roof. By the mid-tenth century most of the cliff had been used and hundreds of caves, linked by wooden walkways and steps, honeycombed its yellow rock. Often old caves were reworked, sometimes being extended or simply overpainted, and several additional cave sites had come into use around the town.

The conglomerate from which the cliff was formed was

extremely friable and not difficult to excavate: only picks and shovels were needed. The workmen started at roof-level and worked into the cliff and downwards, the debris being taken away in baskets. The work was hot, dirty and tiring and the workmen were hampered by the wind which swept across the cliff face, bringing down sand from the slope above the rock. As part payment for their services they were fed in the monastery on the valley floor. Monastery officials visited every few days to survey progress and decide on the eventual size of the cave. The king was their most important patron and they wanted to ensure that the work was well executed, and within budget.

Once the preliminary excavation work had been done, the roof and walls were chiselled out further by stonemasons, and the floor was tamped to make it flat and smooth. The cave consisted of a small antechamber, joined to the main chamber by a short passage. The uppermost walls of the main chamber sloped towards a coffered roof and in the centre of the chamber a wall of stone with a U-shaped platform in front was left standing.

Once the excavation was complete, a team of plasterers took over, covering the rock walls with a thick straw and clay stucco, overlaid with a fine slip. In the desert heat this did not take long to dry. The paintings were to be murals rather than frescos, painted on a dry surface. The labourers and stonemasons were paid off with grain and a meal and the plasterer additionally received three litres of hemp oil.

Various paintings had been commissioned by wealthy individuals to adorn the walls and ceiling: there were to be several on the main register of each wall, including various paradise scenes, events from the *Guanshiyin sutra*, and the story of the monk Śāriputra subjugating demons. This last was very popular at the time: there were similar depictions in other caves and Baode had only to look through his files to find guide sketches for the composition. Before starting work he spent a morning in the cave, measuring its dimensions and, in his head, laying out the various scenes. He then ordered his young apprentices to mark up the wall. To do so they dipped string in red powder, held it taut near the wall and then flicked it so that the powder transferred itself from the string to the wall, thus defining the limits of each horizontal register and of each main composition. The most important events of the story of Śāriputra occupied nine panels on the lower register of the south wall, while other scenes from the story were shown on the west wall.

The story tells of the chief minister of a kingdom in southern India whose 'moral purchase is as important as salt and pepper are for cooking', but who is not yet a Buddhist. He has several sons, the youngest of whom has yet to marry. In order to find his son a wife he dispatches a trusted servant with gold, bracelets of fine jade, bolts of silk brocade and gauze, and a hundred elephants: 'Even when the stars come out at night you must not rest . . . should you gratify my son's wishes a handsome reward awaits you.' A suitable girl, the daughter of the premier of another kingdom, is duly found and the chief minister goes to stay with the girl's family to discuss the marriage. Here he learns of Buddhism and, filled with a desire to know more, sets out to find Buddha guided by a light sent by Buddha himself: thereupon 'he suddenly awakens to a state of enlightenment'. Buddha designates a fellow countryman, the young monk Śāriputra, to be his guide and the two return to their kingdom to find a place where they can invite Buddha to preach. After some searching they locate a suitable park which they purchase, at great cost, from the crown prince. But the Six Masters of the heretical doctrines of the kingdom are not happy. In the words of the storyteller:

> Filled with anger,
> They puffed up their cheeks, arched their eyebrows,
> Gnashed their teeth and bared their gums.
> They were extraordinarily irate.

They inform the king, and the chief minister is detained for interrogation. The king, hearing his chief minister's eulogy of Buddha, decides that the question can only be decided by a competition between the two religions. The chief minister is delighted: 'The youngest of Buddha's disciples', he asserts, 'will be able to withstand the heretics', and he volunteers Śāriputra as the Buddhist protagonist.

A great arena is constructed south of the city for the contest.

The king announces that if the Buddhists win then he and all his countrymen will be converted. If they lose then Śāriputra and the chief minister will be executed. The chief minister is, not unnaturally anxious, but Śāriputra reassures him: 'This contest between the heretics and myself is like taking a fish and giving it to an otter.' Nevertheless, Śāriputra disappears just before the contest. The chief minister is distraught and rushes out to find him: this is not difficult, for Śāriputra is the only shaven-headed man in the kingdom and is found in meditation, calling on Buddha to invest him with the necessary powers for the contest. They proceed to the arena, the Buddhists sitting to the east, the heretics to the west, the king to the north, and the commoners to the south.

In the contest each side in turn conjures up extraordinary visions. The heretical monk starts with a precious mountain whose peak reaches to the Milky Way and which is covered with sightseeing immortals. Not surprisingly, the spectators gasp in amazement. Śāriputra responds by calling up a Diamond God, his feet a thousand miles square and his eyebrows 'as bushy as the twin summits of a forested mountain'. The spectators decide in favour of the Diamond God. The next two visions are of a water buffalo and a lion respectively, again both enormous. The lion seizes the water buffalo and snaps its spine, at which the buffalo breaks into pieces.

The heretical monk then creates a vast lake, but Śāriputra conjures up an elephant which sucks up all the lake water in its trunk. By this time the heretical monk 'is flushed and flaxen, his lips and mouth parched, and his innards feel as if a knife is being twisted in them'. But he is determined to beat Śāriputra and, using all his magical powers, he conjures up a poisonous dragon which blocks out the sun and makes the earth tremble. The spectators are terrified but Śāriputra remains calm, for his part conjuring up a bird which repeatedly attacks the dragon from the air, eating it bit by bit until nothing remains.

Despite these defeats, the contest continues with the heretical monk calling up two monsters. Before Śāriputra can decide how to counter them, one of the Heavenly Kings, Buddha's attendants, arrives of his own accord to confront the monsters. They throw themselves to the ground in awe and beg for their lives. Undeterred, the heretical monk calls up a giant tree. Śāriputra

*The story of Śāriputra: The Buddhist lion devouring the heretics'
water buffalo. From a ninth-century illustrated manuscript from
Dunhuang*

counters with a God of Wind who opens his bag and lets the wind
blow until the tree is destroyed. At this, the king finally declares
that the Buddhists have won. The heretics are tonsured and
obliged to embrace Buddhism.

The story of Śāriputra was a mainstay of the travelling storyteller
who set up his pitch in the marketplace and at temple fairs. As he
told the story he would remove the appropriate scrolls from his
rucksack and unfurl them one by one, pointing at the scroll as he
spoke and embellishing various details. All except the very young
knew what was going to happen next, but they none the less
enjoyed the retelling.

The depiction of the story on the cave wall was, of necessity,
different in format. The narrative was enclosed in frames all visible
simultaneously and not revealed in stages as in the scrolls of the
storyteller, but the paintings offered great scope for movement,
drama and imagination. Sketches stored in the Painting Academy
provided the overall design, with rough blocks of each scene and
various marks to show their order and placement. There were also
rough sketches of the two main protagonists. However, the detail
was left to the imagination of the artist. Dong Baode had worked
on this story since he was a young apprentice and knew it well, but

younger, less experienced artists would do much of the work, and the sketches were vital for them.

Once the measuring was complete, Baode and other artists sketched the outlines of the first main design with animal-hair brushes and carbon-black ink. They drew freehand, some using the sketches as guides. The next stage was to fill in the detail and colour. Baode had already checked the atelier's stock of paints, powder, brushes and other materials and had ordered in new supplies, leaving the actual preparation of the paint to more junior artists. The paints were made from mineral pigments, most of them mined in China. Azurite and malachite, the basic carbonates of copper, were traditionally used for blue and green, although in caves further west, near Kucha, lapis lazuli was also used. The pigments came in several grades, but a basic distinction was made between the dark, coarse grinds and the lighter, fine grinds. Cinnabar and minium were used for red; litharge, orpiment and ochre for yellow; and ceruse for white. Vegetable dyes were not common, except for indigo and gamboge, a yellow tree-sap imported from Cambodia.

Before noon the group of artists would stop work and descend to the dining-hall of the monastery on the valley floor below the cliff. Here they were given a meal in part-payment for their services. They worked hard and it was not long before the colouring of the main figures was complete: Śāriputra sitting on a lotus throne under a large canopy, with the heretical monk facing him across the arena. Baode then took a fine brush and ink to overpaint the figures. The rest of the scenes were completed in the same way, although by more junior artists. The donors were portrayed at the bottom of the composition and the painters left cartouches for explanatory text to be written by a local scribe.

The other major compositions were similarly painted on the remaining walls and the Heavenly Kings of the four directions were depicted on the corner segments between each sloping walls. Then Baode had to consider the lower registers and the coffered ceiling. It was common to use pounces for the latter in order to ensure that the design was repeated uniformly. The outline of the design was drawn in an ink wash on squares of thick, coarse local paper and then pricked through with a needle. Next, the artist would fill a cloth bag with red cinnabar powder, tie it up and attach it to the end of a long stick; scaffolding had been erected inside the cave so that the ceiling was accessible. With one hand holding the paper pounce in place on the ceiling, the artist would bang the powder bag against the paper so that, on impact, powder leaked through the rough cloth and the holes in the paper on to the ceiling behind, leaving a faint red outline. This process was continued until the whole ceiling was covered in red lines. For this particular ceiling Baode had ordered an apprentice to prepare new pounces of small Buddha figures, each sitting on a lotus throne, and decorative lotus flower motifs. The pattern was composed in tiers: on the outside several rows of the seated Buddha figure, then flying musicians and the lotus, and finally, in the very centre of the ceiling, a pair of intertwined dragons. Each artist worked with a different coloured paint, tracing around the designs and then filling them in with a few strokes until the whole was complete. The lower registers of the walls were also filled with repeating designs but there was no need to use pounces for these as they were easily accessible.

The monk administrator in charge of the commission visited the site regularly to see how the work was progressing, and other monks and nuns would also come to have a look. One day newly ordained monks and nuns, distinguished by their pale, freshly shaven heads, paid a visit. Baode showed them the painting of the heretics being tonsured and they giggled: most were still only children.

While the artists were working on the inside of the cave, carpenters, sculptors and stonemasons were brought in. The carpenters erected a wooden awning resembling the tiled roof of a temple over the entrance to the cave. Planks on either side of the entrance emulated columns. The stonemasons worked on the central U-shaped platform inside the cave, chiselling lotus designs on its two steps. The sculptors measured the platform and went away to their studio to prepare the central statue grouping. It was usual to have a grouping of three, five or seven figures with Buddha in the centre flanked by his two disciples, the youth Ānanda and the old man Kāśyapa. Additional figures were of bodhisattvas and the Heavenly Kings. The local stone was too friable to be used for sculpture and so statues were modelled instead from clay stucco on an armature of wood or tamarisk. Once prepared,

*Pounce, ink on paper with pricked outlines from a design on the
other side: Buddha on a lotus throne, Dunhuang, mid-tenth century*

they were put in position and painted. This cave, because of its size
and importance, contained three statue groupings, each with a
different manifestation of Buddha in the centre. The main grouping, with its back to the curtain wall, faced the cave entrance.
Bodhisattvas were painted on the curtain wall, to either side of the
Buddha figure. The placing of the statue grouping enabled worshippers to walk right round the image, and the rear of the curtain
wall was also painted with elaborate designs.

The Mogao caves did, however, contain a stele made from stone
commemorating Hong Bian, the most important Buddhist in the
area west of the Yellow river in the previous century. He had been
especially active in Dunhuang in the late ninth century after the
Tibetans were ousted, and was awarded the 'Honour of Wearing
Purple' by the Chinese government. After Hong Bian's death in
862, a memorial chapel was excavated from the side of another
cave and a statue of him was commissioned by General Zhang, a
great patron of Buddhism. The painted stucco statue, showing the

monk sitting cross-legged in a patched robe, was placed on a low, painted platform. The painting on the wall behind showed his two attendants, and his leather satchel and water bottle hanging from trees. In Baode's time the statue was still *in situ*, but several decades later it was removed so that the small cave could be put to another use. Bundles of manuscripts on paper, printed documents and silk paintings from the Dunhuang monasteries' libraries were carefully placed in the chamber and its entrance sealed and painted over. It was not reopened until 1900, when the finds included prayers and paintings commissioned by King Cao.

In contrast to the statues, the cave walls and silk paintings contained many portraits of local individuals who had acted as donors, among them members of wealthy local families, other local dignitaries, and monks and nuns. But the primary donors at this time were Dunhuang's rulers. King Cao had been depicted as a young man in a cave commissioned by one of his numerous brothers-in-law: this particular one had married his sixteenth sister. In the same cave one wall of the corridor leading to the main chamber showed King Cao's father at the head of all his sons, each holding offerings to Buddha.

Cao Yuanzhong had become ruler shortly after this portrait was finished, following the death of his two elder brothers who had in turn each ruled for only a few years. Their father had been ruler before this, and Cao Yuanzhong expected his son to succeed him. The Dunhuang court sent regular embassies to the various dynasties that had ruled parts of China since the end of the Tang in 907 and accepted the honours awarded them by successive emperors, but to all intents and purposes they were autonomous. This remained the case even after the Song dynasty reunited China in 960. King Cao had more regular contact with neighbouring kingdoms: Khotan to the west, Kocho to the north-west, and Ganzhou to the east. Relations with Khotan were excellent. Embassies passed back and forth, and Khotan's royal family sometimes visited Dunhuang. They were fervent Buddhists and had even patronized the Mogao caves, their portraits being painted by an academician on a cave wall in commemoration of their donation. There, the king, his queen and numerous princesses all appear with elaborate coiffures, much jewellery and dressed in richly decorated silk robes.

Kocho and Ganzhou were both ruled by Uighurs, the descendants of those refugee families forced to move south after their defeat by the Kirghiz. One group had moved first to Beshbaliq, north of the Tianshan, but then had migrated across the mountains to the Turfan basin and settled in Kocho, though they continued to use Beshbaliq as their summer capital because it lay within the rich pastures of Dzungaria and was cooler then the low-lying Turfan basin. Many of the Uighurs married local people and embraced Buddhism. Kocho also had a Manichean community, mainly comprising Sogdians who had long served the merchants from their country who passed along the Silk Road in great numbers in previous centuries. But in recent decades their numbers had been swollen by refugees from Sogdiana, families who were unwilling to convert to Islam. Kocho did not enjoy good relations with its increasingly intolerant Islamic western neighbour. Both Manicheans and Buddhists patronized local cave temples near Kocho and commissioned new works in a Uighur style, distinct from the Chinese–Central Asian style of earlier caves. There was also a Nestorian Christian community, and they, too, had caves painted with scenes from their religion, one showing worshippers arriving at church on Palm Sunday. Buddhist, Manichean and Nestorian texts were also translated into Uighur from various languages: a Uighur version of *Aesop's Fables* was written during this period.

Relations with Dunhuang's Uighur neighbours were difficult, despite outward signs of friendship. King Cao maintained an uneasy peace with them during his reign, but only a few years after his death in 975, Uighurs attacked Dunhuang and forced the submission of his son, the Uighur kaghan declaring himself the legitimate ruler of Dunhuang and sending an embassy to China. He continued the long tradition of Chinese–Uighur diplomatic relations by supplying horses for the Chinese cavalry. The Chinese historians made a point of noting that they were 'good horses', probably a veiled reference to the nags that the Chinese had been forced to buy two centuries previously when Uighur fortunes were at their height.

Even before the Uighur take-over of Dunhuang, the kingdom's large Uighur population retained their own clan organizations and their influence was felt at all levels of society from the court down. Cao Yuanzhong's father had both Chinese and Uighur wives, and after the death of his principal Chinese wife in 935, his Uighur wife became the dowager queen. This increasing Uighur influence was also evident in the art of the period. Dong Baode painted in what was considered a regional Chinese style, based on the metropolitan style that had been perfected in the Tang dynasty which had itself absorbed Indian and Persian influences. From the height of the Tang in the late seventh and early eighth centuries, the style filtered back along the Silk Road, where it was absorbed into local styles and itself absorbed new styles. In the eighth century six Chinese artists travelled to Turkic lands to paint a portrait of the dead kaghan. His brother was so pleased with the likeness that he sent a gift of fifty horses in return. Chinese artists were also requested by the Tibetan court, and here a distinct style also developed, influenced initially by Indian, Nepalese and Chinese artists and then, from the late tenth century, by Khotanese artists.

The Dunhuang Painting Academy was the beneficiary of these cross-cultural influences and of the region's unsettled history over the past century. Tibetan artists had been resident since the Tibetan occupation, and Uighurs since the end of the Uighur kingdom, and in the tenth century these new influences started to be seen in the Mogao cave paintings, some donors even requesting certain artists and styles. The artists were professional and able to distinguish between genres, but motifs and some small stylistic features crept across the divides. Earlier styles were reworked as caves were renovated. One painting, which still exists, shows the main Buddha figure in traditional Chinese Silk Road style, with secondary figures in Tibetan style.

The Great Buddha Temple was the largest cave among the hundreds in the complex. Its huge statue of Buddha had been erected early in the eighth century, when Dunhuang was under the control of a Chinese dynasty at the height of its powers, and before the rebellion of Rokhshan. The Buddha figure was in typical high-Tang Chinese style, moulded from clay on a rock core which was left when the rest of the cave had been excavated. The workmen of the time also excavated a tunnel around the back of the figure and carpenters built a wooden staircase leading up to the head of the Buddha and a four-storey pagoda jutting out from the cliff face to protect the statue from the elements.

By 966 the cave was in need of repair. It was the end of the fifth month and King Cao and Lady Zhai were visiting the caves to perform pious acts following a month of fasting. Two of the wooden platforms around the colossal Buddha were rotten and when the king and his wife were approached, they readily agreed to fund the restoration. The work started on the nineteenth day and was completed in less than ten days. New timber was obtained from stores in the town – the poplar wood in the valley itself was too dry – and workmen were also hired in Dunhuang, the monastery at the cave temples providing them with food and wine. During this initial work, additional problems were discovered. The cave temple administration approached Cao again and he agreed to provide more funds for a second stage of restoration on which fifty-six carpenters and ten plasterers were employed. The end of the work was celebrated with a great banquet.

King Cao and Lady Zhai were not Dong Baode's only patrons. As the phrase had it, 'his brush was moistened' by most wealthy members of the community at one time or another, as well as by visiting royalty and ambassadors. He was often asked to prepare silk paintings and banners for display at Buddhist services or for use in the numerous festivals which punctuated the year. One of the most profitable of these for Dong Baode was the procession of the Buddha's image.

Dunhuang had adopted his ceremony from Khotan where it had been immensely popular since the fifth century. It was held on various days throughout the year, such as Buddha's birthday and the Moon Festival. A large statue of Buddha was placed in a cart and decorated with gold and silver, garlands and banners. The cart was followed by others containing statues of bodhisattvas and the Heavenly Kings. Before the procession started on its journey out of the city to the cave temples the streets were swept and sprinkled with water, the gates of the city were closed off with vast curtains and the statues were washed with fragrant water by the monks.

The procession made its way along the dusty track towards the cave temple. The carts were followed by all the monks and nuns, led by the king, who was wearing a new cloak and burning the finest incense in a long-handled gilt incense-holder inlaid with gems. In Khotan there had been fourteen days of processions attended by all the monks in the region, and each day the statue of a famous local monk was part of the procession. There, the carts carrying the Buddha statue were constructed into five-storeyed pagodas, and there were twenty or more carts. In Dunhuang the celebrations were shorter and less elaborate but it was still a major event, and everyone who could afford it paid for offerings and decorations. Many of the numerous banners held aloft by the monks and hung from the carts were Baode's work. The banners usually depicted a bodhisattva or a Heavenly King and were made from one strip of silk, which came in standard widths of about 2 feet. Once the painting itself was complete, a triangular head-piece of bordered silk was sewn on to the top of the painting with a loop from which to hang it. The base was stiffened with a piece of bamboo or wood. Two long, thin strips of dyed silk were then sewn down each side of the painting, and three or four long strips added at the bottom. Another stiffener was fixed between these and the bottom of the painting itself. Banners on hemp were commissioned by those who could not afford silk, but Baode did not take these commissions.

Up to three widths of silk were used for the larger paintings enabling Baode to compose elaborate scenes of Buddhist paradises, with the central Buddha figure on a lotus throne, surrounded by his attendants and with scenes from Buddha's former lives on the outer register. Baode would make a careful full-size sketch of the whole composition before starting to paint. A space was left at the bottom for donor portraits, but increasingly he was being asked to make the portraits much larger so that they encroached into the main scene itself. Sometimes the donor figures were almost as large as the subject of the painting.

Baode's contemporaries in Chang'an, the Song dynasty capital, regarded Dunhuang as little more than a provincial backwater, forgetting the great heyday of the Silk Road and the debt they themselves owed to Silk Road art and culture. The new Chinese emperor was a keen patron of the arts and the imperial painting academy attracted cultured individuals versed in literature and painting, able to draw on the works of the past masters and painting manuals held in the imperial collections, certain of the moral and artistic superiority of their works over all others. Their names are known, but most of their works have been lost. The works of Baode and his contemporaries on the Silk Road, however, though their names have long been forgotten, are still admired today.

Epilogue

THE STORIES OF the Silk Road do not end with the artist Dong Baode in the tenth century, but from the eleventh century onwards the culture of the region changed. China's influence was felt less and less, even in Dunhuang which was relatively close to Central China, as Islamic culture and religion spread from the west. And although trade continued, the maritime route from southern and eastern Chinese ports became dominant. Whether because of a drop in the water table or a decline in population, many of the Silk Road towns were gradually abandoned, to be reclaimed by the desert sands. Not until a later imperial age did the Chinese once again colonize the Western Regions, calling them the 'New Territories' (Xinjiang). For many Chinese the area then became a place of exile.

The discovery by European archaeologists of the riches of the Silk Road at the end of the nineteenth century and beginning of the twentieth was characterized by competition, each vying to excavate newly discovered sites. Aurel Stein was only the first to reach Dunhuang because a German expedition, unable to decide whether to go to Dunhuang or Kocho, flipped a coin. The coin decided the latter. There is, however, some hope that archaeology in the next millennium will be characterized by co-operation. A Chinese government decree of 1992 allowed foreign archaeologists to work together with Chinese on digs, and Japanese and French archaeologists have since excavated various new Silk Road sites. An exhibition held at the Shanghai Museum in 1988, which displayed 142 objects dating from 1000 BC to AD 1200 unearthed during various recent excavations in China's Xinjiang province, suggested the wealth of material yet to be discovered.

Greed is now a greater threat to the preservation of these objects than competition. Silk Road artefacts fetch high prices in the antique market and many items are being looted by locals, sold to middlemen and smuggled out of the countries in question to dealers abroad. This is particularly the case in areas of conflict, such as Afghanistan, but it is also happening in China. In trying to piece together the story of the past it is imperative to know the provenance of the items of evidence: without that knowledge, they tell us little. Those who steal such artefacts are, of course, concerned to hide provenance, and each piece looted is thus a piece lost to the historical jigsaw. Added to this is the fact that many such pieces are bought by private collectors and are never put on public display or made available for scholarship. Whatever one may think of the actions of Stein and others at the start of this century, the items they removed are now in public institutions and have always been available for study. Even so, much of what was taken to Germany, particularly many wonderful wall fragments, was destroyed during the bombing of Berlin in the Second World War, although the more portable objects that had been moved to safer locations survive. War has not been the only cause of loss. Count Otani, the leader of Japanese expeditions to Central Asia at the time of Stein, experienced financial difficulties some years later and many of his finds were sold. His manuscripts are now divided between private and public collections in several countries. Scrolls have been remounted and colophons added by their new owners, rendering it impossible to determine the provenance or verify the authenticity of many pieces.

Another group who are intent on confusing the story are the forgers. Forgers exist wherever there is a market for items which are either too little understood or are easily reproducible. Islam Akhun was only the first of those who exploited a lack of knowledge of the Silk Road's history. Subsequently, both buyers and forgers had access to genuine manuscripts and, though the forgers therefore had to become more skilled, if they copied the originals in all particulars, detection was unlikely.

As scientific methods to provide objective tests for authenticity have developed, so forgers have become ever more sophisticated. A recent sale of ancient Egyptian paintings by a leading auction house was cancelled after it was discovered through scientific analysis that the pigments used were based on chemicals that had only been synthesized in the nineteenth century. Other reports suggest that forgers of Chinese pots are now using ground-up shards from ancient pots, so confusing any thermoluminescence test. It is inevitable that this competition between those who wish to mislead and those who are intent on discovering the truth will continue.

But this is as it has always been: Nanaivandak, the merchant of the first tale, managed to deceive the buyers of his cargo of wool by letting sand seep into the bales, thus increasing their weight. Though much change has come to the Silk Road since his time, its people still represent the diversity of human life and experience.

Further Reading

THE PRIMARY SOURCES used for this book are manuscripts found in the ancient oasis towns and Buddhist sites along the Silk Road. The largest cache, over 40,000 items, comes from Dunhuang in the province of Gansu. Of the hundreds of caves hollowed out of the friable cliff face there between the fourth and eleventh centuries (described in 'The Artist's Tale'), one particular cave was sealed in the mid-eleventh century and remained hidden until its accidental discovery in 1900. The manuscripts (and some printed documents and paintings) from this and other sites are now scattered around the world, with major collections in the National Library of China, Beijing, the British Library, London, the Bibliothèque nationale de France, Paris, the Institute for Oriental Studies, St Petersburg, and the Staatsbibliothek, Berlin. The importance of these manuscripts cannot be overstated and is elegantly discussed in articles by Professor Denis Twitchett, 'Chinese Social History from the Seventh to Tenth Centuries' (*Past and Present*, 35, December 1966, pp. 28–53), and Professor Fujieda Akira, 'The Tunhuang Manuscripts: A General Description' (*Zinbun*, ix, 1966, pp. 1–32, and x, 1969, pp. 17–39).

Many of the manuscripts have been catalogued and translated. For a general description see Lionel Giles's early catalogue of the London collection, *Descriptive Catalogue of the Chinese Manuscripts from Tunhuang in the British Museum* (London, British Museum, 1957). For elegant translations of some of the stories told in the manuscripts see Arthur Waley, *Ballads and Stories from Tun-huang* (London, Allen & Unwin, 1960). More recently Victor Mair has translated many of the Buddhist stories, such as that of Śāriputra ('The Artist's Tale') and Mulian rescuing his mother ('The Nun's

Tale'): see Victor Mair, *Tunhuang Popular Narratives* (Cambridge, Cambridge University Press, 1983).

The International Dunhuang Project, based at the British Library in London, was founded in 1994 to bring the manuscripts back together using computer technology. Many thousands of the manuscripts, and details of their contents, can now be viewed on the Project website (http://idp.bl.uk). The site also gives links to other sites containing images of the paintings on the cave walls which have also been an important source for many of the characters in these stories. For details of these finds, an excellent read is Peter Hopkirk's *Foreign Devils on the Silk Road* (London, John Murray, 1980). Peter Hopkirk has also written on the machinations of the British and Russian spies who preceded the archaeologists in this region (*The Great Game*, London, John Murray, 1990). The British Museum publication by Roderick Whitfield and Anne Farrer, *Caves of a Thousand Buddhas* (London, 1990), provides a clear background to the Dunhuang site and its finds. The Getty Conservation Institute, which has been working on the Dunhuang site for several years, has also recently published a well-illustrated overview.

Mention has already been made in the Preface of four major secondary sources. General scholarly books on the history of the Silk Road are still comparatively few and usually rather daunting to even the scholarly reader, because of the plethora of peoples and places cited. Luc Kwanten, *Imperial Nomads* (Leicester, University of Leicester, 1979) and Rene Grousset, *The Empire of the Steppes: A History of Central Asia* (New Brunswick, Rutgers University Press, 1970) provide general histories, although both their works have been subject to much criticism and are now somewhat out of date. A more recent history is Richard Frye, *The Heritage of Central Asia* (Princeton, Markus Wiener, 1996). However, volumes 3 and 4 of a series published by UNESCO, *The History of Civilizations of Central Asia* (6 vols) cover the period under discussion here and provide the most detailed and up-to-date scholarship. For sound one-volume works, see Denis Sinor (ed.), *The Cambridge History of Early Inner Asia* (Cambridge, Cambridge University Press, 1990) and Richard C. Foltz, *Religions of the Silk Road* (New York, St Martin's Press, 1999).

For more detailed accounts of the four great empires discussed in these stories, see Christopher I. Beckwith, *The Tibetan Empire in Central Asia* (Princeton, Princeton University Press, 1987); Colin MacKerras, *The Uighur Empire According to T'ang Dynastic Sources* (Canberra, Australian National University Press, 1972); Bernard Lewis, *The Arabs in History* (Oxford, Oxford University Press 1993); and Jacques Gernet, *A History of Chinese Civilization* (Cambridge, Cambridge University Press, 1996). Gernet's *Daily Life on the Eve of the Mongol Invasion* (London, 1962) gives a fascinating glimpse into Chinese life in the Song dynasty, just following the period covered here. He is also the author of a valuable work on the life and role of Silk Road monks – *Buddhism in Chinese Society* (New York, Columbia University Press, 1995, English translation). For a sound and clear discussion of the doctrines of Mahāyāna Buddhism I would recommend Paul Williams, *Mahāyāna Buddhism: The Doctrinal Foundations* (London and New York, Routledge, 1989).

Several good travel guides to the Silk Road have been published in recent years which introduce some of its history. See, for example, Kathleen Hopkirk, *Central Asia: A Traveller's Companion* (London, John Murray, 1993). For a history of trade along the Silk Road, see Irene M. Franck and David M. Brownstone, *The Silk Road: A History* (New York and Oxford, Facts on File, 1986). There are also several excellent accounts of travels through Central Asia, starting with that of the fourth-century monk, Faxian, and the seventh-century Chinese monk, Xuanzang. The latter's journey is discussed by Sally H. Wriggins in her recent book *Xuanzang: A Buddhist Pilgrim on the Silk Road* (Boulder and Oxford, Westview Press, 1996). In the nineteenth century, two French Jesuits, Abbés Huc and Gabet, travelled across the northern fringes of China and into Tibet, keeping a detailed record of their journey (*Travels in Tartary, Thibet and China during the Years 1844–5–6* (London, Kegan Paul, 1900, rpt. Dover Publications, 1987)). Evangelism also inspired Mildred Cable and Francesca French, Protestant missionaries who travelled across Chinese Central Asia in the 1920s (*Through Jade Gate and Central Asia* (London, Hodder and Stoughton, 1927)). And in the 1930s, Peter Fleming and Ella Maillart travelled to Kashgar and Kashmir (Peter

Fleming, *News from Tartary* (London, Jonathan Cape, 1936, rpt. Abacus, 1987) and Ella Maillert, *Forbidden Journey* (London, Holt, 1937)). All their books are worth reading and give firsthand and perceptive accounts of travelling the Silk Road before the developments of the late twentieth century.

Apart from these, Aurel Stein himself wrote lucid accounts of his first three expeditions. See *Sand-Buried Ruins of Khotan* (London, Fisher & Unwin, 1903) and *Ruins of Desert Cathay* (London, Macmillan, 1912, 2 vols; reprinted by Dover, 1987). Stein has been the subject of two biographies, of which the second, by Annabel Walker (London, John Murray, 1995), is still in print.

I should also mention one more. Professor Edward Schafer whose works include exhaustive articles on the Bactrian camel and whose book on everything Central Asian – from art to animals – has been an indispensable aid: *The Golden Peaches of Samarkand* (Berkeley, University of California Press, 1985).

Finally, for a polemic on the importance of Central Asia for world history, Andre Gunder Franck has written an excellent short work that is both accessible and provocative: *The Centrality of Central Asia* (Comparative Asia Studies: 8) (Amsterdam, VU University Press, 1992).

Table of Rulers, 739–960

FRANKISH Carolingians	BYZANTINE Isaurians	ARAB Umayyads	TIBETAN	TURKIC/UIGHUR Eastern Turkic	CHINESE Tang
Carl (714–41) (Charles Martel)	Leo III (717–41)	Hisam (724–43)	Khri lDe gtsug b(r)tsan (Mes Ag tshom (705–55)	Bilga Kaghan (716–34)	Xuanzong (712–56)
				I-jan Kaghan (734)	
				Tengri Kaghan (d. 741)	
Pippin III (741–68) (Pippin the Short)	Constantine V (741–75)	Al-Walid II (743–4)		Ku-to Yabghu Kaghan (d. 742)	
		Yazid III (744)		Ozmis Kaghan (d. 744)	
		Ibrahim (744)		Hulongfu Bomei Kaghan (d. 745)	
		Marwan II al Himar (744–50)		Uighurs	
		Abbasids		Mo-yen Cur (747–59)	
		Al-Saffah (750–4)			
		Al-Mansur (754–75)	Khri sron lDe b(r)tsan (755–c. 799)	Bogu (759–79)	Suzong (756–62)
Karol (768–814) (Charlemagne)					Taizong (762–79)
	Leo IV (775–80)	Al-Mahdi (775–85)		Tun Bagha Tarqan (779–89)	Dezong (779–805)
	Constantine VI (780–97)	Al-Hadi (785–6)			
		Harun al-Rashid (786–809)		Talas (789–90)	
	Irene (797–802)		Mu ne btsan po (c. 799–c. 800)	Kutlugh Bilga (790–5)	
	Nikephoros I (802–11)		Khri lDe srong b(r)tsan (Sad na legs, mu tig btsan po) (c. 800–c. 815)	Huaixin (795–805)	Shunzong (805)
	Staurakios (811)	Al-Amin (809–13)		Kulug Bilga (805–8)	Xianzong (805–20)
				Alp Bilga Baoyi (808–21)	

Byzantine	Carolingian	Abbasid	Tibetan	Uighur	Chinese	Dunhuang (as 'Returning to Allegiance Army District')
Michael I Rhangabe (811–13)	Hludowic (814–40) (Louis the Pious)					
Leo V (813–20)		Al-Ma'mun (813–33)	Khri gTsug lDe b(r)tsan (Ral pa can) (c. 815–36)			
Amorians Michael II (820–9)	*The following ruled as emperors over only part of the old empire*			Kuclug Bilga Chongde (821–4)	Muzong (820–4)	
	Lothar I (840–55)			Kazar Zhaoli (824–32)	Jingzong (824–7)	
Theophilos II (829–42)		Al-Mu'tasim (833–42)		Alp Kulug Bilga Zhangxin (832–9)	Wenzong (827–40)	
Michael III (842–67)		Al-Wathiq (842–7)	Khri U'i dum brtsan (Glang dar mae) (836–42)	Wudu Gond (839–40)	Wuzong (840–6)	
	Louis II (855–75)	Al-Mutawakkil (847–61)	*End of Central Tibetan Kingdom*	*End of the Uighur Empire*	Xuanzong (847–59)	Zhang Yichao (848–67)
		Al-Muntasir (861–2)			Yizong (859–73)	
		Al-Musta'in (862–6)				
Macedonians Basil I (867–86)	Charles the Bald (875–7)	Al-Mu'tazz (866–9)				Zhang Huaishen (867–?86)
	Charles the Fat (881–7) *End of the Carolingian Empire*	Al-Muhtadi (869–70)			Xizong (873–88)	
		Al-Mu'tamid (870–92)				
Leo IV (886–912)		Al-Mu'tadid (892–902)			Zhaozong (888–904)	Suo Xun (c. 886–c.893)
						Zhang Chengfeng (c. 893–910)
		Al-Muktafi (902–8)			Aidi (904–7)	
		Al-Muqtadir (908–32)			**Five Dynasties (907–960)**	Cao Yijun (c. 910–40)
Constantine VIII (913–59)		Al-Qahir (932–4)				
		Al-Radi (934–40)				
		Al-Muttaqi (940–4)				Cao Yuande (940–2) Cao Yuanshen (942–6)
		Al-Mustakfi (944–6)			**Song (960–1290)**	Cao Yuanzhong (946–74)
Romanus II (959–63)		Al-Muti (946–74)				

Index

Abbasid Caliphate (Arab), 6, 13, 27, 33, 51, 54, 142; *see also* Arab empire

aconite, 115

acrobats, 46–7, 61, 143

Aesop's Fables, 218

Afghanistan, 8, 10, 11, 12; *see also* Bactria

Africa, 7, 16

agate, 200

agriculture, 8, 11, 13, 23, 27, 35, 39, 50, 53, 56, 57, 58, 59, 61, 70, 74, 78, 82, 83, 102, 105, 123, 124, 125, 131, 150, 160–1, 176–7, 178, 180–1, 182, 184, 188, 190, 191, 195

Ahura Mazda, 18; *see also* Zoroastrianism

Akhun, Islam, 4, 224

Aksu, 24, 43, 63

al-Saffah (Arab caliph), 27

alchemy, 93

Alexander the Great, 8, 9, 37, 118

alfalfa, 23

almanacs, 5, 114, 178, 195–7, 198, 201–2, 205

almonds, 106, 142

almsgiving, 19, 39, 44, 203

aloeswood, 96, 183

Altai mountains, 8, 22, 25, 40, 87, 88

altitude sickness, 42

alum, 149

amber, 38, 95

America, 9

Amitābha Buddha, 155

Amu Darya *see* Oxus river

Amur cork tree (*Phellodendron amurense*), 208

An Lushan *see* Rokhshan

Ānanda, 215

Anatolia, 8

Angra Mainyu, 18; *see also* Zoroastrianism

animal husbandry, 11, 25, 39, 56, 59, 83, 87, 111, 144, 169, 182

Anityatāsūtra, see The Sutra of Impermanence

antaravāsaka (monk's shirt), 163

antelopes, 47

Anxi, 47, 49

aphrodisiacs, 79, 96

Arab empire, 1, 6, 12, 13, 14, 15, 30, 33, 34, 36, 51, 53, 97, 115, 142; lent money by Sogdian merchants, 14, 34; medicine in, 115; occupation of Sogdiana, 34, 51; paper-making in Damascus, 30; relations with Chinese, 13, 14, 30, 53; *see also* Abbasid Caliphate, Umayyad Caliphate

Aral Sea, 63

Archaeological Survey of India, 3

archaeology, 1–2, 3–4, 8, 61, 223–4

archery, 35, 55, 64, 68, 72–3, 88, 93, 111

architecture, 28, 35–6, 43, 58–9, 70, 78–9, 83, 105, 123, 127, 128, 129, 134, 136, 163, 175–6, 179, 197, 199, 201, 209–10

arhats, 16–17

armour, 55, 60, 68, 72, 93, 94, 100, 193

arsenic, 73

arsenphyrite, 115

asbestos, 22

Aśoka (Mauryan king), 17, 119, 120, 200

asses, 47, 166; *see also* donkeys

astrakhan fur, 22, 40

astrology, 74, 194–6; *see also* almanacs, divination

astronomy, 118, 194–6, 201–2

Atlantic Ocean, 9

Attila (king of Huns), 8

aubergine, 181

Avalokiteśvara, 132, 146, 159, 171, 182, 185, 191–3, 196, 204, 207, 210

Avīci Hell, 169–71; *see also* hells

Aza people, 12, 56, 61–2, 70, 144, 176, 182, 186

azurite, 214

Babylon, 18, 20

Bactria, 8, 10, 11, 20, 25, 30, 37; *see also* Balkh

Baghdad, 14, 27, 33, 51

Balkh, 22, 25, 33, 37

balsam, 149, 181

Baltic Sea, 38, 95

bamboo, 21, 56, 73, 105, 181, 208

bandits, 6, 39, 44, 45, 48, 50, 176, 183, 186, 203; *see also* law and order

Baramula, 118

barley, 56

Baroghil pass (Hindu Kush), 63, 65, 66, 122

basil, 149

beacon forts, 60

Bedal river (Tianshan), 42–3

Beishan, 50

Beiting, xiii, 91; *see also* Beshbaliq
Beshbaliq, xiii, 25, 91–2, 93, 94, 153, 218
board games *see* double-sixes, mah-jong
bodhisattva *see* Buddhism
Bon, 20
book production, 114; *see also* libraries, printing
border controls, 39, 90, 91, 99, 125, 136, 152
Borneo, 79, 183
brass, 38
Britain, 1, 2, 4, 10, 226, 227
Broussonetia papyifea see mulberry
bSam yas monastery (Tibet), 136
Buddha *see* Amitābha, Buddhism, Śākyamuni
Buddhism, 2, 7, 11, 14, 15, 16–17, 19, 44, 52, 82, 95, 101, 113–37, 142, 143, 144, 145, 146, 155–73, 189–90, 191–4, 199–202, 203, 210–13, 220; arhats, 16–17; art, 5, 38, 119, 156, 186, 219; banners, 221; bodhisattvas, 17, 117, 119, 132, 156, 159, 220, *see also* Avalokiteśvara, Kṣitigarbha, Mañjuśrī; Chan, 142; charity, 203; clothing of clergy, 156, 159, 163, 172, 217, *see also* antaravāsaka, kāṣāya, uttarāsaṅga; extreme practices of, 116, 120; founder of, 16; Four Noble Truths, 16; funerals, 133, 155, 164–6, 167, 186; Heavenly Kings, 128, 220, *see also* Dhṛtarāṣṭra, Vaiśravaṇa, Virūḍhaka, Virūpākṣa; hell, 164–6, 169–71, 185; Hīnayāna, 11, 17, 141; iconography of, 128, 216–17; in Khotan, 127–9; in Takṣaśīlā, 118–19; in Tibet, 14–15, 120, 136; karmic debt, 16–17, 163–4, 169–71, 202, 203–4; King Aśoka's support of, 17, 119, 200; Mahāyāna,. 11, 14–15, 17, 120, 141, 159, 200; medicine in, 115, 176; meditation, 16, 120, 142, 162, 209; monastic rules (vinaya), 158–9, 164, 166, 172; monks, 113–37, 172, 194; nirvāṇa, 16, 158; Noble Eightfold Path, 16; non-duality, 200; nuns, 155–73; ordination, 115, 136, 156, 158–60, 161, 162, 215; rebirth, 16–17, 166, 169–71, 185, 202, 203–4; Red Hat sect, 120; ritual, 119, 120, 133, 156, 163–4, 167, 176, 192–3, 220–1; saṃsāra, 16; stupas, 119; suppression of, 101, 133–4; Tantrism, 14–15, 17, 120, 159; Third Council, 17, 200; women in, 158–9, 185–6; Zen *see* Chan
Buddhist canon (Tripiṭaka), 163, 201–2; monastic rules (vinaya), 158–9, 163, 164; sutra commentaries, 163; sutras, 3, 6, 17, 117, 120, 133, 136, 141, 155, 162, 163, 167,

173, 183, 199–202, 203–4, 208, 217; sutras, non-canonical, 163; *see also Sutra of the Ten Kings*; written in blood, 120
Buddhist monasteries and nunneries, 52, 114, 115, 119, 120, 125, 128, 129, 134, 136, 142, 163–4, 167–8, 191–3, 194; agriculture in, 160–1; industry in, 161, 168; moneylending, 161, 166; libraries, 194, 199, 208; other income of, 161, 167, 168, 184; property of, 171–2
Burma, 95, 140
butter, 90

Cable, Mildred, 228
calcium, 85
calendar *see* almanacs
Cambodia, 140, 214
camel sage, 24
camels, 31, 32, 37, 42, 43, 44–7, 48, 49, 76, 82, 87, 90, 95, 100, 103, 104–5, 126, 131–2, 143, 176; Arabian camel, 46; Bactrian camel, 46, 95; Bright Camel Envoy, 46, 79; dung, as firewood, 90; wild camels, 46
camphor, 79, 183
camphorwood, 106
Cannabis sativa see hemp
Canton *see* Guangzhou
Cao Yijun (ruler of Dunhuang), 167, 199
Cao Yuanzhong (ruler of Dunhuang), 167, 206–22 *passim*, 217, 218–19, 220–1
caravanserai, 28–9, 36, 37, 43; *see also* inns
Carolingians, 6
carpets, 96, 104, 105–6, 131, 163
Caspian Sea, 2, 18, 97
catalpa, 207
catapults, 72–3, 100
Celts, 8
censorship, 135, 196–7
centipede, 115, 191
Central Asia: geography of, 2–3; history of, 7ff; movement of peoples in, 8; problems with sources on, 9–10; Soviet occupation, 8
ceruse, 214
Chach (Tashkent), 22, 23, 25, 32, 33, 34, 37, 39, 40, 41
Chang'an, 2, 13, 18, 21, 22, 26, 27, 29, 38–9, 40, 41, 51–4, 55, 62, 70, 76, 80, 81, 82, 84, 85, 89–91, 96–7, 98–100, 102, 107, 109, 117, 123, 134, 135, 140, 146–52, 154, 156–7, 195, 196–7, 201–2; courtesan quarter, 90, 96–7, 146–8; Eastern Market, 90, 146, 197; foreign communities in, 40,

Chang'an (*cont.*)
78, 84, 89–91, 135; Imperial City, 90, 146,
201–2; plan of, 52; restaurants, 31–2, 51;
sack of, 150–2, 156–7, 190; Western
Market, 29, 89–90; Zhangjing Temple, 112;
Zoroastrian temple in, 18
Charklick, 131
cheese, 90
childbirth *see* pregnancy and childbirth
Chiman-tagh, 57
China: army, use of foreign soldiers, 44, 53, 72,
see also Gao, General; Koso Khan, General;
Rokhshan; calendar as legitimization of
rule, 195–7; civil service, 38, 190, 202;
customs, 29, 125, 178; Jewish community
in, 18; first history of, 10; foreign
communities in, 18, 78, 85, 135; influence
of Central Asia on, xi, 9, 10, 62, 85, 100–1,
149–50, 221–2; position of women in, 109;
rebellions, 6, 72, 150–3, *see also* Rokhshan;
relations with Arabs, 13, 14, 30, 53, *see also*
Talas River, battle of; relations with Eastern
and Western Turks, 77–8; relations with
Tibet, 13, 14–15, 38, 44, 53, 55–75 *passim*,
79, 90, 99, 122, 131; relations with Turghiz,
53; relations with Uighurs, 14, 77–112, 123,
141, 144, 218; religions in, 11, 17, 18, 20,
135, 163, *see also* Buddhism, Confucianism,
Daoism; Turkic communities in, 78, 135;
see also Chang'an, Han dynasty, Song
dynasty, Sui dynasty, Tang dynasty
Christianity, 18, 20, 116; *see also*
Nestorianism
chrysanthemums, 104
cinnabar, 115, 147, 214, 215
cities along the Silk Road, 7, 9, 11, 12, 13,
15–16, 20, 21–6, 27–8, 31, 33, 38, 39, 40,
47, 56, 57, 91–2, 123, 131, 223; as city-
states, 11, 12; Chinese control of, 15, 50,
53, 56, 61, 80, 91, 123, 131, 144, 145, 146,
155, 218; culture of, 14, 15; foreign
communities in, 7, 15–16, 177; markets and
trade in, 9, 11; religions of, 14, 15, 19–20,
223; Tibetan control of, 13, 53, 56, 61, 91,
123, 131, 144, 145, 146, 155; Uighur
control of, 123, 143–4, 153, 218; *see also*
Aksu, Anxi, Beshbaliq, Chalch, Chang'an,
Dunhuang, Hami, Kashgar, Khotan,
Kocho, Kucha, Merv, Panjikent,
Samarkand
citragandha, 181
climate, 23–5, 27, 28, 39, 40, 41–2, 49, 67, 71,

76, 86, 103–4, 105, 122, 123–4, 126, 136,
169, 174
clothing, 9, 21, 30, 31–2, 39, 41, 60, 76, 79, 85,
89, 95, 96, 106–8, 118, 126, 135, 138, 148,
150, 159, 166, 172, 178; Chinese, 95, 106,
107; Japanese, 106; Korean, 106; of
Buddhist clergy, 135, 156, 159, 166, 172; of
dancers, 31–2, 79, 96, 150; of Manichean
clergy, 108, 135; Sogdian, 29, 30–1, 96;
Turkic, 106; Uighur, 76, 85, 107–8
cloves, 147
clubs, women's, 185–6, 188
Confucianism, 15, 146, 188, 190, 198, 201–2
conjurers, 143
contortionists, 143
copper, 134, 141, 147, 166, 176, 214
coral, 38
corn, 121
cornelian, 200
cosmetics, 138, 143, 148, 149
cotton, 21, 22, 172, 193
courtesans *see* prostitution
Crete, 17
crickets, 191, 192, 194
crossbows, 93, 100
croton seed, 115
crows, 170, 194
crystal, 106, 200
cucumbers, 19
currencies, 21–2, 39, 43, 118, 147, 161, 172–3,
177; *see also* gold, silk, silver
cyclamen, 118

Damscus, 6, 12, 14, 30, 33, 51, 54
dance, 26, 31, 61, 79, 90, 96, 131, 139, 140,
143, 145, 182, 193; Kuchean dance, 44, 90,
139, 140, 143; Sogdian dance, 96, 140;
'whirling' dance, 79, 96, 140
Dang river (Dunhuang), 24
Daoism, 52, 99, 101, 109–10, 127, 146, 148,
158, 198
Darkhot pass (Hindu Kush), 63, 65, 66, 67, 68,
69, 122
death, 73–4, 111, 157, 169–71, 176, 186, 188,
197, 203; Buddhist rites of, 133, 155,
163–6, 203–4; Chinese rites of, 157, 188;
Uighur rites of, 94, 110; *see also* medicine,
post-mortems
deer, 88, 106
demons, 35, 104, 115, 142, 164, 165, 170, 185,
191
desert storms, 44, 131–3

Index

desert travel, 44–6, 47–8, 126–7, 131–3
Devashtich, 34
Dharamarajika stupa (Takṣaśilā), 119
Dhṛtarāṣtra, 128; *see also* Buddhism, Heavenly
  Kings
Diamond Sutra, The, 155, 162, 199–201
diamonds, 127, 199–200, 212
disease, 74, 86, 87, 142, 147, 174–5, 176, 183,
  188, 191; colic, 87, 175; plague, 176;
  rheumatoid arthritis, 74, 174–5, 188;
  sexually transmitted, 147; *see also* medicine
divination, 44, 114, 173, 178, 191, 194–6, 197
Divine Prestige Army, 72
divorce, 180–1
dogs, 41, 80, 138, 149, 171
donkeys, 156, 191; *see also* asses
double-sixes, 80, 183, 207
dragons, 94, 97, 142, 212, 215
drink *see* food and drink, tea, wine
drums, 94, 139, 151, 179, 193, 194
drunkenness, 198–9
Du Huan (Chinese prisoner-of-war), 54
Du Yu (Chinese writer), 55
dumba sheep, 40
Dunhuang, xi, 2, 3, 5, 16, 24, 57, 113, 131, 133,
  134, 136–7, 144–5, 155–222 *passim*, 223,
  226, 227; Buddhist caves near, 5, 114, 134,
  136, 145, 183, 190–3, 209–21, 226, 227;
  Buddhism in, 156, 158–9, 209; Chinese in,
  155, 190–1, *see also* Zhang Yichao;
  educational system, 198–9; government of,
  156, 158, 161, 176, 186–8, 189–222; library
  cave, 4, 5–6, 217, 226; Painting Academy,
  206, 213–14, 217, 219; Printing Bureau,
  206–7; relations with central China, 202,
  221–2, 223; relations with Uighurs, 218–19;
  Rites Academy, 198–9; Tibetans in, 155,
  190–1, 208, 216–17, *see also* Zhang Yichao
duophysites, 20; *see also* Nestorianism
dye, 4, 89, 208
Dzungaria, 22, 25, 26, 34, 76, 83, 87, 88, 91,
  93, 218

eagles, 89
Eastern Market (Chang'an), 90, 146, 197
Eastern Turks, 40, 77–8
edelweiss, 118
education, 4, 189–90, 194, 198–9, 201, 202, 208
Egypt, 17, 224
elephants, 200, 211, 212
elms, 24, 209
emeralds, 21

entertainment, 139, 143, 147, 173; *see also*
  acrobats, board games, conjurers,
  contortionists, dance, festivals, fire-eaters,
  jugglers, music, tightrope walkers
Equus przewalski see horse, tarpan
ermine, 76, 106
Esoteric Buddhism *see* Buddhism, Tantrism
*Essential Teachings for the Instruction of Young
  People*, 190
etiquette, 105, 198–9
Europe, 7, 8, 9, 30, 116, 223
Eurasian steppes, 28

falconry, 41, 76, 88–9
Family Teachings of Taigong, The, 190
famine, 82
Faxian (Chinese pilgrim monk), 228
felt, 41, 78, 88, 95, 131, 166, 172; making of, 88
fengshui see geomancy
fennel, 87
Ferghana, 10, 13, 14, 23, 33, 34, 97–8
festivals, 35, 105, 143, 169, 171, 173, 188, 207,
  220–1; Dragon Festival, 190–2; Ghost
  Festival (Buddhist), 169, 171, 173, 204, 207;
  Moon Festival, 220; New Year (lunar), 105,
  143, 208; procession of Buddha image,
  220–1
fir trees, 118
fire-eaters, 143
fish, 46, 51, 178, 180, 212
flora and fauna *see* individual entries
flute, 139
food and drink, 26, 31, 46, 47, 85, 87, 90, 103,
  104, 115, 124, 134, 138, 147, 163–4, 168,
  179, 186; religious proscriptions on, 19,
  134, 163–4, 186; *see also* individual entries
footbinding, 109
footwear *see* shoes and boots
forgeries, of artefacts, 4, 224–5
Four Noble Truths, 16
France, 2, 5; expeditions, 223
fruit, 19, 23, 31, 43, 49, 50, 87, 90, 102–3, 106,
  115, 118, 119, 120, 123, 127, 142, 149, 186
funerals *see* death, Buddhism, funerals
fungus, 87
furniture, 104, 105–6, 172, 183
furs, 76, 95, 106, 166

gamboge, 214
games, 147, 183; *see also* double-sixes, mah-
  jong, polo
Gandhāra, 118

Index

Gandhāri, 4, 118
Ganges river, 119, 200, 202
Gansu corridor, 2–3, 9, 10, 13, 14, 22, 24, 49, 72, 91, 100, 112
Gansu Province, 5, 226
Ganzhou, 112, 123, 217, 218
Gao, General (Chinese army), 53, 63–70 passim, 72, 79, 122
Gautama, Prince see Śākyamuni
gazelle, 47, 103
gecko lizard, 147
gemstones, 21, 22
gentian, yellow, 118
geomancy (fengshui), 178, 197
gerbils, 47
Germans, 8; expeditions, 2, 5, 223
Germany, 224
Gilgit river, 10, 63, 66–8, 69, 70, 118, 122
ginger, 87
glass, 22
goats, 124
Gobi desert, 12, 24, 49–50, 91, 100, 103–4, 112; Black Gobi, 49–50
gold, 8, 10, 21, 22, 38, 44, 49, 51, 78, 85, 93, 105, 106, 107, 108, 109, 119, 130, 141, 142, 166, 182, 200, 211, 220; covering Uighur tent, 78; Tibetan ornaments, 38; Turkic belts, 38, 108
gonorrhea, 147
goose, 104
goshawk, 76, 139
gourds, 45
Great Game, The, 1, 9, 227
Greeks, 7, 8, 115, 118
Guang (king of underworld), 203
Guangzhou (Canton), 7
Guanshiyin sutra, 171, 210; see also Lotus Sutra
Guanyin see Avalokiteśvara
Guazhou, 207
gunpowder, 100
Gupta dynasty, 11

hairstyles and ornaments, 41, 95, 96, 106, 107, 109, 127, 138, 145, 146
Hami, 23, 24, 25, 47, 49, 144
Hamlet, 190
Han dynasty (China), 8, 10–11, 12
hare, 106
harp, 139, 182
Heaven's Mandate, 195
hell, 164–6, 169–71, 185, 186, 203–4
hellebore, 115

hemp, 161, 168–9, 177, 208, 210, 221
Herodotus, 8, 47
Hezhong, 102
Himalayas, 2, 70
Hīnayāna Buddhist see Buddhism, Hīnayāna
Hindu empires, 116, 120; see also Karkota dynasty, Sunga dynasty
Hindu Kush, 3, 9, 10, 11, 25, 42, 63
Hinduism, 11, 17, 20, 116, 139
Hittites, 7
homosexuality, 117
honey, 183
Hong Bian, 216–17
horses, 41, 47, 76–88, 89, 93, 94, 95, 97, 103, 109, 142, 143, 151, 187, 191, 200, 218, 219; Arab, 47, 85–6; as pack animals, 42, 117, 122–3, 132, 133; Ayran, 97; breeding in China, 85, 86, 95; cavalry, 8, 9, 59, 63, 68, 79, 86, 93, 94, 97, 98, 193, 218; for ceremonial use, 97; dancing horses of Chinese court, 98; diseases among, 86; domestication of, 8; Equus przewalski, 76, 77, see also tarpan; Ferghanan, 23, 47, 95, 97–8; fodder for, 117, 168; horsemeat, 87; horseriding as sport, 97, 142, 183; legends about, 97–8; mares' milk, 90; Nisean, 97; post horses, 100, 109; shen (Samarkand), 27; tarpan, 47, 76–7, 85–6; trade between Uighurs and Chinese, 82, 85, 86–7, 98, 100, 110, 218; Turkic, 47, 97; wild, 47; see also polo
hospitals, 119; see also medicine
hot springs, 80
Huainan, 196
Huang river, 62
huangbo, 208; see also dye
Hund, 119
Hungarian expedition, 3
hungry ghosts, 171, 185
Huns, 8; see also Attila, Xiongnu
hunting, 41
Hunza river, 122

Imperial City (Chang'an), 90, 146, 201–2
incense, 115, 119, 126, 133, 155, 156, 174, 191, 193, 221; recipe for, 183
India, 2, 3, 7, 8, 9, 11, 14–15, 16, 17, 21, 22, 25, 44, 53, 61, 63, 96, 115, 118, 130, 136, 139, 140, 159, 197, 200, 203, 211, 219; Jewish community in, 18; religions in, 11, 14, 16, 17, 37; trade in, 21, 44; see also Gupta dynasty, Mauryan dynasty, Sunga dynasty

Index

indigo, 149, 214
Indo-Greek kingdoms, 10
Indo-Malayan traders, 7
Indus river, 8, 67, 70, 118, 119
inns, 43, 45, 146, 175–6; monasteries as, 134–5;
    see also caravanserai
International Dunhuang Project, 227
Iran, 9, 11, 18, 20; religions of, 11, 18, 20
Iron Blade, 62, 72–3
iron, 22, 51, 141, 170; casting of, 22
irrigation, 23, 28, 49, 57–8, 168, 177, 203
Islam, xi, 2, 7, 12, 14, 15, 16, 27, 33, 37–8,
    223
Islamabad, 9
Issuk-kul, 25, 38, 39–40, 41, 109
ivory, 22, 166

jade, 22, 44, 95, 108, 117, 123, 127, 131, 140,
    142, 163, 170, 211; as medicine, 127; source
    of, 127; working of, 127
Japan, 5, 106, 136, 139; expeditions, 2, 223
Jaxartes, 23, 25, 39
jewellery, 21, 30, 95, 121, 127, 143, 211; see also
    hairstyles and ornaments
Jhelum valley, 118
Judaism, 7, 11, 16, 18, 33; persecution, 17–18
jugglers, 143
jujube, 193, 207
juniper trees, 58

Kara-kash river, 127
Karabalghasun, 14, 25, 78–9, 81, 82, 83, 84, 85,
    89, 91, 94, 98, 99, 105–9, 141
Karakorum Highway, 118
Karlik pass, 124
Karkota dynasty (Kashmir), 12, 116, 136–7
kāṣāya (monk's robe), 163, 172
Kashgar river, 25
Kashgar, 4, 13, 23, 25, 38, 43, 63, 122, 125, 141,
    228
Kashmir, 3, 10, 11, 12, 16, 26, 42, 63, 70, 113,
    115–16, 117–18, 119, 121–2, 125, 126, 130,
    133, 137, 228; legends of, 121–2; religion
    of, 115–16, 130
Kasyapa, 215
Katmandu, 16
Khan-Tengri, 42, 43
kharoṣṭhī script, 4, 118
Khazars, 18
Khitans, 15, 80, 100, 111
Khotan, 11, 24, 43, 44, 56, 95, 123, 125,
    126–30, 131, 141, 172, 217–18, 219, 220,

221; founding of, 128; legends of, 128, 130;
    products of, 131; religion in, 127–30
Kirghiz, 14, 111, 123, 141, 142, 218
Kocho, xiii, 20, 24, 31, 48–9, 91, 93, 94, 102,
    112, 123, 142, 143–4, 145, 153, 217, 218;
    Manicheism, eastern diocese of, 20, 48–9,
    218; Uighurs in, 141–2, 143–4, 145, 153,
    218
Koko-nor, 12, 26, 56, 61, 62, 70–5, 144, 145,
    176, 186, 187; battle site, 61, 70–5
Korea, 53, 68, 72, 106, 136, 139
Koso Khan, General (Chinese army), 62, 71–3,
    79, 80, 81, 141
Kṣitigarbha, 204
Kucha, 11, 15, 24, 40, 43, 44, 48, 56, 90, 96,
    138, 141–2, 152, 153, 157, 199, 214;
    Buddhism in, 44, 141, 199; Chinese in, 44,
    142; Tibetans in, 56, 142; Uighurs in,
    141–2, 153; see also dance, Kuchean
Kuchean, 44, 141
Kufa, 14
Kumārajīva (Kuchean monk-translator), 141,
    199
Kunlun mountains, 23–4, 25, 57, 58, 74, 127,
    131
Kushan empire, 1, 17, 22

Lady Weng (Chinese poetess), 95
Lady Yang (Chinese imperial consort) see Yang
    Guifei
Lady Zhai (Cao Yuanzhong's wife), 208, 220
Lady Xu (Chinese poetess), 97
Lan Yanmei (Dunhuang printer), 206–7
languages of the Silk Road, 32, 36, 44
Lapchuk, 144
lapis lazuli, 22, 30, 38, 95, 107, 200, 214
law and order, 4, 6, 39, 50, 90–1, 146, 147, 161,
    165, 176, 183–5, 186–8
lead, 141, 149
letters, 4
Lhasa, 26, 56, 62, 70, 99
Li Yu (Chinese emperor-poet), 80
Liangzhou, 22, 103, 146
libraries, 120, 136, 194, 195, 199, 208, 217
Lidai minghua ji see Record of Famous Artists
    Through the Ages
linen, 21, 113
lion, 212, 213
liquorice, 75, 181
literacy, 114, 157, 162, 167, 184, 185, 190, 197;
    see also education
litharge, 214

Index

Little Balur, 15, 38, 56, 63–70, 71
Liu Yuxi (Chinese poet), 103
Liu Zongyuan (Chinese writer), 189
lizards, 47, 49, 147
Loćzy, Count Lajos, 3
longbow, 93
Lop desert, 57, 131
Lop-nor, 23, 24, 57
Lotus Sutra, The, 116
lotus, 108, 163, 214, 215, 216, 221
luohans *see* arhats
Luoyang, 13, 80, 81–2; sack of, 81–2

mah-jong, 183
Mahāmaudgalyāyana, 169; *see also* Mulian
Mahāyāna Buddhist *see* Buddhism, Mahāyāna
Makam river, 120
malachite, 214
Malakand pass, 120
Mani, 17–20, 32, 36
Manicheism, 4, 7, 11, 13, 16, 17, 18–20, 32–3,
    36–7, 39, 48–9, 52, 82–3, 103–4, 135, 218;
    persecution of in China, 135; script, 37
Mañjuśrī, 117
manufacturing, 8; glass, 22; silk, 8, 22
manuscripts, 4
Mar Ammo, 19–20; *see also* Manicheism
Mara, 16
maritime trade route, 7, 21, 223
marmot, 124
marriage, 19, 74, 95–112, 121, 157–8, 178–81,
    197
martagon lilies, 118
massicot (yellow lead), 149
mathematics, 118
Mauryan dynasty (India), 9, 10, 17, 119,
    200
Medea, 97
medicine, 4–5, 30, 44, 60, 109–10, 113–15,
    118, 119, 125, 128, 130, 133, 137, 142, 145,
    173, 174–5, 181, 202; acupuncture, 114,
    115, 174; charms, 113, 114, 118, 181;
    exorcism, 115, 174, 183; for animals, 60, 87,
    119; for childbirth, 181; for children, 115;
    herbalism, 114, 125, 174, 181; massage, 174;
    of Arabia, 115; of China, 115, 181; of
    Greece, 115; of India, 115, 181; of Tibet,
    115, 175; surgery, 114, 115
Mediterranean Sea, 38
Meng Chang (Chinese ruler), 97
menstruation, 110, 179
merchants along the Silk Road, 2, 4, 6, 7, 11,
    14, 18, 21–2, 26, 27–54, 131, 135, 152–3,
    203, 218
Merv, 14, 20, 37
metallurgy, 8, 22, 142; gold, 8, 142; iron, 22
Miaofalianhuajing see The Lotus Sutra
Mihr, 20; *see also* Manicheism
military campaigns, 12, 13, 14, 15, 30, 33–4, 37,
    40, 44, 47, 52, 55–75, 98, 99, 100–1,
    111–12, 123, 131, 135, 138–54, 155, 182,
    190, 193, 207, 218
military service, 150, 161
Milky Way, 212
millet, 168, 177
milling, 35, 161, 168; water, 35
mining, 8, 141; of gold, 8
Ministry of Education, Beijing, 5
minium, 214
Miran, 4, 55–75, 131; irrigation at, 57–8, 131;
    population, 57, 131; Tibetan control of, 57,
    131; Tibetan fort at, 55–61, 131
missionaries along the Silk Road, 11, 17, 18
Mogao Caves, 209–21, 215, 219; *see also*
    Dunhuang, Buddhist caves
Moguls, 2
money *see* currencies of the Silk Road
moneylending, 51, 101, 158, 166–7, 188
Mongolian steppes, 2, 10–11, 12, 13, 14, 22, 25,
    34, 51, 76, 90
monophysites, 20; *see also* Nestorianism
Mount Mug, 34
mourning rituals *see* death
mulberry tree, 30, 124, 208
Mulian, 169–71, 174, 186, 204, 226
murals *see* paintings
music, 26, 46–7, 51, 96–7, 104, 138, 139, 140,
    144, 146, 147, 148, 149–50, 152, 153, 179,
    193, 215; Chinese, 96–7; Kuchean, 96, 139,
    149–50; musical dramas, 139; transcription
    of, 144; Uighur, 153
musk, 96, 183
Mustagh-aga, 125
Muzaffarabad, 118

Naga Apalala, 121
naga legends, 121–2, 130
Nana, 35, 36
Nanshan (Gansu corridor), 24, 25, 50, 57
Natural History (Pliny the Elder), 21
Nepal, 16, 219
nephrite *see* jade
Nestorianism, 7, 11, 16, 17, 20, 33, 218
Nestorius, 20

Index

nirvāṇa *see* Buddhism, nirvāṇa
Noble Eightfold Path, 16
nomads, 2, 7–8, 13, 33, 49, 56, 78, 83, 87–8, 95, 101, 119, 124, 187, 195, 227; *see also* Celts, Germans, Greeks, Hittites, Mongols, Scythians, Slavs, Tibetans, Turks, Uighurs
noodles, 90

oboe, 139
ochre, 214
oil, 161, 166, 168–9, 185, 210
onycha, 149, 183
Ordos, 9, 11, 12, 14, 78, 100, 103
Orkhon river, 25, 78, 105–6, 141
orpiment, 138, 214
otter, 212
oxen, 153, 166, 168, 178; *see also* yaks
Oxus river, 2, 9, 12, 14, 25, 27, 28, 33, 37, 63, 64, 68, 69, 122, 124

Pacific, 2
Padmasaṁbhava, 120, 136
painting, 114, 128, 130, 134, 136, 140, 145, 153, 186, 193, 203, 206–22; Buddhist banners, 114, 119, 128, 156, 186, 206–22; Buddhist cave murals, 134, 136, 145, 153, 186, 193, 203, 209–21; Chinese imperial tombs, 107, 140; Chinese style, 219; forged, 224–5; Manichean, 218; Nestorian, 218; royal portraits, 217–18; Sogdian murals, 6, 35–6; Tibetan style, 219; *see also* pigments
Pakistan, 8, 9, 10
Pamirs, 2, 3, 10, 11, 12, 15, 22–3, 25, 27, 28, 37, 38, 42, 53, 56, 61, 63–8, 71, 98, 122, 124, 125, 201; campaigns in, 63–8, 122; *see also* Little Balur, Wakhan
Panjikent, 6, 27–9, 32, 33, 34, 35, 36; Arab siege of, 34; houses in, 35; *see also* Sogdiana
paper, 4, 30, 45, 120, 127, 201–2, 207, 208, 214–15, 217; Chinese, 30, 201–2, 208; production of, 4, 30, 127, 208
papyrus, 30
parchment, 30
Parsees, 37
Parthian empire, 9, 11, 22
pawnbrokers, 51, 187
pearls, 200
Pelliot Paul, 5
Perfection of Wisdom Sutra, The, 200, 208
perfume, 96, 147, 148, 149, 183, 188
Persia, 2

Persian empire, 7, 38, 97, 106, 115, 219; religions of, 52
Persian Gulf, 7
Petra, 7
Phellodendron amurense see Amur cork tree
physiognomy, 114
pigments, 138, 214, 225
pine trees, 120, 181
Piti springs, 103
plague *see* disease
Pleiades, the, 195
Pliny the Elder, 21
Plough constellation, 201
plums, 142
Poems of Brahmācārin Wang, 190
Poetical Essay on Supreme Joy, 116–17, 145–6
poetry, 73–4, 104, 110, 145, 147, 157, 198, 202; anti-war, 73–4; erotic, 110, 145–6; of courtesans, 147, 148
poll tax, 33
polo, 97, 123, 139, 183, 198
Polonius, 190
poplar trees, 4, 23, 58, 89, 124, 127, 176, 177, 191, 209, 220
post-mortems, 115
pounces, 214–15, 216
Prajñāpāramitasūtra see The Perfection of Wisdom Sutra
Prakrit, 4
pregnancy and childbirth, 181–2
printing, 51, 130, 196–7, 206–7, 217
prisoners-of-war, 30, 54, 71, 143, 146, 147, 182
prostitution, 31, 51, 60, 90, 96–7, 138–54; in Chang'an, 51, 146–52
Punjab, 9, 11, 118
puppets, 143

Qianziwen see The Thousand-Character Classic

Rahu, the Star God, 174, 175
Ramaṇyā, 122
rats, 130, 178
realgar, 115
Record of Famous Artists Through the Ages (Lidai minghua ji), 206
Red Sandy Wastes, 24–5, 39
Red Sea, 7, 21
refugees, 152, 156–7
rehmannia, 181
religions along the Silk Road, 11, 16, 17–20, 21, 36–7, 83; spread from Iran, 11, 19; *see also* Bon, Buddhism, Daoism, Hinduism,

Index

religions along the Silk Road (*cont.*)
  Judaism, Nestorianism, Manicheism,
  shamanism, Zoroastrianism
restaurants, 51, 146, 150
revolutions in Silk Road empires, 6–7
rhubarb, 87
rice, 171, 179, 182
Richthofen, Baron Ferdinand von, 2
Rokhshan, 13, 53, 72, 79–81, 86, 98, 99, 134,
  150, 194–5
Roman empire, 7, 11, 21–2
romanization, xiii
ruby, 121, 200
Russia, 1, 2, 4, 227
Rustam, 35, 39

sable, 106
Saddharmapuṇḍarīkasūtra see The Lotus Sutra
saffron, 120
Śākyamuni (Buddha), 16–17, 116, 119, 130; his
  death, 17, 119; his enlightenment, 16, 116;
  his previous lives, 116, 118, 120–1; *see also*
  Buddhism
Śākyas, 10, 16
sal ammonia, 142
salt, 22, 25, 49, 50, 176
Samarkand, 2, 8, 13, 17, 20, 21, 22, 24, 25, 26,
  27, 28, 30, 31, 32–7, 38, 39, 42, 43, 51, 54,
  55, 80, 82, 140; battles against Arabs, 34,
  37–8; *see also* Sogdiana
Sampson, T., 103
saṃsāra, 16; *see also* Buddhism
Samye monastery, 136
sand jujube, 193
sandalwood, 130, 183
sanderswood, 106
Sanskrit, xiii, 4, 118, 139, 141, 162, 167,
  199
sarakaul, 126
Sarhad, 63–4, 68, 69, 124
Sarikol, 125
Śāriputra, 210–13, 226
Sassanian empire, 11, 17–18, 20; religions of,
  18–20
schools *see* education
Scythians, 7, 8, 9, 16; *see also* Śākyas, Yuezhi
sedan-chair, 178, 179
Selenga river, 78–9
Serindia, 2
sewage disposal, 60–1, 160
sex, 19, 80, 109–10, 116–17, 143, 145–6,
  151–2, 159, 179–80, 186

Shakespeare, William, 181, 190
shamanism, 16, 20, 83, 87
Shanghai Museum, 223
Shapur I, 18, 20
Shatou Turks, 92, 111, 152
Shazhou *see* Dunhuang
sheep, 30, 40–1, 87, 88, 95, 184; dumba, 40
ships, 7
Shiwangjing see The Sutra of the Ten Kings
shoes and boots, 30–1, 32, 39, 45, 76, 106, 107,
  108, 166
'The Shrewish Young Wife', 180–1, 184
Sichuan (China), 196
silk, 8, 10, 21–2, 29, 30, 31, 41, 49, 85, 87,
  105–6, 107, 108, 109, 117, 131, 143, 149,
  150, 163, 166, 172, 182, 183, 186, 211, 220;
  Arabic silk, 30; as currency, 85, 87, 110; as
  tribute, 10; Chinese silk, 30, 106, 130;
  Chinese silk found in Bactria, 8, 21;
  furnishings, 41; in Buddhist ritual, 119; in
  Rome, 21–2; manufacture of, 8, 22, 106,
  110; paintings on, 5, 186, 220–1;
  production of, 30, 130; Sogdian, 29, 30
Silk Road: antecedents, 8, 9; definition, 2–3;
  naming of, 2; *see also* Central Asia, trade
  routes
silver, 21, 31, 32, 51, 85, 93, 106, 140, 166, 173,
  177, 182, 200, 220
silver birch, 118
Sima Qian, first historian of China, 10
Śiva, 139
slavery, 35, 143, 160, 168, 171, 182, 197
Slavs, 7
snakes, 191
Sogdian letters, the, 4
Sogdiana, 2, 4, 6, 11, 12, 14, 19–20, 22, 26,
  27–9, 30, 32–4, 35, 37–8, 53, 55, 63, 72, 79,
  97–8, 140, 218; agriculture, 35; cities in, *see*
  Panjikent, Samarkand; clothing, 29;
  languages of, 36–7, 83; merchants, 44, 83,
  103, 218; rebellions against Arabs, 33–4,
  37–8, 39; religion, 32–3, 35, 37–8
Song dynasty (China), 15, 152, 155, 205, 217,
  221–2
Southern Tang dynasty (China), 80
Soviet Union, 6, 8
Spice Route, 7; *see also* maritime trade route
spices, 28
spiders, 191
sport *see* falconry, hunting, polo
Sri Lanka, 17
Srinigar, 118

Index

Stein, Sir Marc Aurel (archaeologist), 2, 3–4, 5, 207, 223, 224, 228–9
Stone Fort, 62
storax, 183
storytellers, 61, 142, 143, 170, 173, 213
Subhūti, 162, 200
Sui dynasty (China), 12
Sunga dynasty (Hindu), 10
Suśravas (Kashmiri naga), 121–2
Sutra of Impermanence, The, 155
Sutra of the Ten Kings, The, 163, 164–6, 204
Sutra on the Prophecy Received by King Yama see The Sutra of the Ten Kings
Swat river, 10, 120–1, 122, 136
Swedish expeditions, 2
syphilis, 147
Syr Darya see Jaxartes river
Syria, 17

Taigong jia jiao see The Family Teaching of Taigong
Taiyuan, 102, 135
Taizong (Chinese emperor), 83
Taklamakan desert, 23, 24, 27, 43, 49, 58
Takṣaśilā, 9, 12, 118–19
Talas river, battle of (751), 13, 14, 39, 53–4
tamarisk, 23, 24, 58, 59, 126, 175, 177, 181, 215
Taming of the Shrew, The, 181
Tang dynasty (China), xii, 6, 9, 12, 13, 14, 15, 27, 77–85, 101, 107, 139, 140, 144, 145, 152, 155, 156, 167, 190, 196, 199, 217, 219; see also China
Tanguts, 15, 100
Tanim ibn Bahr, 109
Tantric Buddhism see Buddhism, Tantrism
Tārā, 159, 160
Tarim basin, 2, 8, 10, 11, 12, 13, 15, 22–4, 25, 41, 42, 47, 49, 112, 122, 124, 125, 141; cities in, 47; see also Aksu, Charklick, Dunhuang, Kashgar, Khotan, Kocho, Kucha, Miran
tarpan see horse, tarpan
Tashkent see Chach
Tashkurgan, 125
tax, 33, 101, 134, 135, 146, 150, 161, 168, 173, 177, 182, 184, 189
Taxila see Takṣaśilā
tea, 51, 90, 104, 106, 167, 183, 207
tents, 41, 78, 87–8, 104, 105, 106, 107, 109, 124; golden tent of Uighur kaghan and Tibetan emperor, 105, 109; Tibetan yak-hair tents, 70–1; Turkic felt tents, 41, 87–8, 124, 141

Terek Davan pass, 23
Theravada Buddhism see Buddhism, Hīnayāna
Thousand-Character Classic, The, 189–90
Tianshan (Heavenly Mountains), 23, 24, 25, 34, 39–42, 44, 53, 55, 78, 91, 93, 94, 141, 142, 153, 218
Tibetan empire, 1, 4, 5, 6, 9, 10, 11, 12, 13, 14, 42, 44, 51, 55, 55–75, 84, 91, 115, 118, 122, 123, 131, 136, 141, 155, 156, 207, 219; army, 55–75, 131; founding of empire, 56; relations with Arabs, 38; relations with China, 12, 13, 14–15, 38, 53, 55–75, 86, 91–4, 99, 122, 131, relations with Turghiz, 40, 51; relations with Uighurs, 14, 55–6, 91–4; religion of, 14–15, 20, 120, 136, 156, 159; trade routes through, 21, 22, 25–6, 63
tightrope walkers, 143
Tigris river, 7
tin, 141
toads, 191
toilet paper, 201–2
toilets, 60–1, 160, 202
Tongdian, 55
tortoiseshell, 95
toys, 193–4
trade, 7, 13, 21–6, 27–54, 166–7, 175, 183, 223; development of, 9, 11; trade routes, 21–6, 39–51, 61
Transoxania, 12, 14, 22, 28, 34, 37, 39, 43, 53, 109; see also Sogdiana
transport see asses, camels, donkeys, horses, sedan-chair, yaks
Tripiṭaka see Buddhist canon
trumpets, 94, 193
Tsaidam, 26, 75
Turfan basin, 49, 218
Turfan see Kocho
Turghiz, 12, 14, 33, 34, 39–41, 51, 53; kaghan, 41; relations with Arabs, 38, 39, 40, 51, 53; relations with China, 40, 51–2, 53; relations with Tibet, 40, 51; relations with Turks, 40
Turkey, 8, 77
Turkic empires, 1, 12, 13, 14, 40, 51, 77–112, 115, 120, 124, 219; see also Western Turks, Uighur empire
Turkic (languages), xiii, 76
Turks, 8, 12, 15, 20, 25, 29, 30, 40, 44, 45, 53, 72, 77–8, 87, 92, 93, 101, 106, 124, 139, 141, 177; legend of origin, 78; religions of, 20; Shatou Turks, 92, 111
turmeric, 175

Index

Uḍḍiyāna, 118, 121
Uighur empire, 1, 6, 13–14, 51, 55, 76–94, 103–4, 123, 135, 141–2, 153, 218; language of, 76, 83, 218; origins of, 77–9, 87; position of women in, 109; refugees from, 141–2, 218; relations with Arabs, 109; relations with China, 14, 77–112, 123, 135, 141; relations with Kirghiz, 111; relations with Tibet, 14, 55–6, 91–4, 141; relations with Turkic tribes, 55–6, 78, 87, 90–2; religions of, 14, 82–3, 103–4, 135, 218; Sogdians in, 78–9, 82–4
Uighurs, 14, 15, 71, 87, 141, 153; as moneylenders, 85; equine skills, 86–7; in China, 85, 135; in Silk Road cities, 141, 153, 218
Ulan Bator, 12
Umayyad Caliphate (Arab), 6, 12, 14, 33, 51; see also Arab empire
Urumqi, 25
uttarāsaṅga (monk's garment), 163
Uzbekistan, 2

Vajracchedikāprajñāpāramitāsūtra see The Diamond Sutra
Vaiśravaṇa, 128, 130, 142
Vietnam, 95
Virūḍhaka, 128
Virūpākṣa, 128

wages, 43, 70, 133, 136, 147, 168, 173, 176–7, 189, 209, 210, 214, 220; see also currencies
Wakhan, 15, 38, 56, 63–9, 71
walnuts, 106
Wang fanzhi shiji see Poems of the Brahāmcārin Wang
water buffalo, 180, 212, 213
weapons, 41, 47, 55, 60, 64, 68, 72–3, 74, 75, 93–4, 100–1, 108, 183; see also catapults, crossbow, longbow, sword, whirlwind gun
Western Market (Chang'an), 29, 89–90
Western Turks, 13, 40, 51, 77–8
Western Xia see Tanguts
wheat, 58, 168, 177, 182
'whirling' dance, 96, 140; see also dance, Sogdian
whirlwind gun, 47
willow trees, 49, 58, 127
wine, 31, 32, 76, 85, 102–3, 106, 148, 150, 178, 179, 181, 182, 183, 185, 186
wolves, 47, 78, 88, 89; as ancestors of Turks, 78

woodslips, 4
wool, 21, 29–30, 38, 40–1, 88
wormwood, 87
Wu Daozi (Chinese artist), 206
Wuchangjing see The Sutra of Impermanence
Wudi (Chinese emperor), 9
Wular lake, 118
Wutai mountain, 117, 134, 135–6, 145, 163

Xian see Chang'an
Xian'an (Chinese princess), 98
Xianbi, 11–12; see also Aza people
Xinjiang Province (China), 223
Xiongnu, 8–9, 10–11, 77–8; see also Huns
Xixia see Tanguts
Xuanzang (China, Buddhist monk), 3, 27, 113, 228
Xuanzong (Chinese emperor), 27, 53, 61, 79–81, 98, 106, 139
Xue Fang (Chinese poet), 76

yaks, 41, 42, 43, 56, 59, 70–1, 87, 90, 124
Yama (king of the underworld), 169, 204
Yang Guifei (Lady Yang), 79–81, 106
Yangi-hissar, 125, 126
Yanluowang shoujijing see The Sutra of the Ten Kings
Yarkhand, 126
Yarkhun valley, 122–4
Yarlung valley, 12, 61, 65, 70
year animals, 178, 197
Yellow river, 13, 14, 62, 71, 84, 100, 102–3, 112, 216
Yin hills, 112
Yong'an (Chinese princess), 98–9
Yuezhi, 9, 10, 11, 21; see also Kushan empire, Scythians
yurts see tents
Yurung-kash, 127

Zangpo river, 70, 136; see also Yarlung river
Zarathustra see Zoroaster
Zerfashan river, 28, 36, 39
Zhang Qian (Chinese envoy), 9, 10, 21
Zhang Yizhao (ruler of Dunhuang), 144, 145, 146, 155, 163, 190–1, 193, 201, 216–17
Zhangjing Temple (Chang'an), 112
Zoroaster, 18, 37
Zoroastrianism, 11, 16, 17, 18, 32, 33, 52; see also Parsees